The African Liberation Reader

Edited by Aquino de Bragança
and Immanuel Wallerstein

Farewell at the Hour of Parting

My Mother
   (all black mothers
   whose sons have gone)
you taught me to wait and hope
as you hoped in difficult hours
But life
killed in me that mystic hope
I do not wait now
I am he who is awaited
It is I my Mother
hope is us
your children
gone for a faith that sustains life

Today
we are naked children in forest villages
school-less children playing with a ball of rags
in the sands at noon
we ourselves are
contract workers burning lives in coffee plantations
ignorant black men
who must respect the white man
and fear the rich
we are your children
in the black neighbourhoods
beyond the reach of electric light
drunk men falling down
abandoned to the rhythm of the battue of death
your children
hungry
thirsty
ashamed to call you mother
afraid to cross the streets
afraid of men
We ourselves

Tomorrow we shall sing anthems of freedom
when we commemorate
the day of the abolition of this slavery
We are going in search of light
your children Mother
   (all black mothers
   whose sons have gone)
Go in search of life.

Antonio Agostinho Neto
President, Movimento Popular da Libertacao de Angola (MPLA)
In commemoration of the 10th Anniversary of the Angolan armed struggle
for Independence (1961-1971)

The African Liberation Reader

Volume 3

The Strategy of Liberation

Edited by Aquino de Bragança and Immanuel Wallerstein

Zed Press, 57 Caledonian Road, London N1 9DN

The African Liberation Reader was originally
published in Portuguese; first published in
English by Zed Press Ltd., 57 Caledonian
Road, London N1 9DN in 1982.

Copyright © Aquino de Braganca and
Immanuel Wallerstein

Copyedited by Beverley Brown
Proofread by Stephen Gourlay, Rosamund
    Howe, Liz Hasthorpe and Anna Gourlay
Typeset by Jenny Donald
Cover design by Jacque Solomons
Cover photo courtesy of Associated Press
Printed by Krips Repro, Meppel, Holland

U.S. Distributor
Lawrence Hill and Co., 520 Riverside
Avenue, Westport, Conn. 06880, USA

British Library Cataloguing in Publication Data

The African liberation reader.
   Vol.3: The strategy of liberation
   1. Africa, Sub-Saharan — Politics and
   government — Addresses, essays, lectures
   I. Braganca, Aquino de II. Wallerstein,
   Immanuel
   320.9'67   JQ1872
   ISBN 0-86232-069-0

The African Liberation Reader

Publisher's Note

Zed Press gratefully acknowledge a grant from the WCC Programme to Combat Racism towards the cost of typesetting this project. Zed Press also wishes to thank the Swedish International Development Authority for making possible the gift of copies of each of these 3 volumes to the liberation movements of Southern Africa.

Contents

Preface

This collection of documents was originally assembled by the editors in 1973-74 and completed just as the revolution in Portugal broke out in April 1974. This event, completed in 1975 by the independence of all the former Portuguese colonies in Africa, transformed the political situation in Southern Africa. We decided to proceed with the publication of this book in its Portuguese version, since independence in the former Portuguese colonies constituted a clear turning-point in the historical development of their national liberation movements.

We hesitated however about an English-language version. The struggle was continuing in Zimbabwe, Namibia, and South Africa. Should the story stop in 1974? If today we have decided to publish this collection as it was constructed in 1974, it is because we believe that the Portuguese Revolution and the Independence, particularly of Angola and Mozambique, constituted an historical turning-point for the national liberation movements of Zimbabwe, Namibia, and South Africa as well.

Indeed so much has happened in those three countries since 1974 that all of us are tempted to forget the historical evolution of the movements in these countries as well as the importance of the early intellectual debates within the movements and their continuing relevance today. We wish to reinvigorate this historical memory which hopefully may serve as a tool of the ongoing struggle itself. It is in this spirit that we have decided to publish today the English-language version of this collection.

Introduction

National liberation movements do not emerge one fine day out of the mind of some superman or at the instigation of some foreign power. They are born out of popular discontent. They emerge over long periods to combat oppressive conditions and express aspirations for a different kind of society. They are, in short, the agents of class and national struggle.

Neither the classes nor the nations, however, have been there forever. They, too, are creations of the modern world and, in the case of Southern Africa, they were born in the crucible of the colonial experience. To understand the national liberation movements, we must first understand the social forces they represent and the ways in which these social forces were shaped by their historical circumstances.

The capitalist world economy came into existence in Europe in the 16th Century. Its internal functioning — the endless drive for capital accumulation, the transfer of surplus from proletarian to bourgeois and from periphery to core, the cyclical pattern of alternating phases of economic expansion and stagnation — combined to make necessary the regular, albeit discontinuous, expansion of the outer boundaries of the world economy. Slowly, over several centuries, other historical systems were destroyed and incorporated into this ever-growing octopus.

The forms of incorporation into the world economy have varied both according to the strength of the political systems in place in the zones undergoing incorporation and according to the internal configuration of forces among core states within the world economy during the period of incorporation. Sometimes incorporation involved direct colonial overrule, sometimes 'informal imperialism', and sometimes first this indirect mode of conquest followed by a later phase of direct colonialism.

Incorporation has everywhere involved two major changes for the zone being incorporated. First, the production structures were reorganized so that they contributed to the overall division of labour in the world economy. Secondly, the political structures were reorganized so that they facilitated the flow of factors of production in the world economy. In the case of Southern Africa, the reorganization of production structures involved the development both of cash crops and of mining operations for export on the world market. The reorganization of political structures meant the creation of colonial

states in the region, the eventual boundaries of which were a function primarily of the struggles among the various European imperial and settler forces.

It is this reorganization of production structures which created the new
classes and this reorganization of political structures which created the new
nations. These classes and nations are institutional consequences of the
development of the capitalist world economy. They are, in fact, the principal
structural outcome of its hierarchical relations. They are at one and the same
time the mode of social imposition of these hierarchies and the mode of social
resistance to the inequalities bred by the system.

The object of imperialist expansion is to utilize the labour-power of the
peoples of the newly incorporated peripheries at rates of real remuneration
as low as possible. Securing such a labour force requires the establishment of
a three-part geographical division of peripheral areas: a first zone to produce
the export products, within which there is initially often forced labour, later
low-paid wage labour; a second zone to produce surplus food to feed the
labour force of the first zone, within which there tends to be household
production; a third zone to serve as a manpower reserve to produce the labour
force for the first zone (and even occasionally for the second), within which
there tends to be so-called subsistence production. (The three zones do not
necessarily have to fall within a single colonial state.)

It is this three-zone system, with its large component of migrant labour
(persons, largely men, leaving the third zone for limited periods, sometimes
only once in a lifetime, and returning afterwards to that zone), which permits
the super-exploitation of labour in the first (or wage labour) zone. The
'migrant' workers located in such a zone participate in extended households,
and over their lifetime the costs of reproduction are disproportionately borne
by the work done in non-wage sectors. Thus the employer of wage labour can
in effect pay *less than* the minimum necessary wage (that is, the wage assuring
the reproduction of the labour force).

It is clear, then, why the conceptual categories which evolved in the context
of the core zones of the capitalist world economy — concepts such as proletarian (meaning by that a life-long industrial wage labourer living in an urban
area with his whole household) and peasant (meaning a life-long agricultural
worker with some kind of hereditary rights to land utilization) — do not seem
to fit exactly when we look closely at the peripheral zones of the world
economy. The work-force there is not divided into 'traditional' peasants
owning the means of production and 'modern' proletarians who have been
expropriated from the means of production. Most (or at least many) workers'
households are in fact composed of *both* 'proletarians' and 'peasants', the
same individuals often being both for part of their lives. It is this combination
of roles which defines the relationship of these workers to the world economy
and permits the particular extreme form of exploitation they encountered in
the colonial era.

The pattern of the creation of the work-force, with its institutionalized
interaction between rural 'home' areas and the urban (or mining or cash-crop)
areas, favoured the continued recruitment to wage employment through

'family' or 'ethnic' channels, and hence the emergence in the urban and commercialized zones of an 'ethnic' consciousness (called by the colonial overlords 'tribalism'), an ethnic consciousness which was in fact very much the expression of the emerging class position of the various groups integrated into the wage work-force.

The ambiguous relationship of class and ethnic 'membership' is hence a structural reality, indeed a structural creation, of the colonial situation, of colonies located within the capitalist world economy. The initial subjective confusions of large segments of the new work-forces were reinforced deliberately by the colonial authorities with their classic divide-and-rule tactics. It is within this framework and against this definition of the situation that the movements of resistance are born. While awareness of the real inequalities of the colonial situation was central to the demands of these movements from the very beginning, the complexities of the class-ethnic structures were a hindrance to their development. These movements evolved amidst contradictory consciousnesses of class and ethnicity and incorporated these contradictions into their very structures — sometimes in the form of competing movements, more often within a single national liberation movement, and frequently in both ways (as this whole collection of documents illustrates).

The history of each individual political unit (colony) is complex and these histories vary from colony to colony. Generally speaking, however, the story of anti-colonial resistance is the story of the construction of a national liberation movement, more or less unified, more or less representative, which seeks to incarnate the class and national struggles of the majority of the work-force. These histories cannot be appreciated or analysed in isolation. The emergence of such a movement in a particular country is itself the function in part of the political evolution of the world system as a whole.

Beginning in a modest way in the 19th Century, and achieving great force in the 20th, the contradictions of the capitalist world economy have led to the rise of a network of anti-systemic movements. These movements have taken different forms, sometimes emphasizing their class character, sometimes emphasizing their national character, usually doing a bit of both. They have sought to counter the oppressions of the world system and, in their more radical versions, to destroy it.

To build an anti-systemic movement, it is necessary to mobilize popular force, and usually it is politically necessary to mobilize this force initially within the confines of particular states. This narrow geographical definition of anti-systemic movements has been at once their strength and their weakness. It has been their strength because it has forced them to remain close to the concrete grievances of the working classes — urban and rural — they have been mobilizing. It has made it possible for them to achieve political power in some preliminary way — in the case of colonies, to obtain independence. But this narrow geographical focus has also been their weakness. Their enemy, the world bourgeoisie, has seldom hesitated to combine *its* strength on an inter-state level. In the case, for example, of the former Portuguese colonies in Africa, the movements in the separate colonies faced a single colonial power, and one that was in turn widely supported by other imperial powers. Furthermore, when such anti-colonial movements have come to power, they have found that juridical state sovereignty is in part a fiction since they were still bound by the constraints of the inter-state system, the political superstructure of the capitalist world economy.

The movements have not been unaware of these contradictions which have posed dilemmas, both strategic and tactical, for their operations. This book seeks to organize in a coherent manner their reflections on the dilemmas and their perspective on the solutions they might find. These solutions are not facile ones, and it is in the quality of these reflections and the action consequent upon them that we can distinguish those movements which have been truly anti-systemic in their impact and those which have fallen by the wayside, to become open or hidden agents for the maintenance and further development of the capitalist world economy.

The hard thinking of the movements in Southern Africa has been of great consequence for the struggle in that part of the world. But it is of great consequence for movements elsewhere as well. The reinforcement of the worldwide network of movements is in fact the great task of our times, a task in process but far from completed.

1. The Enemy's Plans

Editors' Introduction

In a strategy of liberation, one of the crucial things for a national liberation movement to do is to understand the operations of the enemy – both strategic and tactical – in order to adjust their own operations to this reality. The national liberation movements of Portuguese and southern Africa were in agreement on one fundamental consideration. The enemy was subtle and complex. Moreover the enemy was multi-headed, and their plans of operations had to operate simultaneously at the political, economic and military levels. But this also caused some of the differences among the movements. There were difficulties in defining who at various periods was the *primary* enemy. And the disagreement about this led to the second difference of opinion: what was the most effective means of responding to tactical shifts that occurred?

The exact form of these questions varied, too, according to the particular country. In the analysis of South Africa, the central strategy, as seen by the movements, was the creation of client states. This emerged of course from internal economic needs (as explained in the section 'Economic Interrelations of Southern Africa'), but it served immediate political and military ends as well. Oliver Tambo analysed this strategy of using aid and investment 'to entrench dependence' and argued its links with historic economic policies and contemporary military needs. The internal parallel to neighbouring client states was the creation of Bantustans in South Africa and Namibia. We include the ANC's denunciation of this 'complete fraud'. We also include Robert Mugabe's assessment in 1963 that Zimbabwe was going down the same Bantustan path under the name of 'Community Development'.

A bigger problem for Zimbabwe was, however, assessing the role of Great Britain. The movements argued that 'Britain is the real enemy' and that it should not be allowed to pose as the moderate middle between the white settler regime and the movements. The ZAPU memorandum argued that Britain was 'deliberately misleading and deceiving' the UN and the world with regard to sanctions. As for the various attempts to resolve the issue 'peacefully' by an accord between Great Britain and the Rhodesian government, the African National Council saw this as a 'vicious and subtle device' to betray the Africans. And, ZAPU went on, behind the 'shadow' of the British government, lay the 'actual power' of British corporate interests.

The movements in Portuguese Africa had to face one tactic of the enemy which was not as serious a problem in the other areas: decapitation. Furthermore, this tactic went way back. We reproduce a letter Agostinho Neto wrote from forced residence in 1961 in which he sought to alert the world to the possibility of his murder. Later three major figures were in fact assassinated: General Humberto Delgado, the leader of the Portuguese underground opposition; Dr. Eduardo Mondlane, president of FRELIMO; and Amilcar Cabral, Secretary-General of the PAIGC. We reproduce a tribute to Delgado published in a PAIGC organ in 1965. And we reproduce a remarkable document: the detailed prediction by Cabral of how and why he would be assassinated, a year before it occurred.

The movements in Portuguese Africa also had to face the issue of 'reformism'. When Marcelo Caetano replaced Antonio Salazar as Prime Minister of Portugal in 1968, the initial reaction was prudent. Cabral saw possibilities of changes in Portuguese internal policy and expressed the thin hope that Caetano, 'more attuned to the historical realities of our days, would come to understand the irreversible character of our struggle for national liberation'. It was not to be. Rather, Caetano combined intensified repression, corruption and pseudo-negotiation, as explained by Iko Carreira and Agostinho Neto of the MPLA. For FRELIMO, 'Caetano's reforms sink in a sea of contradictions'.

Lastly, we come to the fundamental strategy of coordination among the white rulers of southern Africa. How this operated from the perspective of one territory is told in the analysis of Mozambique by José Oscar Monteiro.

Apartheid — A Threat to Africa's Survival
Oliver Tambo

From the address by the Acting President, ANC (South Africa)
to the Nigerian National Committee on Apartheid in Lagos,
18 March 1971.

The strategic objective of the South African racists with regard to the African continent is both short term and long term. It is to create client states among the independent African countries, with the aim of cutting off the South African national liberation movement from all sources of assistance; to compel such client states actively to participate in campaigns aimed at our destruction and the destruction of the faith of our oppressed and revolutionary people in the inevitability of liberation; and to ensure the preservation of *apartheid* by destroying the African National Congress (ANC), the decisive force on whose shoulders falls the task of liberating the African people of South Africa.

The strategy of creating client states is further aimed at cutting short

Africa's strivings to establish for herself an independent and equal position in the world's economy and the international political system; at using these client states against other African states; and, ultimately, at maintaining Africa as South Africa's exclusive political and economic preserve. In this connexion, special mention should be made of the attempt of the South African regime to establish a so-called 'Southern African Common Market'. A white South African apologist of *apartheid* has written: 'If allowed to proceed unhindered, developments in this area could lead to the creation of a new multinational giant, the Europe of Africa, which will one day exercise a profound influence on developments in Africa, if not in the world.' The centre of gravity of this combination would be the white South African minority regime.

White South Africa uses many and diverse means in the attempt to fulfil her objectives. To begin with, South Africa is economically the most powerful country in Africa. On the other hand, the peoples of Africa, especially in the sub-Saharan part, on the basis of continental comparisons, have the lowest standard of living in the world. The South African racists seek to exploit this situation to their advantage.

Trade Relations to Make Africa Dependent

In the first instance, they seek to expand trade relations with the rest of Africa. South Africa's exports to Africa more than doubled between the years 1964 and 1968, while her imports from Africa grew by about a third.

We need to draw attention to two points regarding these trade relations. First, relative to the rest of the continent, South Africa in the period mentioned – and, I am certain, up to the present – enjoyed a favourable balance of payments. This, of course, necessitates that the African countries must find foreign exchange to settle their debts. South Africa takes advantage of this situation by offering credits to these countries to buy South African goods. The African countries are then faced with the task of periodically servicing their debt to South Africa.

Second, South Africa uses Africa as her market for manufactured goods. If, for instance, we take three categories of South African exports, namely, chemicals, machinery and transport equipment, and miscellaneous manufactured goods, we find that by 1968 Africa was taking 75 per cent of South Africa's total exports in these categories. On the other hand, in the same year, Africa exported to South Africa only about 1.5 per cent of South Africa's requirements of goods in these categories. This means that South Africa maintains the classical trade relations between an imperialist country and its colonies. The African countries serve South Africa as sources for cheap raw materials and markets for her expensive manufactured goods.

In all, these trade relations increase Africa's dependence on South Africa and help maintain the African economies at a low level of development. The South African racists further strive to entrench these trade relations by signing agreements, binding on both signatories for an agreed period, as they have done in the case of Malawi.

Aid and Investment to Entrench Dependence
In the second instance, the South African policy of aid and investment has also been designed to entrench these tendencies of perpetual dependence. Funds exported by South Africa go first to the development of raw material extraction and secondly to the development of the infrastructure.

South Africa already has large investments in mining in all the countries of southern Africa. Her companies have reached even as far north as Mauretania where, in co-operation with French capital, South African money and technique is used in the mining of copper. South African companies are already prospecting for bauxite and other minerals in Malawi. Newspaper reports have also stated that South African companies, again in co-operation with French capital, are investigating mining possibilities in Malagasy. South Africa, again in co-operation with France, is wooing Mauritius and dangling the prospect of big loans and investments before the Mauritian Government. Mr. Sean Gervasi, an economist at Oxford University, has stated: 'Total [South African] investments in Africa were in the hundreds of millions at the beginning of the 1960s. They have probably more than doubled since then.'

I have said that South Africa is helping with the financing of the infrastructure in some of these countries. Currently, of course, the most notable of such projects is the Cabora Bassa Scheme in Mozambique which is not only largely South African-financed and designed to generate electricity for a host of countries in the area, including Mozambique, Angola and Malawi. But the Governments of Zambia and Tanzania have both condemned the scheme and taken steps to preclude any Zambian or Tanzanian participation in the scheme.

South Africa also lent Malawi £6 million (US $16.8 million) for the construction of a railway line terminating at Port Nacala in Mozambique. She is building an important road through Namibia to Angola's seaport, Luanda, and a gas pipeline from Mozambique to South Africa. Further, she has signed an agreement with Malagasy to open an air route between the two countries, as well as maintain and fly Malagasy's aircraft on that route. If I may quote Sean Gervasi again: 'All these changes create new links which are essentially ones of dependence for those with whom South Africa deals.' And, let me add, dependence means absence of independence.

Apartheid Needs Expansion
It is necessary to point out that the economic processes I have just described, dealing with South Africa's external economic relations, are organically linked with *apartheid* in so far as it is an internal, South African system of economic relations. As a system, one of whose central features is the super-exploitation of the African people, *apartheid* results in certain economic consequences.

One of these is that since the earnings of the African majority are kept at the bare minimum level, the internal market for industrial goods is extremely limited. This is particularly important in the situation which obtains today wherein manufacturing contributes more to the gross domestic product than mining and agriculture.

4

Mining and agriculture have, of course, been traditionally export-oriented. A limited home market was therefore of no material significance to their development. The contrary is however the case with regard to manufacturing. The restricted nature of the home market acts as a fetter on the development of this sector. Hence the necessity for South Africa to find external markets for her manufactured goods.

The second of these economic consequences is that very low wages mean very high profit rates. South Africa, therefore, generates the bulk of her investment funds internally. In 1969, for instance, the ratio of net capital flow from the rest of the world to gross domestic investment was only 3.2 per cent. Over a period of time, however, the influx of capital from abroad adds up to large amounts. In the period from 1956 to 1968, direct investment from abroad alone amounted to about two billion dollars.

What attracts such large funds is the factor of very low wages, and correspondingly, very high profit rates. During the years 1960 to 1965, for example, returns on British investment in South Africa were consistently 'almost 50 per cent higher than those on the average British direct investment overseas'. The same can be said of United States investments in South Africa.

Given the high savings rate in South Africa, the vast inflow of foreign capital and the restricted internal market, a situation arises in which South Africa finds herself burdened with an 'embarrassment of riches'. She, therefore, exports her 'excess' capital. Thus it is that South Africa's internal economic processes are organically linked with the external. The super-exploitation of the Black people in South Africa is at once the basis of the South African economy and the objective reason for South Africa's quest for external markets for her 'excess' capital.

The external relations are clearly the relations of domination and exploitation because, firstly, they are dictated by the objective requirements of the most powerful economy on the African continent; and, secondly, because they are designed and intended to serve the exclusive economic and political interests of the white South African racist minority and not those of the African people, inside or outside Africa. If we take the nature and duration of the economic relations between the United States and South America as a timely parallel to South Africa's relations of domination and exploitation in Africa, then we cannot possibly ignore the stern warning already sounded by the French author, Dumont, that the objective of the South African racist regime is to 'South Americanize' Africa. And God forbid that Africa, in whole or in part, should be surrendered to these heartless racists and condemned to such a horrifying disaster by any African leader or group of leaders.

Import of Black Manpower

It is worth remembering that South Africa 'imports' manpower from Africa. In mining alone, last year, Black workers from outside South Africa constituted 70 per cent of the total African labour force. This system of 'importation' of African labour, at highly exploitative wage rates, is as cruel as it is a criminal

5

rape of Africa's manpower. The youth is seized from developing African countries in its prime; it is used mercilessly in the interests of South Africa's mining magnates; and it is then returned home a spent force, as poor as it had left and bringing no wealth for the development of its countries and peoples. As a system which 'is leading away from industrialization and not towards it', and which does not create job opportunities in the countries of origin, it condemns not only the present, but also the future generations to dependence on South Africa. Small wonder that Zambia has decreed against Zambians working in the South African mines.

We are familiar with the definition of war as the continuation of politics by other means. I have already said that South Africa's policy in Africa is that of creating client states, of making Africa her own sphere of political and economic domination. The white man in South Africa has been preparing and continues to prepare for war, for a continuation of his political policy by other means.

The racist regime's military strategy falls into two parts. Firstly, the regime has adopted a military posture aimed at keeping the white-dominated south of Africa intact, while simultaneously pushing the regime's military defence line far to the north, thus creating a system of buffer states around itself. Secondly, it has made preparations to strike against the independent countries to the north, in terms of what the Israelis, who maintain military contacts with racist South Africa, call 'the doctrine of anticipatory counter-attack' or 'carrying the war into enemy territory', to quote General Allon, Israel's Deputy Prime Minister. The parallels between Israel and South Africa are, of course, obvious. The difference, however, is that whereas Israel needed to go to war in order to capture and occupy Arab territory, South Africa did not have to do so in the case of Namibia, which she now stubbornly refuses to relinquish despite the United Nations decision terminating her mandate. South Africa's military presence in Zimbabwe, Mozambique and Angola is by agreement with the sister colonial and racist regimes of Portugal and Rhodesia, members with South Africa, of the economic, political, military and intelligence Unholy Alliance. Just as Israel has been conducting acts of aggression against the Arab countries, using captured territory as her base, so will South Africa use her buffer states for 'anticipatory counter-attack'.

She has furthermore built a major military base in the Caprivi Strip, in the northernmost tip of Namibia, one thousand miles from her own borders with Namibia. From this base she can strike, quickly and suddenly, at countries far to her north, as President Kaunda has repeatedly warned. Only last year, the world was informed by a South African Cabinet Minister that the new airport being built in Lilongwe, Malawi, would be open to aircraft of the South African Air Force. The Minister subsequently published a diplomatic denial of the statement. But South Africa openly maintains a military attache's office in Malawi.

The Bantustan Fraud
ANC

Article in Sechaba *(ANC), III, 5 May, 1969.*

The fraudulent Bantustan scheme was launched by the racist South African regime in 1963 after many years of preparation. Long before its implementation and ever since then the African National Congress consistently exposed the scheme as a sham and a facade. Recently (October) the people of the Transkei, the first Bantustan, went to the polls to elect a new legislative assembly. In view of the results of these elections and the publicity this has received it is pertinent at this juncture to review the political and economic position in the Transkei in the light of the fascist regimes theories of race. It goes without saying that the oppressed people of South Africa led by the ANC have totally rejected the Bantustan fraud along with all forms of racism. Our express purpose here is to show that the scheme is a total failure even by the racist standards of the white minority regime. It is necessary first of all briefly to examine the Bantustan theory.

Bantustan Theory

The ruling Nationalist Party came to power in 1948 on the platform of apartheid or separateness. At that time this was a somewhat vague and nebulous concept designed to cover up naked racism and elevate it to the rarified atmosphere of political philosophy. From time to time long tracts were churned out expanding voluminously on apartheid as being in keeping with 'natural law', as being based on the word of God, etc. Examples were (and still are) assiduously sought in any part of the world where there is racial friction to 'prove' that the policy of apartheid is the ideal solution.

To satisfy the theorists and purists of the South African Bureau of Racial Affairs, the intellectual wing of the Nationalist Party, the Tomlinson Commission was set up in 1951 to go into the whole question of separate development with special reference to the geographical separation of the African people into various tribal units. The commission laboured for several years and eventually produced a report which glaringly underlines the deep poverty, utter desolation and eroded barrenness of the reserves to which so many millions of Africans were confined by law and from which only the most able-bodied and strong are allowed to leave to work on the farms, the mines and the towns which the White man regards as his personal and private preserve. Needless to say it is the very poverty of the reserves which compelled this clamour to leave the reserves to seek work at pitiful wages under miserable conditions. The Tomlinson Report pointed out that if the reserves, comprising only 13% of South Africa were fully developed they would be able to accommodate ten million Africans by 1987 still leaving more than half in the towns and the farms of the Whites. But even such development 'necessitated the expenditure of £100 million over the next ten years' (from 1956). There were other recommendations about the setting up of industries, improvement of agricultural methods, etc., which the racist regime found totally unacceptable. It was all very well to talk about self-governing Bantustans in order to dupe the world and to appear to be 'solving the native question'. But to spend such vast sums of money on 'kaffirs' was preposterous. The report was quietly shelved.

However, in the '60s the ever mounting struggle of the oppressed, the increasing pressure from the international community and pressure from its own intellectuals the government was compelled to show apartheid to be some kind of serious and meaningful doctrine. And so, in 1963, the Bantustan scheme was launched promising self-government and eventual independence to the people of the Transkei.

Transkei

At no stage were the people of the Transkei consulted as to whether or not they wanted Bantustans though they often expressed their opposition in various forms of protests. At scores of meetings peasants from all over the Transkei expressed their opposition to the establishment of a Bantustan. Some Chiefs, like Matanzima and Botha Sigau, capitulated. Others were deported. But, the peoples wrath cannot be contained. In Pondoland following an unprovoked attack by the police during which eleven tribesmen were killed at a peaceful meeting at Ngqusa Hill, the Pondos rose in revolt almost to a man. The months that followed saw yet another glorious chapter in the history of an enslaved people rising in revolt against the best equipped army and police force in Africa, in support of their just demand for full freedom and democracy in the land of their birth. A meeting of chiefs was convened in 1962 but even here Sabata Dalindyebo, Paramount Chief of the Tembu, the largest group in the Transkei, was not allowed to voice his courageous opposition to Bantustans. The racists apparently thought they knew what was best for the 'child-like' Blacks. It must not be forgotten that in theory, at least, it was promised that the Bantustans would eventually become democratically governed, economically viable, independent states.

In practice, despite all the promises of the racists, the Transkei Bantustan was launched under the most inauspicious circumstances, such as:

1) The extreme poverty and economic backwardness for there were no plans whatsoever except that White capital would never be allowed in.

2) The Emergency Regulations proclaimed in 1960 at the time of the Pondoland uprising and still operative. Under this regulation opponents of apartheid are still being hounded.

3) Out of a total of 109 legislative assembly seats 64 were to be filled by chiefs nominated by the central government. These chiefs depended on the racist government not only for their titles but also for their salaries. Only the unusually dedicated would dare to go against the wishes of the Pretoria regime as such opposition almost invariably resulted in the withdrawal of the chieftainship as happened in the case of the late Chief Albert Lutuli.

4) The most dedicated and progressive of the people's leaders were either in gaol, in restriction, exiled or banned as was the only mass

organisation the ANC.

Nevertheless, despite all these restrictions the Transkei electorate voted overwhelmingly for the Transkei Democratic Party (TDP) which stood for a non-racial South Africa and opposed Bantustans. Matanzima's Transkei Independent Party (TNIP) won only 25 per cent of the seats and was only able to form a government with the support of the nominated chiefs.

Who Governs the Transkei

> From the point of view of real, legal power which rests solely on the control and exercise of the parliamentary franchise, the ballot papers in a Bantustan election might as effectively be dropped in a well as into a ballot box. (O.D. Schreiner *The Nettle*).

Despite the farce of elections and despite the fact that the Transkei has been granted 'departments' of Chief Ministry, Finance, Justice, Agriculture and Forestry, Interior, Education and Roads & Works, real power continues to be wielded by the Pretoria regime. All laws and decrees have to be sanctioned by the racist government. Matanzima's faint talk of replacing Bantu Education with genuine education was quickly silenced. Similarly his claims to more land have been frowned upon so much so that Matanzima is now very quiet about them. In 1966 Matanzima appointed Curnick Ndamse, formerly of Fort Hare, as professional assistant to his 'Department of Education' but shortly thereafter the Pretoria regime imposed severe banning orders on Ndamse which, among other things, prohibited him from entering educational institutions. It took months of negotiations to have the banning orders sufficiently relaxed to permit him to enter educational premises. But the Bantustan way is indeed a strange one. Ndamse was last month made a member of Matanzima's new Cabinet. The Emergency Regulations imposed by the central government continue to terrorise the people of the Transkei. In 1966 alone almost 100 banning and banishment orders were issued against Transkei citizens. Matanzima's so-called government is powerless to prevent this even if it desired to do so. Despite conditions of terror, arbitrary arrest and banishments, opposition to the Bantustan scheme still manifests itself. Several people have been detained and jailed for alleged plots to kill Matanzima, including two opposition M.P's Jackson Nkosiyane and C. Nogcantsi who are currently serving a seven year prison sentence.

A few months before the recent elections several senior African civil servants were quizzed by the Special Branch (political police). Recently five men were detained under the Emergency Regulations among them Ezra Sigwela, Secretary of the Transkei General Workers' Union and Jongabantu Joyi, executive member of the union. The latter has been an outspoken critic of Matanzima describing him as a 'bossboy' of the Whiteman. This attitude perhaps explains these detentions just prior to the elections.

We have quoted only the most glaring instances to show that real power continues to be wielded by the central government and is being used to hound even the mildest form of opposition.

The Rule of Chiefs

We have already pointed out that chiefs depend on the racist regime not only for their titles but also for their salaries. However, since the implementation of Bantustans the powers of the chiefs have been enormously increased. Their vested interest in maintaining the present system has been given additional incentive by their right to conduct Chiefs' Courts popularly named 'Bush Courts'. They are able to enrich themselves by taking a share of the damages granted to a plaintiff with the result that they are very interested parties even when they themselves conduct trials. It is well-known that chiefs often appoint their own agents to bring complaints against relatively wealthier peasants in order to aggrandise themselves. Opponents of the Bantustans are also brought to these courts on trumped up charges and heavily fined to fill the chief's coffers. To show how wealthy chiefs can get from all this, we quote from Govan Mbeki's book *The Peasants' Revolt*.

> One attorney has been appointed a Chief at an official monthly salary of £30. He will compensate for the loss of his practice by making more money. And in addition he can readily surround himself with comforts by calling upon the people to impose a levy upon themselves for such purposes as to buy the chief a car . . .

Also peasants have to have permits from chiefs to cut wood, to cut thatching grass, to brew beer, to hold initiation rites, etc., and for all this chiefs have to be paid. Chiefs also have powers to allocate land and to issue trading licences, again at a price. It must be borne in mind that aside from enriching themselves chiefs have the authority to refuse to grant permits, licences or land. Thus enormous powers have been placed in the hands of chiefs to influence the people by means of terror.

The Transkei Civil Service

The Pretoria regime boasts of the rapid Africanisation of the Transkei civil service. Impressive figures of Africans who have replaced Whites in the police force, prisons, etc. receive wide publicity. Four prisons are now headed by Africans. Two men, Lennox Mbuli and Donald Stofile, who have had long years of civil service in various dummy institutions set up by Pretoria, have been appointed district magistrates. The racist government has, however, made it clear no Whites would ever stand trial before Africans nor would any prison headed by an African be allowed to admit White prisoners. Needless to say African magistrates will administer laws in which Africans have had no say.

It must be pointed out that much of the so-called 'Africanisation' is due to the acute shortage of Whites who find conditions in the civil service unattractive. On the other hand Africans find so many avenues of employment closed and those that are available are vastly inferior to those of Whites with similar qualifications and experience.

Obtaining these jobs with enticing prospects of promotion these men and women also begin to develop a vested interest in the Bantustan system. It gives them an opportunity, no matter how degrading, to escape from the general poverty that surrounds them. Having had some chance of acquiring an education these men are not without influence irrespective of the nature of that influence.

Political Development
On the political front, too, significant changes have taken place. Political authority, no matter how limited, once tasted cannot but generate stronger demands. In the context of Bantustan politics this can only mean demands for greater freedom from Pretoria. In both the TNIP and the TDP such agitation has grown over the years, resulting in several vocal members from both parties breaking off to form the Freedom Party which demands immediate independence. Matanzima has been able to meet this challenge on its own merits by such phraseology as 'The road to freedom is a long one and has to be negotiated carefully step by step . . . we cannot be political dreamers'. The TDP with its total opposition to the Bantustans has found itself hamstrung not only by government terror but by its insistence on a peaceful solution in the face of such terror. The real opposition has been driven underground and is not in a position to influence electioneering and elections. In the recognised (by Pretoria) political parties the ultimate goal of freedom from White rule has become the dominant feature cutting the ground from under the feet of the TDP.

Conclusion
In this brief analysis we have tried to show that the Bantustan scheme of the racists is a complete fraud. We have also attempted to explain why it was possible for Matanzima's TNIP to win a majority of elected seats in the recent elections. We will reiterate the factors involved:

1) The strict control by the central government which has used its powers to attack opponents of the racist regime.

2) The increased powers and vested interests in the chiefs.

3) The Transkei civil service which is beginning to have a vested interest in the system and which, in an educationally backward society such as the Transkei, has considerable influence.

4) The understandable inability of the TDP to have any real impact has caused some people to think in terms of freedom from White rule, even if this is in a Bantustan.

It must be remembered that real opposition not only to the Bantustan scheme but also to the whole policy of racism rests not among those who are playing the parliamentary game but among the broad masses of the oppressed peasantry and the urban workers led by the ANC. These people have opted out of Bantustans in various ways and ultimately it is they, guided and led by the ANC who will solve the problems of South Africa.

The Path of No Return
Robert Mugabe

*From a statement by Mugabe, on behalf of ZAPU, to the 1442nd
Meeting of the Fourth Committee of the UN General Assembly,
in New York on 8 October 1963. (The ZAPU-ZANU split
occurred only in 1964.)*

The settlers have chosen the path of 'no return'. Every day that passes without
a solution is a day in their favour. Already they are in forcible possession of
most of the land and monopolize the country's resources and the instruments
of production. They have consolidated their hold by erecting prisons and
detention camps into which those who criticise them and agitate for the right
of self-determination are thrown, often under the pretext that they have
violated the innocuous repressive laws enacted in the name of law and order.
Aware that their political iniquities are bound to recoil on them by ultimately
arousing the African masses to action, they now seek a whole Army and Air
Force with which to carry out a ruthless campaign of suppressing African
nationalism.

These are not all their evil intentions, for as they make these military
preparations, they are at the same time engaged in working out the most
subtle plans to effect apartheid thinly disguised under the name 'Community
Development' – a less suspicious name under which the scheme is being
implemented.

Community Development is known to most people and Governments of
developing states where it is a genuine attempt to facilitate development
through self-help schemes. In Southern Rhodesia however, the Rhodesia
Front reactionary government gives it a different connotation and, indeed,
seeks to apply it differently. Mr. Jack Howman, the settler Minister of Local
Government and African Education, who is charged with the responsibility
of effecting the plan, has described 'Community Development' as a 'political
philosophy' based on the existence of different culture. Again in the words
of the same Minister, this political philosophy recognises 'that the social
integration of people differing in race and culture does not conduce to
harmony; indeed lessons have been drawn from social studies which show
that in such circumstances racial friction and intolerance are inevitable.'

The Rhodesia Front pamphlet entitled 'Community Development – What
it Means and How it Works' clearly advocates apartheid when it states, 'Community Development involves the process whereby each community, whether
European, African, Euroafrican or Asian, defines its needs, makes its plans
and carries out these plans with its own resources and secures outside assistance where this is needed.' This might very well have come from Verwoerd.

According to this theory, rigid racial communities are to be carved out,
demarcated by rigid social, economic and political barriers with the sole
object of preventing social, political and economic encroachments by Africans on the present privileges and rights enjoyed by the settler minority.

Already 350 Africans, previously agricultural assistants, have been diverted from their normal occupation and placed in preparation for a country-wide implementation of the separate-development schemes. The total number of people to be trained is 600, who, it is sad to say, will be trained with American (mark you, not South African) technical assistance.

Mr. Jack Howman's speech reported in the Hansard containing the Debates of the Southern Rhodesia Legislative Assembly, of 23rd August 1963, removes any doubts as to the intentions and machinations of the settler government. Mr. Jack Howman, the Minister of Local Government, is reported as saying: 'But let me make it abundantly clear that we are going to implement these policies, we are going to put them through whatever the oppositions may be.'

When asked whether his Government would do it by force, he replied, 'There will be no question of trying to soft-pedal these policies to not implement them because of ignorance of certain persons,' and he added that if the African people did not want the Community Development schemes they would be deprived of their schools, clinics and hospitals. 'Well,' he said, 'the people cannot have it both ways.'

What further evidence do we require to prove that the settlers left to themselves will definitely turn the country into a second South Africa. These are not the men to be appealed to through reason, for they have lost all sense of judgement on vital political issues and behave as well-conditioned reactionaries, always with an exaggerated notion of their racial superiority. They talk glibly of 'civilised standards' and, like hypocrites they are, daily chant imperialist Rhodes' dictum, 'equal rights for all civilised men', taking care that they allow no one else but themselves to judge as to who is civilised and who is not. Indeed it is too much to expect that men who have for so long enjoyed monopoly of privilege and political power can on their own accord suddenly turn holy and begin bestowing the same rights and privileges upon the Africans who, they know, outnumber them by 16 to 1. Well, the fact is they have chosen not to do it and now threaten dire consequences if they are compelled to do so.

Britain is the Real Enemy
ZAPU

Article in Zimbabwe Review *(Lusaka), II, 3 June 1967.*

In the face of all this enormous problem, the African people of Zimbabwe continue along their unrelenting course of resisting the oppressive regime. It has been our conviction that the Rhodesian settler regime rests on force and can only be eliminated by the use of force. Towards this end, we are mobilising our people to make the utmost sacrifices of their lives through the prosecution of an armed struggle, in order to defeat the enemy.

The courageous sons of Zimbabwe are engaged in this in ever increasing proportions within the country. In fact, the rigorous measures being taken by the racist regime to repress the African people through the enormous army, is evidence of the regime's awareness of the growing force of the African people against it.

This statement was made on behalf of the Zimbabwe African People's Union in a memorandum submitted to the United Nations Committee on Colonialism.

We do hereby, therefore, call upon the Committee to:

Condemn Britain and her allies for deliberately misleading and deceiving the United Nations over the programme of sanctions against Rhodesia;

To regard Britain as the real enemy to be eliminated in Rhodesia;

Recognise that the sanctions programme against Rhodesia is a fraud, which is failing and can never bring about the required political effect;

Encourage all the nations which genuinely support the African struggle towards the elimination of the racist minority dictatorship and establishment of an African popular government to support, by all means, the African people of Zimbabwe in their measures of an armed struggle to attain their objectives.

On behalf of the struggling African masses of Zimbabwe we wish to extend our thanks to the Committee for having decided to look at the Rhodesian case from close range. We also thank the Committee for its continuous vigilance over the issue and for permitting us to contribute to its task.

Since we presented evidence before this Committee last year on the Rhodesian question, political developments have indicated a worsening of the situation. The settler regime has taken upon itself a more defiant attitude to the international world and has introduced far more oppressive measures on the majority inhabitants of the country. Moving along this disastrous path, the regime has established a constitutional commission whose task it is to devise a constitution for permanent entrenchment of minority dictatorship and racism. Once again, in the familiar pattern, this proposed constitution is being framed up with the assistance of South Africa and the connivance of the British Government. The Commission is carrying out a fake exercise of receiving evidence from all over the country but the Commission has not, and cannot get, evidence from the genuine leaders of the African people of Zimbabwe. We wish this Committee to note that, in a way, this Constitutional Commission is an instrument for the implementation of an idea born out of the British Government in seeking means to impose the Tiger conspiracy of last December. Therefore, the Constitutional Commission, as presently instituted by the Ian Smith regime, cannot be divorced from the imperialist tactics of the British Government.

Police State

In measures to oppress and suppress the undaunted uprising of the African people, the regime is taking upon itself powers to make Rhodesia a permanent police state. The Law and Order Maintenance Act, through which brave sons of Zimbabwe have been massacred, imprisoned, lined up in death-cells and thrown into detention camps all over the country, is an Act familiar to this Committee. The regime is now adding to these brutal powers what it calls a Preventive Detention Amendment Bill. Under this measure, the regime can detain any number of people for any allegation imagined by a policeman and for any length of time, without the regime having to declare a State of Emergency or report to Parliament.

Education
The regime is, further, whittling African education at a brutal pace. The expenditure on African education is now pegged to two per cent of the gross national product. African teachers are being dismissed in hundreds. This throws thousands of African children into the streets and thrusts work on the remaining teachers to about three classes for each teacher. There is a restriction on the development of any new schools for the Africans and missionary bodies are being deprived of several schools that they have been running. It should be noted here that more than 75% of the schooling for the African people has long been undertaken by missionaries, at their own initiative and at considerable cost to themselves. It is this development that the regime is taking measures to stifle. The intention of the regime is, clearly, to increase suffering among the African people, and widen the pliable cheap labour reservoir.

The African people are being displaced from types of employment which are graded for the white workers. This is a measure to get every white person in the country employed, eliminate discontent among them, pass it over to the Africans who are then met by measures of force for suppression.

The most significant political development undertaken by the regime is the open introduction of apartheid. The mask of multi-racialism used by the British Government for many years, has been removed and the regime has declared the provision of direct separate facilities for various tribal and ethnic groups in the country. This is a direct copy of the Group Areas Act and the Bantu Authorities Act of South Africa. Under the scheme of the Rhodesia regime, Africans settled in towns will be provided for, in their housing, according to the areas of their original villages and their chiefs. Education is planned to be provided in accordance with the language and cultural habits of the tribal group. But the syllabus for education will be planned on the advice of industrialists in terms of the cheap labour they want. In the rural areas, further measures are being implemented to increase the punitive powers of the stooge chiefs. To give them a semblance of authority, a Local Authorities Act has been introduced to authorise chiefs to collect taxes from their people, out of which some little budget will be made available to the chiefs for implementation of certain of the regime's measures. These stooge chiefs are given the protection of the settler army and police. Through this, the chiefs are instructed to deport out of their areas anybody who disagrees with the regime and hand them over to the regime.

Military Expansion

The regime has continued to lay emphasis on expansion of its armed forces.
It spends a total of eleven million pounds (Sterling) towards this purpose,
which is an increase of five million pounds above its expenditure for the same
in 1965. It is in this field that international conspiracy in support of the
regime is very evident. West German, Turkish and Taiwan military experts of
various fields have been brought in to train the regime's armed forces in their
war preparations against the African masses of Zimbabwe. The Rhodesian
army is equipped largely with British arms, British spares for these arms pour
into Rhodesia.

Under the now familiar alliance between South Africa, Portugal and
Rhodesia, there is a clear interchange of security officers for various operations. Indeed, South African regular troops have been brought into Rhodesia
to reinforce the regime's offensive line along the Zambezi border. As recently
as March 19th to March 23rd this year, 525 South African soldiers entered
Rhodesia in civilian clothes and changed into Rhodesian military uniform at
Bulawayo before they were sent to points on the Rhodesian side of the
Zambia-Rhodesia border. Of these men, 225 under Colonel Dries Kotzenberg
are stationed near Chirundu, and the remainder, 300 men, are led by Daan
Pretorius in the Zambezi Valley. In addition to these, another five South
African army officers were seconded to the Rhodesian armed forces during
the first three weeks of April. They are Colonels J.A. du Plooy, H.F. van der
Spuy, T.M.C. Diederichs and Commanders M. Rupert and H.P. Brand. During
this same period, 317 South African recruits entered the Salisbury Police
Training Depot for para-military training for the Rhodesian fascist minority
dictatorship.

In considering measures to solve the Rhodesian problem, which is a threat
to international peace, the United Nations has been led by Britain along the
path of economic sanctions. These measures have been based on the assumption that Britain, as one of the great powers and a member of the United
Nations, would, finally, respect the UN resolutions and implement these
resolutions honestly. It has now been demonstrated beyond doubt that these
assumptions were wrong from the very start, and, therefore, the programme
of sanctions could never be a success. In fact, Britain and her allies piloted the
programme of sanctions as a decoy to the international forces away from the
target into the wilderness. Britain contrived this as a device to give herself
sufficient time to make a success of the UDI which is her creation. Britain
and her allies have deliberately piloted the idea of sanctions, with the full
knowledge that these will not only fail in themselves but would ensure
measures to foil them.

In the meanwhile, the economy of Rhodesia continues to flourish, without
the slightest sign of collapse and certainly without any possibility of bringing
about a political change. The Rhodesian regime has South Africa to back all
its international trade and South Africa is a base for British money and trade.

Besides, trade between Rhodesia and British firms has been going on.
The British commercial banks, Barclays, National and Grindlays, Standard
Bank and Ottoman, are continuing to operate in Rhodesia. Britain is permitting the entry of capital into Rhodesia under the cover of necessary items,
like the University of Rhodesia and other schemes.

Two weeks ago, the British-Dutch combine, Unilever, based in and controlled from London, authorised the expenditure of £135,000 (Sterling) for
extension work to its Rhodesian subsidiary. Sixty per cent of the ships carrying oil to the port of Lourenco Marques in Mozambique are British ships. The
British Petroleum Company (BP) supplies oil to Rhodesia and continuing its
business. It is clear, therefore, that the first defaulter in the programme of
sanctions is Britain herself. In short, she is piloting a programme of sanctions
at the United Nations and piloting measures of undermining these very
sanctions in Rhodesia itself.

Our conclusion is that, in fact, Britain introduced sanctions with the full
knowledge that they would not harm Rhodesia but would harm the economy
of Zambia. If we add to this the conspiracy of big international capitalistic
combines to prop the economy of Rhodesia, it becomes clear that Britain,
with all her allies, is set to foil any possible success of the sanctions against
Rhodesia for the simple reason that, after all, the economy of Rhodesia is
not so much that of the settlers as it is of these international financial
combines.

For example, the Standard Oil Company of New Jersey digs oil in the
Middle East, hands it over to the French Company, Total, which carries the
oil to Rhodesia through depots in Lourenco Marques, and Total passes the
oil to British Petroleum, Shell and Caltex for direct sale to Rhodesia. This
indicates a pattern for many companies dealing in various lines.

Foreign Capital

In fact, if the question were asked, 'who is sustaining the Rhodesian dictatorship by revenue?' the answer would be: such companies like Lonrho, Anglo-
American, Rio Tinto, Union Carbide Corporation, and so on; all of which are
British or American based companies. Since it is impossible for these companies to refrain from expanding the economy of Rhodesia or diversify it, it
is therefore impossible for the sanctions to have the required political effect.
The regime has on its own established agencies to handle the sale of its products to the international markets, some based in Rhodesia and others based
in Mozambique, Angola and South Africa. The Manica Trading Company, for
example, is connected with several shipping lines and sends out Rhodesian
goods. Sugar is sent out to Mozambique and there given a Portuguese label to
conceal the source and attempts are made to sell it even to African countries.
Perhaps the best indication of the strength of the Rhodesian economy, in
spite of the sanctions, is a loan of £7½ million it floated in April. The loan
was over-subscribed within minutes. It is clear that the programme of sanctions has neither a chance of being fully and effectively applied nor a chance
of bringing about a political change in Rhodesia, which was supposed to be

the original objective of sanctions. Since Rhodesia continues to be a threat to international peace, a change of strategy is now imperative on the part of the progressive nations that continue to be determined to support the objective of liquidating the racist dictatorship and establishing a popular African government in the interests of justice and peace in the area.

The Anglo-Rhodesian Proposal: A Betrayal of the African ANC

A press statement signed by Bishop Abel T. Muzorewa,
National Chairman of the African National Council
(Zimbabwe) and eight other members of the Executive,
released in Highfield (Zimbabwe), on 16 December 1971.

The Anglo-Rhodesian proposals for a settlement have been critically studied analysed and found to be a vicious and subtle device for the recognition of the UDI by the British government. These proposals are a constitutional 'rape' of Africans by both the Rhodesian and British Governments, which is tantamount to a sell out of African majority of this country to a perpetual oppression and domination by the privileged white minority. The simple fact that a racist Rhodesian Government has accepted them is a measuring stick pointing to their dangerousness for Africans.

The sensible African people of this country deplore and condemn the manner in which the British Government conducted the negotiations that resulted in the constitutional proposals now before the country. It is sad that the African leaders were excluded from talks until after Her Majesty's Government had reached an agreement with the Rhodesian Government.

We are convinced that the only reasons why the British Government consulted African opinion were to give respectability to an already concluded deal and deceive the world that the agreement was a result of negotiations with European and African leaders in Rhodesia. The proposals as contained in the White Paper do not reflect a single suggestion made by African leaders. Their views were completely ignored.

The $10 million 'development programme', 'employment opportunities' in public service and elsewhere, and the ending of discriminatory legislation all vaguely promised nakedly stand as mere appetizers and baits to induce Africans into accepting the settlement proposals now before us.

The African feelings and opinion so far assessed and voiced repeatedly have called for a united front composed of all African people of various sections, organizations, political parties (including the banned African Nationalist parties) of this country to take a concerted action in making a decision that can save us from pitfalls into which we may be blindly led.

As a result, responsibility and patriotism have challengingly compelled us to organize ourselves into a body that represents the voice and will of the silent African Majority throughout the country. This National Organization shall be called The African National Council (or ANC). It has a national executive of ten people and committee members that represents all regions, districts and areas of our country.

The ANC aims and objectives are:

1) To call our people to realize the essential power of unity now. And move on as one people for the sake of achieving our ultimate goal of freedom.

2) To explain, advise and expose the dangerous implications that would result if we accepted the Anglo-Rhodesian constitutional settlement proposals.

3) To raise funds for the promotion of the organization. It is a temporary body to execute the Task before us.

We apologize for the delay in presenting this. However, we feel it was necessary to study the proposals intelligently in consultation with political, legal and economics experts. We also needed time to assess informed African feeling and opinion.

We are happy to inform the public that the African feelings and opinion we purport to represent have been freely expressed, unlike the so-called African opinions which have been sought and expressed under pressure of blackmail, bribery with money and employment to vote in favour of the proposals. This experience compels us to distrust the 'Yes' which may be expressed by civil servants and conducted by civil servants.

Following the views we have advanced above and the details of our analysis of the proposals which we will release soon for the public's information, we are convinced beyond doubt that acceptance of these proposals by Africans would be betrayal of the Africans, dead, living and yet to be born. We cannot be vendors of our own heritage and rights. Therefore, the African's responsible answer should be an emphatic *'No'*.

A Challenge

I wish at this point to call upon all the African people — sons and daughters of the soil, at home and abroad, poor or rich, educated or uneducated, young and old to stop now quarrelling, bickering and division which continue to cripple our struggle for freedom. Remember, whether we are poor or rich, educated or non-educated, chiefs or not, civil servants or not, whether we dwell in the King's domain or not, we are all condemned as *Black People*. We must and it is a big million *must* be united and work for a common *good Independence*. It must be realized with grave concern that our enemies have thrived and continue to capitalize upon our disunity and apathy. We must not be like brothers who go out for hunting and on the way stop to fight for a beast safe and alive in the bush. We need to be purpose-centred rather than personality centred. This is a time to forget recognition, positions, credit and start to aim high. We must realize that we will fight a losing battle until we are united and form one active front of dedicated leaders and loyal followers.

I call upon the youth to be active, obedient, disciplined and continue to work for a common good, joining hands with the adults and our allies, the coloured, the Indians and white Liberals and Christians and *reject* these proposals with unqualified *'No'*.

Actual Power and the Shadow
ZAPU

> *Article appearing in* Zimbabwe Review *(Lusaka), I, 4, October-November 1969.*

The revolutionary struggle these days faces more problems than ever. Not least among these is the enemy's use of its extensive propaganda machinery to confuse the fundamental issues of the struggle. Learning from a series of defeats in Asia and a large part of Africa, the traditional colonisers are trying to perfect the skill of lying and diversion. This, of course refers to Britain, Portugal, South Africa and their allies.

We have the experience of Britain which, earlier on, using such spent forces as Welensky, Whitehead and those of their ilk, used to emphasise that what the African requires is good shelter and good food but not politics. The South African Boers indulge in the fantasy that the Africans there would like to live in separate areas according to lingual or tribal groups. Then comes Portugal's hallucination that the African countries she has imposed herself upon are part of Portugal: that is jumping the Sahara desert and crossing the Mediterranean to be physically annexed to that tiny foreign land.

These and many other foolish claims and statements often made by these colonisers rebounce and cause mental harm to the white followers of these regimes. These regimes do of course console themselves on the few collaborators — the assimilados in Portuguese territories, the constitutionalists in Rhodesia and the Bantustan participants in South Africa. This is indeed logical since the whole exercise of colonisation is adventurism and self-deception. What needs to be pinpointed thoroughly is, who the enemy is and how complex he is.

Very often, and also in this issue, we expose the economic combines of the western countries which silently but ruthlessly forge ahead with extraction of the country's resources at the expense of the natural owners, the Zimbabwe people. What must be emphasised is that these economic structures germinate on their native soils and, like grass-creepers, spread their arms in a wide range of countries and digging their roots deeply wherever soft ground can be found. They interlace and intertwine to an extent (like grass) that one can never be sure of their source, their direction and depth of their suction roots. Graphically this is the exploitation complex.

To take one simple and common example, the British Petroleum Company, BP Shell. In Rhodesia its section assumes a local name. It does the same in Indonesia and in a host of different countries. In reality it is one company from the drilling point in some Middle East well to the general and local distribution lines. The centre of control and convergence of profits is London. Today BP is merging with the United States colossal company, Standard Oil of New Jersey which is dominating in the United States and in South and North America. When these companies succeed to merge, they will be controlling a very large section of the international distribution of oil. We must not be misunderstood for expressing the folly that there is something wrong in the oil itself and in its distribution. There are three points we are bringing to the surface by this example. Firstly, the United States Government and the United Kingdom Government are powerless, for the purpose of protecting the smaller companies, to prevent the formation of this gigantic combine. They tuck themselves under the false cover of freedom of association when they are conscious of, but weak, against the injustice, the monopoly will bring about.

Secondly the monopoly puts out of business, almost forever, any possible independent initiative in the same field of enterprise by some other talented persons. Any initiative or talent which will emerge in this field must be a servant of these combines.

A few families, plus some number of shareholders accepted by these family directorates who, in most cases are a clique or class of already rich families. The workers, among whom are hundreds of Zimbabweans for the Rhodesian section, are so many thousands more than the shareholders and the owning directorate. The point here is that it is the workers' talent which goes into production whilst the owner comforts himself in management and coordination of that talent.

Thirdly, BP Shell can, with impunity, devise the modus vivendi of giving itself the local status irrespective of, in fact disregarding, any talk of sanctions by the British or any government. So that virtually these economic structures are governments in themselves and dictate the pace of events to their respective states.

The example of BP Shell and Standard Oil were but a few of the many and large monopolies in these countries which are the actual power behind their governments. They are the core-substance, as it were, and the governments mere shadows. Of course this does not mean these regimes are insignificant factors in themselves. They are aspects of the complex machinery whose weight of exploitation descends so heavily in Zimbabwe. These examples must not appear farfetched. They are very pertinent to the Zimbabwe situation in the real sense.

Here we might illustrate our point taking the example of the abortive sanctions against Rhodesia. The fact that they have always been piloted by the British Government gives better substance to the point. Have you ever asked yourself why Britain nervously hurries on to the method of listing out goods as objects of sanctions? Why does she speak of sanctions against oil, coal, chemicals and so on and not of sanctions against the companies which produce and distribute these goods? Sanctions against companies would immediately bring about confrontation between these imperialistic regimes and the companies which are their backbone. So that Britain's continued initiative on the sanctions programme is a fake; it is just a diversion from the actual issue or, rather, the actual culprits which are the industrial companies behind these regimes.

The logical question then is, if this state of affairs is not as should be, what is the better alternative? The precise answer to this should come through practical implementation as the results of the revolutionary struggle become certain. But nothing commends itself more to reason than the fact that just remuneration can only be assured by elimination of individual or class monopoly through permanent entrustment of ownership to all who share the sweat at production. The state is then neither an instrument nor at the mercy of some such mining director or directors of some such companies because basic power then lies with the people and their labour.

It is possible that one could misconstrue our views as a reformist plea for the survival of small companies as against big sharks like BP. On the contrary, we are destroying the very aspiration of an individual or company to grow to the extent of squeezing the whole nation and other nations out of just livelihood.

We started off by pointing out the skillful psychological devices which the coloniser has developed to survive under the impact of revolutionary change. This characteristic is evidence of the economic forces which put these regimes in power and determine their stay there. Much as it is difficult to isolate the different industrial companies, banks and other financial institutions of the western countries which intertwine and combine their finances to maintain the oppressing settler regime in Rhodesia, so it is difficult to isolate the different western countries, through their governments, which back Britain in maintaining the status quo of entrenching its settler regime in Rhodesia. The same goes for the military alliances which are the background for the intransigence of the Smith-Vorster-Caetano regimes in the unliberated territories of Africa.

This is the nature of the complex enemy we face. But complexity is neither synonymous nor identical with invincibleness. It is largely a revelation of the greater possibilities of contradictions in the system which is an unavoidable condition for total defeat in the long run. Putting the war of words aside, the African people of Zimbabwe are set on a course for the total destruction of the British colonial regime in Rhodesia whatever face it may assume.

On Rumours About My Plan to Escape

Agostinho Neto

> *From a letter sent on 21 March 1961 to friends when Neto was in forced residence on the island of Santa Antao (Cape Verde Islands) and released to the press by the CONCP in May 1961.*

The authorities have put out rumours that I am trying to escape by Russian submarines. At any time the police can kill me and announce that I have escaped. People who are in contact with me are advised to avoid me. Some of them have been threatened with imprisonment if they see me again. It looks that the police has engaged some agents to incite people against me so that a gang may be gathered to provoke and kill me. These and other activities around me make me fear that I may be killed by them at any time.

The Assassination of Humberto Delgado
PAIGC

Article in Libertacao *(PAIGC, Conakry), No. 53, April 1965. Translated from Portuguese.*

The world has just been surprised by the news of the assassination of General Humberto Delgado, one of the best known leaders of the Portuguese democratic opposition.

Everything leads one to believe that General Humberto Delgado, fallen in combat, has been a victim of the murdering fury of PIDE agents.

The Portuguese democrats have always recognized in General Delgado total patriotism and courage, and a complete devotion to the cause of the struggle against Fascism in Portugal. The Portuguese people, which does not forget the arduous fight of 1958 when General Delgado defended with courage his aspirations to freedom and democracy, as a candidate of the opposition to the Presidency of the Republic, rebels indignantly against still one more of Salazar's repulsive crimes.

General Delgado, by condemning colonialism and recognizing the justice of our struggle, has also won the respect and sympathy of our peoples.

By assassinating one of the most intrepid sons of the Portuguese people, Salazar and his agents have just committed a monstrous crime against their own people. But the assassination of General Delgado, like that of thousands of patriots and democrats who have long been fallen victims of the Fascist repression, merely helps to reinforce the hatred which the Portuguese people direct against the regime of Salazar. And it serves as an incitement for the struggle against oppression and exploitation, in order to initiate an era of Freedom, Peace and Progress for every Portuguese.

The Danger of Destruction From Within

From a message sent in March 1972 by Amilcar Cabral, the Secretary-General of the PAIGC, to all those holding posts of responsibility in the Party. Translated from French.

Driven to despair in face of the victorious advance of our struggle and the defeats which they suffer everyday in our country as well as on the African and international fronts; convinced of the difficulty if not of the impossibility of buying or of bribing the leaders by means of work *outside of the party*; frightened by the name and prestige which our party is increasingly acquiring in Africa and the rest of the world; realizing that their policy in Guinea will not bring success, since the population of the urban centres is more and more interested in the struggle and in the party — the Portuguese colonial criminals and their representatives in Guinea have decided to establish a new plan in order to attempt to stop our struggle and in order to ensure the continuation of our people's exploitation: *they now wish to destroy our party from within*. They are determined to do everything — to pay whatever price so that they may sow confusion and division within the leadership of the party, in order to weaken the unity of the party, to destroy the party from within.

What is the plan of the Portuguese colonial criminals and of their representatives in our country?

According to the information which I have received from various reliable sources, this is their plan:

1st stage: Profit from the fact that a large number of our compatriots are presently leaving Bissau and other urban centres in order to join the party, by introducing within us some of their reliable African agents, to whom Spinola promises honours and money, were they to succeed in their mission. These agents, who may be either new or old party members, are trained by the PIDE in the techniques of political sabotage, provocation and the instigation of confusion within an organization. *In the first stage these agents must:*

a) pretend that they are good militants, and be devoted to the struggle of our people against the Portuguese colonialists.

b) make a detailed reconnaissance of the life of the party, its problems, and mainly of the weaknesses of our organization, so that they may be fully exploited; inform the colonialists of the situation within the party.

c) detect who are the 'dissatisfied' militants, and principally who are the 'dissatisfied' leaders; establish bonds of friendship and comradeship with such 'dissatisfied' ones, and always support their point of view in what concerns the leadership of the party, particularly the Secretary-General.

d) take advantage of every occasion to sow confusion in the minds of the militants and leaders, to provoke, and remove authority from and disrespect the leadership of the party, in particular the Secretary-General. In order to do so, these agents must always uphold a position as 'defenders' of the militants' rights, incite them into disrespecting the leadership, and create the spirit of indiscipline and division within the Party.

e) sow misunderstanding within the Party, on the basis of racism and, if possible, on the basis of tribalism, even on religious differences, in an attempt to pit the Guineans against the Cape Verdians, the latter against the former, the tribes one against the other, the illiterate against the intellectuals, the Muslims against the non-Muslims and vice-versa — all this in order to destroy the unity of our party and the unity of our people, which are the main strength of our struggle.

2nd stage: After having created confusion and division within the Party and obtaining the support of the 'malcontents', after being certain that a certain number of militants and leaders would be willing to betray the leadership of the Party, the Secretary-General in particular, these agents would:

a) create an underground network of militants and leaders in every sector of our life and struggle, notably among the armed forces. To do this they would have to contact the leaders the militants, and the fighters who, for whatever reason may be 'dissatisfied' with the leadership of the Party. These contacts would have as their aim sabotaging the action of the real leaders who are loyal to the Party, and subsequently creating confusion and division all over.

b) create a 'leadership' parallel to the real leadership of the Party, composed of one or more agents and several 'dissatisfied' leaders. The agents would do everything in their power in order to make some of the present leaders of the Party participate in this underground sabotage group, in particular those who, on the basis of the errors which they have committed and the criticisms of which they were the object, are not 'happy' with the leadership of the Party, in particular that of the Secretary-General.

c) This underground 'leadership' of sabotage and destruction of the Party would then contact the parties and the governments of the neighbouring countries, notably that of the Republic of Guinea, in order to obtain their support against the real leadership of the Party, particularly against the Secretary-General. They would also, as far as possible, contact some ambassadors of friendly countries, in an attempt to create confusion, to show that there is 'division' within the party and to obtain the support of such countries.

d) At the same time as they are engaged in this work of internal destruction of the party and of its external support, the agents and their accomplices would do everything in their power to provoke and bring into discredit the Secretary-General of the Party, to sabotage his authority and prestige, to prepare the way for the elimination of the Secretary-General from the executive of the party, or even if necessary, his physical destruction. On the other hand, the agents and their colleagues would conduct a major propaganda campaign to popularize among the militants and fighters the names of other leaders (former and current), which they would present as being the sole and true leaders of the party, against the leadership of the Secretary-General.

e) In this second stage, in agreement with prepared plans, the colonialists and their allies will engage in a large campaign at the African and international levels about the 'divisions' within the party in order to discredit the present executive and in particular the Secretary-General. Within the country, the colonial troops, would launch major offensives in order to terrorize and discourage the populations and the combatants.

3rd stage: If the colonialists' agents who penetrated our ranks were not to be discovered and exposed in time, and if they would succeed in accomplishing their mission, above all if they were to obtain the cooperation of

some of our most important party leaders as well as the support of the neighbouring countries, particularly the Republic of Guinea, then there would
begin the third stage during which they would:

a) strike a blow against the present party executive, in order to eliminate
the Secretary-General and all the leaders loyal to the line of our party, to the
unity and struggle of our people in Guinea and in the Cape Verde Islands
against the Portuguese colonialists, for the total independence of our African
country. If they are not able to accomplish this, they will try to assassinate
the Secretary-General as well as some other leaders.

b) form a new party executive based on racism and on tribalism and
religious beliefs if necessary, in order to ensure the division of our people
and its demobilization and capitulation to the colonialists. They would
change the name of our Party.

c) stop all the activities of the struggle both inside our country and
abroad, notably in the Republic of Guinea; take possession of all the goods
of the party, with the support of the traitors, in order to paralyse all the
activities of the struggle and to prevent resupplying the armed forces; arrest
and destroy all members loyal to the party.

d) contact the Portuguese Government, with Spinola as the intermediary,
for the purpose of false 'negotiations', with the aim of obtaining the 'internal
autonomy' of Guinea (Bissau), for a so-called 'self-determination under the
Portuguese flag'. The creation of a puppet 'government' of Guinea, which
would from then on be called 'State of Guinea' and which would belong to
the 'Portuguese Community'.

e) In line with the promises and plans of Spinola and the Portuguese
colonialists, important posts in the political scene and within the armed
forces would be assigned to all those agents who would accomplish this
mission, as well as to all the leaders of the party who would be their accomplices and who would help carry out the plans. Moreover, they would all be
well remunerated for their betrayal of our great party.

Caetano: More Attuned to History?

Amilcar Cabral

> *From a declaration made in Dakar (Senegal) by the Secretary-
> General of the PAIGC, on the occasion of turning over to the
> International Red Cross three Portuguese prisoners on 19 Dec-
> ember 1968. Translated from French.*

Although the political death of the Portuguese dictator has not created illusions in us, because our people and our militants are aware of the fact that
we fight against Portuguese colonialism, which we have never confounded
with the politics of a man, it is nevertheless true that certain political changes

may become possible in internal Portuguese politics, particularly in regard to the style of government and repression. In the long run, these changes might become more significant, as a consequence both of the increasing pressure of new phenomena which have taken place and will continue to do so in the life of Portuguese politics, conditioned and traumatized as it is by a colonial war, and of the need for the progressive affirmation of the personality of the new Prime Minister. From this perspective, some claim that Mr. Marcello Caetano, younger than his predecessor, and more sensitive to the historical realities of our times, will be able to understand the irreversible character of our national liberation struggle and the inevitability of our African peoples' access to national independence, the only possible conclusion of the war which Portuguese colonialism has forced upon us.

Last November 27, in the speech read to the Portuguese National Assembly, the new Prime Minister was able to give a peculiar emphasis to the desperate situation of the war in our country. In so doing, he not only gave indirect homage to our people and our party, whose prestige is a reality on an international scale, but he also showed that he had an acute knowledge of reality. The fact that he resorted to Salazar's jargon, to a certain patriotic demagogy as well as to the dramatized evocation of the scarecrow of 'Communist subversion', does not significantly limit the scope of the speech, and could be explained by the imperious necessity of appeasing the *ultras* and of moderating the action of those Portuguese who, from all strata of society, notably from the students and the youth, have dared to manifest their hostility towards the colonial war. Although proclaiming his decision of maintaining our people under the colonial yoke 'at whatever price', the leader of the Portuguese Government is well aware of the fact that, besides the enormous and irremediable losses in Portuguese lives and supplies, at the worst our people may sweep from the soil of our country any kind of Portuguese presence, too stained by the crimes of the colonial war and the attempts at genocide of our populations. It would be better to be realistic, to face up to the *vultures* of the colonial war courageously, and to obey the demands of history: to negotiate with our party for the accession to independence of our people, who are already in control of over two-thirds of the national territory, and thus preserve the possibility of useful cooperation between our countries.

The Methods of the Portuguese
Iko Carreira

Response of Iko Carreira of the MPLA to interview questions of Aquino de Braganca, published in AfricAsia, 25 April 1971. Translated from French.

Braganca: What did the Portuguese do to try to recuperate the lost territory?

What were their objectives at the time?

Carreira: They tried different methods, one by one. Starting from scorched earth to the systematic use of fragmentation bombs and napalm, they went on to resettlement of the population in 'strategic hamlets', then to the policy of psycho-social recuperation by the corruption of autochthonous elements. Lately, they have made criminal and massive use of defoliants and have destroyed the harvests. Thus thousands of peasants were forced to abandon their *kimbos* (villages) in order to find refuge in neighbouring Zambia or in the savanna of the Centre-South of Angola which became, to a certain extent, a disadvantage to the occupier since these peasants served as a vehicle for 'national subversion' within more inhabited areas.

The aim of the Portuguese army was strategic, of course: to destroy the harvest and the vegetation in the areas controlled by the MPLA in order to bring the autochthonous population under its 'protection'.

But such an action remains a genocide, nonetheless. A committee of doctors from our Medical Assistance Service (SAM) led by Dr. Eduardo Santos noted the consequences of the utilization of these toxic products on the populations of the Moxico area, bordering Zambia, populations which consume fish taken from the waters polluted by the defoliants.

These doctors fear the appearance of congenital anomalies in the newborn, as we have witnessed in Vietnam after the usage of the same kind of defoliants.

We are considering inviting experts to visit the contaminated areas, so that they may lay the crime of genocide before everyone, a crime for which we in Angola hold the Portuguese responsible.

Braganca: Are these reforms (the projection of limited autonomy for overseas provinces) not going to reinforce the 'white power' of South Africa?

Carreira: These constitutional modifications will only reinforce the power of the colonists who hold, at a local level, the levers of economic control. Furthermore, they would not constitute a response to the legitimate aspirations of the Angolan people, and to their right to national independence.

In addition, although stressing these 'autonomistic' fancies, the Portuguese government orders the tribunal to judge the MPLA militants on the grounds of 'subversive activities'. A case of ten Angolan nationalists, among them the honorary president of our movement, Rev. Fr. J. Pinto de Andrade, has begun in Lisbon on February 11. Other nationalists recently arrested in Angola are serving a sentence without judgement, in the dungeon of Tarrafal.

On the other hand, the Portuguese government strengthens its alliances, particularly with the NATO countries and with South Africa.

In connivance with South Africa, Portuguese commandos sabotage and constantly threaten the territorial integrity of the Republic of Zambia.

We are dealing, in fact, with a global plan of destruction of the African national liberation movements, as has been displayed by the simultaneous attack against Guinea and the PAIGC.

But in order to clearly understand the generality of the imperialist plan for the destruction of the national liberation movements, it is necessary to stress the role played by South Africa. It is a very insidious role.

The upholders of apartheid, partners in this vast continental conspiracy, are naturally taking the lead in the establishment of a regional structure for southern Africa. South Africa, having at its disposal an enormous economic, military and energetic potential, meets all the required conditions to act, with respect to the neighbouring countries, as an imperialist 'metropole'. The expansionistic need of its regime stems from a political and economic evidence: it needs, on the one hand, to dismantle the opposition to apartheid and to create external markets large enough to sustain its industrial development, and on the other hand (a South African author has openly proclaimed it) 'the Republic of South Africa dominates the Third World as much, if not more, than the United States dominates the American continent'.

Along with the export of apartheid, the South African regime has for some time obtained the 'understanding' of certain African countries, known as the 'moderates', who are already signing cooperation agreements, or who, as a first step, are advocating dialogue. Such a position is meant to break the unity of the African forces against apartheid, and thus, it aims at weakening the resistance of the liberation movements of the whole southern Africa area. Such is the challenge represented by 'Portuguese power'.

The Use of Material and Moral Corruption
Agostinho Neto

From an interview given by Agostinho Neto, President of the MPLA to FRELIMO, and published in their journal A Voz da Revolucao, *No. 6, November-December 1971.*

Vis-a-vis the masses of the population, the enemy has utilized in Angola exactly the same tactics and has the same strategic objectives as in Mozambique. Recently he has intensified in Angola the attempts to corrupt the population, offering better living conditions, giving them high posts in the public administration, encouraging among our population the belief that sooner or later Portugal must leave Angola and that she will be autonomous. We all know the significance of the law that Marcelo Caetano claims has altered the Portuguese Constitution in the direction of greater autonomy for the colonies. The enemy is using moral and material corruption.

Another method used by them is extremely violent repression. But we should note a difference today from the early days of the war. In the beginning the Portuguese destroyed, massacred, practised an indiscriminate policy of scorched earth. Now they first make use of what they can. For example, they are attacked near a village. They do not immediately destroy this village. First they take some persons prisoner, place others in strategic hamlets, and only later act, and then with great violence, engaging in barbarities, killing those who show themselves to be firm patriots and who do not yield to the methods of corruption used upon them.

The Enemy Have Changed Their Tactics
Agostinho Neto

From the address of the head of the MPLA delegation to a meeting of the MPLA and the FNLA in Kinshasa (Zaire) on 28 February 1973. The object of the meeting was to implement the unity accord of the two organizations arrived at on 13 December 1972.

The enemy have changed their tactics. In order better to achieve their strategy of exploitation, which derives from their very essence, the enemy, who have been brought to bay by the growing vigour of popular resistance, are trying at all costs to find a political way out, having shown themselves to be incapable of finding a military way out. Negotiation is the enemy's present tactical objective. But the negotiations they are so desperately seeking would be with corrupt individuals, and not with a united, organised and armed people. Setting Angolan against Angolan is the key to their new strategy.

In the press, on the radio, in public speeches and in new laws, Portuguese reformism is aiming increasingly at 'autonomy and independence' which would merely be a perpetuation of the system of exploitation and oppression in force in Angola for almost five hundred years.

Leading articles, reports, interviews and polemical debates in the newspapers, and political commentaries, directives and even forced statements on the radio are no longer filled with insults, contempt or arrogant confidence in their alleged military supremacy. The tone has now softened. They are seeking to seduce, to divide people with half-promises, so as to win them over to their neo-colonial policy. The days of the 'old settler' have gone. The present policy is an open door policy to non-Portuguese investments, and pseudo-Africanisation, rural reorganisation (*reordenamento rural*), European settlement and so-called social advancement.

Deputies to the Portuguese National Assembly, government ministers and the colonial authorities openly acknowledge the failure of the traditional policy in public speeches, and give the broad lines of the new policy. And the traditional system of laws has finally been adjusted to sanctify this new line. The constitution itself has been changed, a new organic law promulgated and a new 'politico-administrative statute' introduced.

And the colonialist enemy's change of tactics comes within the framework of the general change of tactics of the imperialist enemy. The present period is one of a massive influx of imperialist capital into Angola. In the mining industry alone, many international companies have embarked upon the exploitation of our sub-soil resources in recent years: Bermann and Krupp (West Germany), and United Steel (USA) for iron; Gulf Oil, Texaco, Mobil (USA), Total (France), Petrofina (Belgium), Bonuskor, General Mining and Tesh Investments (Republic of South Africa) for oil; Diversa & Oestedian (controlled by Diamond Distributors, USA), Diamang (International), Anglo-American Corporation, Diamul (South Africa), and Anchor Diamond Corporation for diamonds; Tenneco and Venneco Corporation (USA), Johannesburg Corporation (South Africa) for sulphur; Nippon Mining (Japan) for copper; Urangesellschaft (Federal Germany) for uranium; International Mineral and Chemical Corporation (USA) for phosphates. And there were further big investments in 1972. The Ranger Oil Company of Wyoming (USA) requested authorisation to prospect for oil, the Great Lakes Carbon Corporation (USA) requested authorisation to prospect for copper, the Companhia Mineira do Lobito doubled its capital by merging it with Japanese capital, the Consolidated Investment Company Ltd. (South Africa) requested prospecting rights for all the minerals in southern Angola apart from diamonds and oil, and a Japanese group was granted a licence to extract and treat 65 million tons of iron in Kassala-Kitungo.

There is the same unbridled rush to exploit in other sectors. There is South African capital in fisheries and manufactures, and capital from many sources in the beverage, cement, canning and shipbuilding industries. And more and more banks are being established in Angola. The interpenetration of colonial and imperialist capital is becoming increasingly complex. Foreign capital in Portugal and the colonies rose from 1,708 million escudos (more than 60 million dollars) in 1969 to 2,267 million escudos (more than 80 million dollars) in 1971, and according to a Bank of Portugal report, foreign investments in Portugal alone doubled during that period.

Angola is becoming a necessary factor in imperialism's economic and political strategy. The territorial extension of the Atlantic Pact to the Southern Africa region is under study in NATO, and they are thinking of establishing naval bases in Angola. The Republic of South Africa, in collusion with Portugal and Brazil, is plotting the establishment of a South Atlantic Pact with Angola as one of the axes.

But imperialist exploitation and oppression in Angola are no longer guaranteed by the permanence of the Portuguese colonial system. Hence the new trend of imperialist votes in the UN, sanctioning 'autonomy and independence' for Angola. Hence the direct or indirect attempts to seek a new type of relations with Angolan nationalist movements. The phase of the open blockade of patriotic movements has already passed. The phase of no direct imperialist pressure on Portuguese colonialism has already passed. Circumstances demand that the neo-colonial manoeuvre in Angola be carried out jointly by Portugal and the imperialist countries which dominate it.

It really is a new situation that we are having to face, and the danger is that much greater in that this change of tactics is definitely having its repercussions within the Angolan Nation. While it is true, on the one hand, that this change has the advantage of consolidating the idea and the hope of national independence in people's minds, it is no less true that it has also given rise to an opportunist attitude towards the neo-colonial manoeuvre in certain sectors of the population. Unlike what existed in the past, today there is a social base, although small, for puppet autonomy and independence in Angola. Only an objective nalaysis of the situation and a serious and patriotic search for popular methods of struggle can successfully avert the threat represented by the enemy offensive now underway.

Caetano's Reforms Sink in a Sea of Contradictions
FRELIMO

Article in Mozambique Revolution *(FRELIMO, Dar es Salaam), 53, October/December 1972.*

When Marcelo Caetano took over from Salazar as Prime Minister of Portugal, there was widespread speculation that 'liberalisation' in the areas of colonial policies, internal economic policies, and the role of opposition would occur. At the same time, it was unclear what the power base inside Portugal for such reforms would be — given the strong role of the ultra-right in the state, corporate, and church machinery — and what the motivation behind such 'reforms' was. Caetano had moved into the top position at a time, when after 40 years of Salazar, some kind of change had to occur. The colonial wars in Angola, Mozambique and Guinea were becoming more and more difficult to finance within the rigid and deteriorating economic structures which characterised the latter years of the Salazar dictatorship. This led to increased economic hardship inside Portugal and spurred opposition to overall government policies. Also, in the international sphere it was important for the Portuguese to gain political and military support from abroad for the colonial wars, and to attract foreign capital into the Portuguese and colonial economies. To be successful in all arenas, Portugal needed an image of 'change'.

But this was certainly not going to mean a change which altered the power relationship within Portugal or in regard to the colonies. The changes that followed were essentially the verbiage of pacification, to consolidate a slightly more expanded power base. Simultaneous with these 'reform' measures, internal opposition and subsequent repression in the Salazarist manner have continued. The political ideology and goals of Caetano and Salazar have been the same. Yet, the methods that Caetano initially attempted to maintain control were more attuned to the internal and external demands of the twentieth century.

However, in viewing the past few years, this strategy has not worked. Caetano has turned in retreat. The inevitable hollowness of his reforms have become obvious to the opposition, and pressures from the right have demanded a continued hard line in order to preserve fascism.

Portugal under Salazar

Portugal was much the same when Salazar died, as when he took power 40 years earlier, except for an increased consciousness and awareness in the colonies and at home of a people that saw a world changing around them that did not include Portugal. Salazar's prime preoccupation throughout his reign was the establishment and maintenance of order and the strengthening of Portugal's finances. Colonial policies were never questioned, and when wars broke out in the early sixties the logical response was the deployment of more and more military force. Gold and foreign reserves may have accumulated, but the economy stagnated trapping the majority of the people into near subsistence existence. A feudal agricultural model, an all powerful church that was a vital part of state machinery, leaderless urban workers strait-jacketed into state controlled unions, and a population that was 40 per cent illiterate all worked together to ensure the maintenance of control by the Salazarist elite. A long history of political repression as the response to any form of political opposition, dealt with any forces that questioned the fascist power structure.

However, because these political and economic structures were clearly not moving, new forces developed towards the end of his rule which emphasised the necessity for some kind of change after his death. The economic standstill, which reduced Portugal to the poorest country in Europe, forced large numbers of workers to emigrate due to the lack of jobs. This eventually created labour shortages, and increased the opposition from those workers who did return. The forced conscription of all men between the ages of 18 and 45, and the drain that the wars had on the economy, led to more frequent questioning of colonial policies and increased support for the liberation movements.

This was the situation when Caetano moved in. Some kind of change was apparent. But the important point about the changes which have occurred is that they have been designed to preserve the status quo. Caetano was the right hand man of Salazar for many years, and had played a vital role in the drafting of the 1933 Constitution which established the fascist 'unitary and corporate republic'. They had their differences, but these were mainly on the tactics and methods of maintaining and sustaining the fascist, corporate state. They were in agreement on ideology. For, in fact, it is Caetano's adherence to this ideology, which in an historical context must be viewed as 'Salazarism', that encouraged modification in tactics in order to ensure the continuance of unitary, state power.

Continuity with Reform — No Liberalisation

Caetano's sensitivity to internal and external pressures, and awareness of more sophisticated tactics can be seen on many levels. First, there are the concrete changes to attack the problems of the economy, to neutralise growing discontent among the politically unorganised social groups, and to divert and stifle opposition to colonial policies. Working with this is the psychological aspect, which attempts to sell to the Portuguese people, as well as to the outside world, that there are, and most important, that there will be 'changes'. Yet as he himself refers to it, it is not liberalisation, but 'renovation'.

The machinery of the state must be remoulded to fit the pressures of the times. But the fascist state will continue to exist. The allocation of power will not change, and the basic contradictions and conflicts within Portugal will still remain. For these cannot be resolved within the context of small modifications in the fascist state. If we examine the first three years of Caetano's rule, we can see the nature of this renovation, the political strategy behind it, and the growing consciousness within Portugal of the vacuous nature of this so-called change.

'Liberal' Reform

From the time that Caetano took office, he tried to avoid strong identification with the previous regime. He barely mentioned Salazar's name, though he was alive for another two years. In his first speech as Prime Minister, his adherence to doctrine while maintaining a flexible strategy became clear, as he emphasised that 'fidelity to a doctrine is not obstinate attachment to formulas and solutions'. Yet in all that was to follow, Caetano also had to be continually aware of the strength of the old guard ultra-rightists (particularly in the army), who were carefully watching his response to colonial policies and opposition, to make sure that his moves did not threaten political order and the existing consolidation of power.

The old guard was hesitant of anything that appeared to be even the smallest change. Caetano had the task of pointing out through the success of his strategies or the reliance on repression, that he was in control. The right had to be shown that his petty reforms did not mean any change in ideology while other social forces were sold the same reforms as the beginning of real change within Portugal. In all practical reforms, the most important aspect is the appearance of change as a mechanism of political manipulation and pacification. To this end, Caetano used the press to a much greater extent than Salazar, and claimed during his first few months of office that a new press law was to be introduced. Widely publicised small changes did occur at first, but were instituted and used in order to consolidate support for Caetano. For example, in the election this so-called increased freedom of the press meant controlling information on the opposition to point out its disorganisation and to show that their demands were similar to what Caetano 'said' he wanted. Any efforts to discuss meaningful freedom of the press were dismissed by familiar arguments that Portugal was not ready for this because a prerequisite was 'proper education of both the press and the public', which of course was difficult in a wartime situation. Accordingly, the new Press Law put into effect on the 1st June, 1972, limits the freedom of the press even more than before. The consistent contradiction referred to above appears clearly in the new Law. Thus, Art. 128 abolishes the Censorship Services, but Art. 129 imposes 'Previous examination for all texts and images to be published in the press'. The reaction to this law in Portugal can be seen by a decision taken by the National Trade Union of Journalists, which in its General Assembly, resolved to 'express to the Government their deep dissatisfaction for the new Press Law, which increases their burden of responsibility without giving them a concurrent right of freedom of expression'.

All his practical reforms, from the start were aimed at alleviating opposition from the various social forces within and outside of Portugal. He immediately issued statements which claimed that economic development and social reforms were priorities. One of his first moves on this front was to move younger professionals who were untainted by office under Salazar, into the ministries in the restless areas of education, social welfare, and the economy. This he hoped would integrate some of the younger, educated and potentially discontent elements into the established order. It would also hopefully, develop more effective internal economic and social policies which could pacify the urban workers and the rural peasantry with slight increase in wages and minimal changes in educational, health and social services. Of course, in the two most important ministries, the interior and the army, two hardliners were kept on, indicating what the fundamental source of power is.

In dealing with students, Caetano attacked the most glaring yet artificial grievances. In response to the realisation that large numbers of educated and skilled manpower would be needed to pull the country out of economic stagnation – and to neutralise student criticism – he announced an investigation into the efficiency of higher education. Caetano's experience in the University as professor and one-time rector, led him to believe that, if possible, it was better not to use crude methods of repression and imprisonment against student leaders, since this often led to more opposition, and turned imprisoned leaders into martyrs. Following this line, his new appointment as Minister of Education, Professor Jose Veiga Simao, cancelled criminal proceedings against some student leaders and sacked the unpopular rector of Coimbra University. Such small concessions he felt would have no effect on the security and stability of the coming change within Portugal. It would also give the state justifiable grounds for interference if the students moved too far into the opposition camp.

The students, however, proved less easy to control than he had imagined. In April and May, 1969, there were large demonstrations against the suspension of some student leaders, culminating in a strike and on May 6th, the University was closed down. Many students were arrested and the following month the cabinet announced that only students with good behaviour would be deferred from military service. In July the students boycotted their exams, and in August the president of the Coimbra students union was brought for trial. The trial was later adjourned, but the following month the elected leaders of the student union were dismissed on orders of the government – so much for their new right to elect their own leaders. The removal of petty grievances within the context of the fascist state, inevitably cannot neutralize opposition – except on the surface and in the short run. For as Caetano assured the ultra-rightists, and as opposition forces such as segments of the students, were quick to realise, the minimal changes in form did not reflect any fundamental change in the political and economic structures.

Caetano's approach to workers organisations was similar. Free elections of leaders in the state controlled workers' syndicates and a national minimum wage were instituted in an effort to combat the growing discontent. Workers outside the syndicates (particularly agricultural workers) were to be organized into syndicates and subject to government protection. This could be sold as increased workers participation, while allowing the state to control the form of organisation that was created. Voting rights were extended when qualifications changed from tax-based criteria to literacy. But since 40 per cent of the population was illiterate, you were still locking out the most oppressed classes. Again these measures were equivalent to the removal of petty grievances at no cost to the control or influence of the state, since the existing unions and the right to vote have very little to do with the allocation of power in the Caetano dictatorship. Their only function is to give the minimal appearance of worker and voter participation.

The abolition of PIDE, the secret police, was another widely publicised reform which helped to confuse people into thinking that 'liberalisation' was taking place. But it was immediately replaced by an identical institution, the DGS. Caetano admits that Portugal cannot be governed without a powerful, all-pervading secret police. There must be such control, in the view of the state, because if the people suddenly had freedoms, 'only chaos would ensue'. But most important, powerful subversive forces threaten the country from within. But abolishing PIDE, the well known secret police, and replacing it with a similar force more directly responsible to himself, Caetano can more easily contain internal opposition. Also, being more closely controlled, the secret police will be less likely to fall under outside influence, from groups like the American CIA, a fear of such rightists. The new DGS is under the Interior Ministry, one of those still dominated by Salazarist hardliners — further indication that no substantive change in policy was intended.

These 'renovations' of the fascist state in the area of moderate practical reforms certainly do not get at any of the basic problems in Portugal: the continuation of the colonial wars and the state of the economy. They could not because, in fact, the problems are the fascist state. The 'renovations' are merely designed to pacify and neutralise various social groups within Portugal; and together with minor changes in the economic structure, to expand the Caetano power base in order to ensure the continued existence of state machinery and ideology.

The Economy

Another aspect of the Prime Minister's renovation attempt has been an attack on the inefficient monopolies of Portuguese industrialists, and the simultaneous encouragement of foreign investment to try to pull Portugal out of its economic lag. Restrictive industrial licensing codes, custom duties, terms of credit, and tax and merger incentives were all revamped. Special funds have been allocated for tourist and agricultural investment, and drastic reforms in the notoriously inefficient and cumbersome Portuguese bureaucracy were promised. All have been viewed as incentives to Portuguese as well as foreign investors.

Caetano's Secretaries of State for Industry have been particularly active in encouraging foreign investments. Important selling points in this campaign have been the ease of transferring profits and the repatriation of capital. An industrial promotion institute specifically designed to encourage an increase of foreign capital penetration in Portugal and the colonies has been set up to facilitate this effort. The Industry's Secretaries have been on several trips abroad to solicit foreign capital, emphasizing that 'liberal renovation' has gotten rid of some of the more distasteful elements of Salazarism. This image building abroad is particularly important since foreign capital would rather be linked to a semblance of change than overt reactionary fascism. But even if there is an upsurge of foreign capital into Portugal and the colonies, it serves primarily to consolidate political power and increase economic profitability for the ruling elite within Portugal and foreign interests more closely tied to the maintenance of fascist rule.

Another serious problem in the economic arena is emigration, induced by the political and economic situation. This has created serious labour shortages, particularly in agriculture, that has led to a subsequent rise in food prices. There are now about a million emigrant workers living outside Portugal, and they are leaving at a rate of about 170,000 a year. These workers generally have above average skills and education, which are greatly needed within Portugal. The wage reforms instituted in the first few years under Caetano, were in large part directed at encouraging this group to remain or return to Portugal.

The economic situation is full of contradictions, and is unresolvable within the context of the fascist, corporate state. All the weaknesses are so intertwined that to alleviate one, merely exacerbates another. On the one hand the economy is stagnant and to get it moving an increase in the labour force is necessary. But, there is an intense labour shortage due to the massive emigrations to Europe and the colonies over the past decade. In turn, the stagnating economy and the labour shortage obviously hurt the Portuguese war efforts in the colonies. However, on the other hand, emigration is also beneficial to Portugal. Settlers are needed in the colonies to aid in maintaining Portuguese control, and Portuguese workers outside the country sending money back have given Portugal its largest source of foreign exchange. So, despite the fact that criminal charges against those illegally emigrating have been loosened, if too many returned it would cut into the valuable foreign exchange that they feed into the lagging economy.

Caetano hopes to avoid the issues raised by these conflicts by importing cheap labour from the colonies. It has been estimated that 15,000 Africans have arrived in Lisbon in the last few months, two-thirds of them from the Cape Verde Islands. But he is locked in. Again, Caetano can try to make petty reforms in the economy, but given the political and economic structures, and the continuation of the colonial wars, these small changes can barely even stabilise the situation.

Foreign Policy

Changes in Foreign Policy have been a response to the growing need to increase support for the colonial wars and to draw more foreign capital into Portugal and the colonies. The new Foreign Minister, Rui Patricio, made it clear at his first press conference in July 1970, that an important aspect of foreign policy making would be the development of a positive national image.

A solid relationship with NATO allies is considered critical by the government as seen in the great importance Portugal gave to the NATO ministerial meeting in July 1971 in Lisbon. But Caetano's strategy within NATO has changed in order to alleviate charges of the misuse of NATO supplied weapons in the war, and to temper the criticisms of some of the NATO allies who oppose the wars. Caetano now lays great emphasis on the fact that Portugal is fighting the colonial wars in Africa without outside assistance, but fails to mention the continuing use of NATO equipment in Africa, a clear violation to NATO regulations. In relation to extending the areas NATO serves to include the South Atlantic, Portugal has carefully refrained from taking any public initiatives. But at the same time, Caetano pushes the strategic location of the colonies for NATO security.

The large scale foreign investment in the colonies that is now being encouraged, will also serve to push these countries to support the Portuguese war effort to protect their growing economic stake. But in order to make the idea of colonialism more palatable to these North American, Western European and Japanese interests, the Portuguese have made very minimal increases in the African wage scale, and slightly expanded the number of schools and hospitals. These token pacification measures, mostly only on paper, are sold under the rubric of 'economic and social development' to increase outside support for the war.

All these programmes and petty changes discussed so far have been aimed at neutralising opposition, pacifying discontent and expanding the power base of Marcelo Caetano. But they are complemented and enhanced by ongoing efforts, to 'split' established opposition groups and render them less effective. Forces which do not respond to the more co-optative method of repression then are confronted with crude force and secret police tactics.

In his first few years Caetano was more successful in his pacification techniques than he has been recently. Increased opposition from the left and heightened pressures by the right have reduced Caetano to the Salazarist tactic of blaming subversive elements for most of Portugal's problems. Then his use of secret police and heavy repression becomes justified.

Pacification and Propaganda

Caetano has pushed himself as a man who communicates easily with the people in hopes of undermining opposition and consolidating a power base, by creating the impression of 'consulting with the people'. He has instituted regular informal T.V. appearances where in simple terms he presses home the same points: the need for social improvements; the importance of defending the colonies, and the threat to Portugal's stability from inside and out. He has also travelled extensively within Portugal and to the three African colonies reinforcing this image. Bringing the question of the colonial wars out into the open for the first time, he hoped to rally support behind the banner of patriotism and duty.

Educated Opposition Groups

The election provided a good opportunity for Caetano to try out these policies. At first these strategies were quite successful, since the groups had little in common except their general opposition to the government, in particular 'Salazarism' and the fact that they had been suppressed. Caetano felt confident enough to permit the return from exile of the veteran opposition leader, Mario Soares, and he met with various opposition leaders to create the impression that he was open to dialogue. This was in part effective, and Soares even stated he would support Caetano in the event of a rightist military coup. Limited criticism in the form of calling for minimal social democratic reforms was allowed, in the early period, as long as there was no serious questioning of the colonial wars. In May 1969, the second Republican Congress was allowed to be held. The press attended, and a 14 point programme for liberal social reform was passed. Many of their proposals were the same measures that Caetano professed to be advocating, thus he could undercut the strength of part of the opposition. By allowing 'free elections', the government brought the rivalries and differences of the opposition groups into the open. But the parties were so harassed and restricted, they never stood a chance in challenging Caetano. That of course, was not the plan. The idea was to make it appear that there was increased freedom, and that the 'people' had decided whether or not to abandon the colonies. Yet, with rigid election controls and a voting population of 1.8 million, success of the governing party was assured. The election made it appear that Caetano was more secure than he had ever been before. He had discredited the opposition, and enhanced his 'liberal reputation' without challenging the political or economic structures. This aided in winning the support of the die-hard Salazarists, a group which had been watching very carefully. Although small, this is a powerful force which must be a part of Caetano's power base.

The maintenance of the colonies with no compromises is a first priority of the old guard, as are related domestic issues such as the necessity of police control. Their basic fears are that even minimal discussion will lead to more serious questioning of the war; that social improvements can only be implemented at the expense of revenue currently going into the war effort, and that growing interest in the European Common Market will adversely affect Portugal's relationship with the colonies. Their strength as a group was first seen by the slight delay in Caetano's appointment after Salazar became incapacitated. All army leaves were cancelled, and troops were recalled to the barracks. The possibility of an army coup existed at that time, but because Salazar hung on for two years, Caetano was given breathing space which allowed him to manoeuvre for stronger support.

Cabinet reshuffles and the replacement of hardliners increased fears of

Caetano's impingement on the old guard's power role. Caetano was forced to move cautiously in some areas. For example, though Nogueira, the Foreign Secretary, was bad for the country's external image, and a subversive force within the government in terms of undermining the new foreign policy, Caetano waited for him to resign rather than dismissing him.

Unorganized Opposition

Caetano tried to integrate opposition from both sides into his base of support. However, this has become increasingly difficult. When he must make a choice, obviously the preservation of the state machinery is primary. Since the strong old guard is more powerful and Caetano does not have basic disagreements with them on goals and ideology, as the internal situation has deteriorated he has moved in alliance with the old Salazar forces against the more 'liberal' social groups. This can be seen most clearly in Caetano's dealing with opposition forces that are not part of 'established' groups, but which comprise the majority of the masses of the Portuguese people.

Early in 1971, large demonstrations took place at the University in Lisbon demanding that Portugal pull out of the colonial wars. These were brutally broken up by the police, and the law faculty was closed down. Along with this, there were widespread arrests among students and members of the opposition. In a strongly worded statement the new secret police, the DGS, attributed the problems to 'communist agitators who stirred up the students against the wars, and wanted to whip up support for terrorist activities'. When asked in an interview about the numerous arrests Caetano replied that the police must act when they have information or suspicion of criminal activity. He indicated that a subversive network had been uncovered in Angola which had links with student groups in Portugal. At that time, about 600 people were known to have been arrested in Angola and about 10 in Portugal. Demonstrations against the trial led to the arrest of 8 of their leaders, and subsequent demonstrations ended with 300 riot police patrolling Coimbra University.

As it increasingly became clear that the social reforms spoken of in the early days of Caetano's rule were hollow, and the colonial wars continued to take its toll in Portugal, more and more people moved into this group of unorganised opposition. Increased repression, designed to silence this group, merely fanned the increasing consciousness.

Opposition to the colonial wars has also increased within liberal church circles. In August 1970, a former army chaplain was arrested after voicing opposition to the colonial wars. Two months before that, the secret police announced that a Catholic publishing group GEDOC had been suppressed because of their circulation of documents and literature against Portuguese colonial policies which violated state security and four people were brought to trial. The Bishop of Oporto has been another vocal critic of the regime. All these activities coming from within the church, coupled with the Pope's meeting with leaders of the liberation movements in the colonies, the withdrawal after 25 years missionary work in Mozambique, of the White Fathers, in condemnation of Portuguese atrocities against the population, and churches outside of Portugal giving overt support to the movements, have created difficulties for Caetano. Subversive priests given the religious traditions within Portugal, could quickly undo Caetano's propaganda efforts, as well as, challenge the charges that only communist forces are behind dissension in Portugal.

Another area of growing discontent and opposition is among labour and in the state controlled unions. There have been several strikes, and demands for wage increases which the acute labour shortage makes inevitable. As a response the Caetano government has dismissed several leaders of the state controlled unions, once they proved disfunctional as puppets of the state.

The emergence of militant underground opposition groups, the Armed Revolutionary Action (ARA), in August 1970 and more recently the Revolutionary Brigade, is of particular concern for Caetano and the rightist elements. The fact that they have been successful in carrying out a number of bombing attacks, and that their targets have been visibly associated with the colonial wars increases their significance and impact. They are also an indicator of what is to come, what is naturally developing out of the internal contradictions in the Portuguese political and economic structures. And their success serves as an example which will and can encourage the large numbers of discontented social groups to act, rather than passively accept.

What Does This Mean For Portugal?

All these developments have reinforced the old guard's accusations that Caetano cannot control the country through liberal 'renovations' and a stepped up propaganda effort. As the number of arrests increased, his liberal sounding statements of the early days are getting fewer and fewer. These are being replaced with warnings of subversion from within and without. The strongest to date has come from his Defence Minister in April 1971, who proclaimed

> In this war there is no front and rearguard. It is everywhere the adversary tries to implant his ideas of defeat, favouring the abandonment of the overseas territories, inciting the young people and soldiers to emigrate or desert from military service, undermining the morale of the youth . . . There is a vast international conspiracy with its headquarters in the UN, but which has numerous obedient followers under the communist command who orchestrate the propaganda against Portugal's overseas territories.

If we view this rhetoric together with increased police repression, a return to Salazarist tactics to maintain Salazarist ideology seems evident. The internal situation, manifested by the increased mobilisation of opposition forces on many different fronts can only be attempted to be controlled through heavy repression. And the focus on the threat of subversive elements is then used to justify this increased and open repression.

In response to questions on the recent changes in his regime, Caetano emphasised that it is necessary to distinguish between long term objectives and short term tactics. Caetano might like to still sell the early days of 'renovation' as his long term goal, but that is now impossible. Contradictions and a new consciousness within Portugal have created forces which are now beyond his control.

Mozambique in the Framework of Southern Africa
Jose Oscar Monteiro

> *From a talk given by J.O. Monteiro of FRELIMO to a collo-*
> *quium held in Berlin in May 1968 and co-sponsored by the*
> *German Committee for the Understanding of Africa, Asia*
> *and Latin America, and Karl-Marx University (Leipzig) and*
> *reproduced in* FRELIMO-Information *(Algiers), July 1968.*
> *Translated from French.*

The conjuncture in southern Africa, notably in respect to Mozambique, cannot be properly understood if one does not take into consideration those tight bonds which unite South Africa, Rhodesia and Mozambique on the economic, political and cultural levels — cultural being here used in the very general sense of the conceptions of life. A simple look upon the map will allow us to see that Rhodesia and the richest areas of South Africa, to wit, Transvaal province where the Rand minerals are located, do not have a proper outlet to the sea: the most economic route goes through Mozambique, specifically through the ports of Lourenco Marques and Beira. This explains the annexationist pretensions expressed by Great Britain at the end of the last century concerning Lourenco Marques, called Delagoa Bay, and which gave rise to a dispute decided under the arbitration of the French Marshall MacMahon.

Later, and taking into consideration the set of other factors of reciprocal interest, there was established a modus vivendi between Mozambique and South Africa, which was consecrated by a series of agreements of which the Convention of 1928, called the Transvaal agreement, and later renewed in 1962, was the most important. According to it the colonial administration in Mozambique pledged to send 100,000 Mozambican workers to the mines in South Africa every year — a base that could be exceeded with the permission of the latter country. In turn South Africa pledged to utilize the port of Lourenco Marques for export traffic from Transvaal, plus a certain quantity of citrus fruit. An identical arrangement was made for Rhodesia, a few of whose contemporary implications we shall have the occasion to appreciate.

In the long run, given the failure of the colonial economy in Mozambique to take off, the result was to create a strong dependence vis-a-vis South Africa and Rhodesia. In 1960, nearly 400,000 Mozambican workers were found in

South Africa and Rhodesia in the framework of the bilateral agreements of Portugal-South Africa and of Portugal-Rhodesia. According to these agreements, the workers' salaries are to be paid to the Portuguese government which would pay the worker in Mozambican 'escudos' at the termination of the contract. This explains how, for instance, 'the output of manpower abroad' could contribute one-fifth of the hard currency income in the budget forecast of Mozambique in 1961.

A quick examination of the balance of payments of Mozambique in 1966 shows on the other hand that transport, railways and ports – not to speak of the fiscal income to which they give rise – represented nearly 42% of total income.

This close dependency also explains the bitterness of the Portuguese complaints about sanctions against Rhodesia which meant, with the closing of the Beira-Umtali pipeline and the decrease in the traffic in Beira and Lourenco Marques ports, a loss of 15 million pounds up to August 1967 (nearly 19 million by the end of the same year), a loss which Portugal claimed in indemnities from the United Nations.

Mr. Nogueira, Portuguese Minister of Foreign Affairs and the maker of this demand, did not however stress that, according to the OECD report, commerce between Portugal and Rhodesia had increased fourfold during the same period, going from $314,000 in the first nine months of 1966 to 1.2 million dollars for the same period of 1967 (imports), and from $111,000 to $493,000 in exports, while industrial production in Mozambique increased to 43% in 1966 from nearly 6% in the preceding year. The refinery in Lourenco Marques, for instance, handled 12 times more oil over the previous year, oil which was going openly to Rhodesia, as was admitted by the above-mentioned Portuguese minister.

These last elements permit us to see that this economic interdependency which we are speaking of does not only belong to historical legend. On the contrary, it is tending to become considerably stronger in a perspective that goes beyond the framework of a transitory political solidarity, but is part of the grandiose projects of economic integration advocated by South Africa.

In our view, that most important item of this integration plan consists in the construction of the Cabora Bassa dam, located on the Zambezi river, in Mozambican territory, in the province of Tete. This dam seems in fact to constitute the cornerstone of the plans of economic cooperation between South Africa and Portugal, and aims at supplying inexpensive electrical energy to South Africa, Mozambique and Malawi, thus accelerating the economic integration of the area. The estimated production amounts to 17 billion KW/h per year while the production of Aswan scarcely exceeds 10 billion. The first stage of the project alone would cost nearly 105 million pounds and three consortia have presented definite proposals:

1. ZAMCO (France – West Germany – South Africa)
2. Cabora Bassa Construction (Great Britain)
3. Cabora Bassa Builders (France – USA).

South Africa has already pledged itself to buy nearly half of the dam's output, energy which will be supplied to it through a line 1,400 kms. long. Even though the first stage of the project has been announced for completion by 1974, it is believed that a certain amount of energy may be produced from 1970 on.

On the other hand, the completed project will make the Zambezi river navigable all along its Mozambican channel, which is 830 kms. long. A port has been planned at the mouth of the river on the Indian Ocean, which could harbour a 40,000 ton ship. Ian Smith's racists are rushing for their part to make the Hunyani, a tributary of the Zambezi, navigable as well, which would give them a means of river communication with the ocean.

The most serious political consequences are to be located however in the settlement scheme made possible by the reclamation of 2.5 million hectares of productive land where the immigration of a million white colonists is projected. No one doubts that this mass of settlers would constitute a formidable human dam opposed to the liberation of this southern region of Africa.

In the framework of economic integration and with the same political aim, there has been the suggestion of a common market for southern Africa, which would include not only the white powers but also the independent countries of Africa. This is the economic aspect of the tentacle-like nature of this white Holy Alliance, and which alternates threats and aggression with seduction and economic infiltration manoeuvres, seeking to create or reinforce economic dependence, and hence political dependence, of the independent African countries of the area.

In face of these overall plans, particularly in view of the acceleration of the process of integration, our answer consists in the development of our political and military action, and its extension to the whole area of the country. Launched in 1964, armed struggle for liberation has already achieved some important successes. In the two northern provinces of Niassa and Cabo Delgado, large areas have been freed from colonial occupation and the people have recovered the exercise of their own sovereignty.

Last March, a new front was opened right in Tete province where the Portuguese are thinking of building the Cabora Bassa dam. The previous successes allow us to forecast considerable difficulties in carrying out the Portuguese plan, if it doesn't make it impossible.

We should now examine the establishment and the development of military cooperation organized among Portugal, South Africa and Rhodesia. The first evidence of this was supplied by an ex-officer of the Portuguese army, Commander Jose Ervedosa, to the Committee of 24 of the United Nations, which met in Algiers in July 1966. According to him, the contacts among the General Staffs of the three armies date from the month of February 1962. Today this cooperation is no longer a secret.

At its origin we find the condition of the white minority in South Africa, without a fallback position, determined to defend its position as a dominator of the African people.

Portugal on the other hand was having to cope with similar problems in Angola and Mozambique, problems which were rendered more acute once

44

armed struggle in Angola had begun in February 1961. Isolated by the old colonial powers – England, France and Belgium – who had preferred to try the more peaceful and less expensive ways of neocolonial domination in place of direct colonization, Portugal turned towards South Africa and Rhodesia to establish joint military plans.

The peculiarity of the Portuguese attitude in the face of the so-called current of 'decolonization' pertains to the structure of its economy, that is to the backward character of its economy, and to the kind of colonial exploitation practised by Portugal which demanded the maintenance of a system of direct domination, the only one which allowed the over-exploitation of natural resources and of local manpower in particular.

This *inability to neo-colonize*, rather than ideological factors, is at the basis of the Portuguese decision to oppose independence, if only of a formal kind, for the colonies.

On the other hand we must emphasize that the social structure in the countries of southern Africa is more or less the same. We are speaking, in each case and despite quantitative differences, of colonies settled by whites where the Europeans are in total control of the political, economic and cultural life of the country, in spite of the often great disequilibrium between the size of the white population and that of the African populations. All this together with the economic and social bonds established from the beginning of the century among the settler minorities in these countries – and this is particularly true of Mozambique – naturally brought them to work together to elaborate a strategy of 'common defence'. It involved at first an exchange of information on the activities of the nationalist forces and of experiences with anti-African repression agreements for the extradition of African and nationalist patriots. To the development of nationalist politico-military action there has corresponded an intensification of white cooperation: South African helicopters of the base at Caprivi were sent to intervene against the Angolan nationalist forces, while the white South African forces openly fought the patriots in Zimbabwe.

In Mozambique our information services signalled the presence of South African troops stationed in Tete province along the Zambezi river, particularly in Chicoa, Mague, Zumbo (several companies) and in Chioco (a battalion); even more recently still, South African troops were said to be in Fingoe and Funrancungo.

In this regard, we should like to emphasize the importance of the participation of South African troops on the fields of combat of the Portuguese colonies, since it tends to remove all autonomous decision-making power from Portugal insofar as 'its' colonial policy is concerned. In effect, by tying its defence, indeed the destiny, of Angola and Mozambique to Rhodesia and South Africa, the Portuguese are willy-nilly taking the path of defence to the death of their colonial territories in a framework whose essential elements have been fixed by South Africa.

We shall finally discuss, if briefly, the situation of southern Africa in the context of world imperialism. Traditionally a source of excess-profits, extremely rich in gold, diamonds and raw materials of all sorts, South Africa, Rhodesia and the Portuguese colonies have been coveted by international imperialism for a long time. The discovery of veins of raw materials of military importance, and of oil only strengthened this interest. The economic exploiters of these regions found zealous and faithful allies in the European settlers in the area. A convergence of interests no longer solely racial but fundamentally economic was established between the settlers and international capitalism. The analyses presented here have abundantly demonstrated, with statistical evidence, that this was so because of the nature of imperialist capitalism itself. We would simply like to emphasize the strategic importance both of South Africa and the Portuguese colonies in the imperialist strategy given the renewed importance of the Cape Route as a central means of international communication. Not only transitory factors, and such as the closing of the Suez canal, but also the technical demands of the giant oilers, and the 'strategic covering' of the Indian Ocean, have led European politicians such as General Bethouart, David Rousset and Sir Alec Douglas-Home to summon the West to protect this vital route, which implies increasing support to Portugal and South Africa. To underline the reinforcement of the ties between the imperialist powers and the white powers in southern Africa, we should also remember the aggravation of the international conjuncture characterized by the escalation of reactionary violence in face of the successes attained by popular forces throughout the world.

Having reached the stage of direct intervention in Vietnam, world imperialism, headed by American imperialism, but involving also Great Britain, Federal Germany and also France — whose role in southern Africa is one of the most notorious — Japan, etc., world imperialism has evolved, we were saying a division of forces and tasks in the framework of a global strategy of choking popular aspirations so as to maintain its domination and its exploitation.

The white bloc of southern Africa is assigned the important task of protecting the reserves of raw materials, of ensuring the exploitation of African manpower and of undertaking an action of re-colonization of the continent, from the South northward.

Before the alternative where we find on one side the exploited popular masses, and on the other the exploiting settlers, the West, i.e. the capitalist countries, has chosen the latter. It could not be otherwise. We note this. We too, we have chosen. We have chosen to be with progressive humanity, with the millions of people who combat oppression, misery, social downfall, those who build a new world and a new man. We are with the forces of progress and social justice; we are with history.

2. The Enemy's Contradictions

Editors' Introduction

In combating the enemy, it is essential for the national liberation movements to discern the contradictions in their camp. It is in the very alliances of the enemy that one set of contradictions are found.

The movements perceived the local white regimes to be part of a larger network of imperialist forces whose centre was in the USA, Great Britain, and western Europe. But the relationship of these core capitalist countries to the local regimes had ambiguities. Up to a point, their interests in suppressing the movements were identical. But there came points where those interests diverged.

Much of the debate within the movements revolved around the role and potential role of the United States government. We illustrate this issue by discussing the relations of the USA and Portugal. Of all the movements in the Portuguese colonies, the one that was reputed to be (accused of being) the most sympathetic to the US was the Angolan UPA led by Holden Roberto. We reproduce two statements of Roberto. One, made in 1961 at the beginning of the Kennedy era, was full of optimism and on behalf of the 'moderate party', the UPA, 'renders vibrant homage' to Kennedy. The second, made in 1968 at the end of the Johnson presidency, suggested deep deception about the US even by Roberto.

The CONCP leaders were more cynical about the US. Their viewpoint is well represented by the denunciation in 1964 by Eduardo Mondlane of the US role, and by an article written by Hugo Menezes in 1965 in which he not only attacked the role of the US but the links of Roberto with the US. However, the CONCP analysis was not simplistic as is indicated by the 1969 FRELIMO article which analysed the ways in which the Portuguese rulers found themselves squeezed between the US and NATO on the one hand and South Africa on the other, with the Portuguese risking losing out in the interplay of the 'contradictions within imperialism'. An ANC article developed some of the differences in international tactics between the South African and Rhodesian rulers.

In addition there are the contradictions among the local rulers themselves. In South Africa, the differences between 'Boer and Briton' are well-known (and analyses of this phenomenon can be found in the section 'The Rule of

White Settlers). But there were strains within the Afrikaner camp itself. The ANC article discussed how important from its standpoint is the conflict between *verkramptes* and *verligtes*. As for the Portuguese, the FRELIMO analysis spoke of three separate groups amongst the rulers, and Neto in his 1969 article indicated that amongst the three, 'the settlers are our most dangerous enemies'. An internal CONCP document discusses the attitudes that might be taken towards the various movements of opposition within Portugal to the fascist regime.

Vibrant Homage to Kennedy
Holden Roberto

> *From a press conference given by the President-General of the UPA (Angola) in Leopoldville (Congo), 24 March 1961. Translated from French.*

The UPA is a moderate party. We would have liked to attain our independence by negotiating with the government of Portugal. The UPA is always willing to negotiate, but unfortunately the regime of Salazar, due to its nature, is unable to do other than obstinately continue to err, even when it may no longer count upon those who had previously supported the colonial wars. We wish, on the other hand, to take advantage of this occasion to render a vibrant homage to the new American administration and to its young and dynamic leader John Kennedy. Our country will have the pride of having contributed to the concretization of a sharp turn in American politics in respect to Africa and decolonization.

Hypocrisy Has Its Limits
Holden Roberto

> *From a statement made by the President of the FNLA (Angola), to the UN's Committee of 24 in 1967.*

We cannot fail to observe that Portugal, being an underdeveloped country with very limited means, is able to lead a war only because of the assistance it gets from NATO. It is this fact that explains its obstinacy in refusing to implement the resolutions of the UN. It is not only in contradiction with the principles of the so-called free world, but also with the wish to defend peace.

To all the Western countries, to all NATO countries and particularly the United States of America, I am constrained to say before this forum that the people of Angola will not forgive the fact that all the means of destruction used against it come from the arsenals of the West.

We are made to believe that the weapons delivered to the Portuguese Fascists within NATO are not destined to accomplish the subjugation of the African peoples. We are also told that the Atlantic pact which allows Portugal to administer an army of 85,000 men in Angola, 40,000 in Mozambique and 30,000 in Guinea-Bissau is not meant to be an alliance directed against these territories and their peoples. This may be true according to the literature, but the facts unfortunately contradict it. The fact is that NATO weapons are being employed in Africa solely, I repeat, solely against us.

Mr. President, there is a limit to hypocrisy. And the 5,000,000 Angolans will never believe that it is by accident that Western weapons are being used against them. The kind of reassurance we want must be matched by counter-measures. We are saying to the USA that they must accept the embargo on the weapons delivered to Portugal, called for in the resolution of the Security Council S/RES/218 of November 23, 1965. We are also saying that they must all realize that they are accomplices of the suffering of our people and that, in our opinion, they share in the abominable crimes accomplished by the men of Salazar in Angola and elsewhere. They must revise their position according to which they proclaim their anti-colonialist position on Sunday and serve as bankers and providers of weapons to the Portuguese colonialists the other days of the week.

The Point of View of the US Government
Eduardo Mondlane

> *Article by the President of FRELIMO, in the New York edition of* Mozambique Revolution, *I, 3, ca. September 1964.*

Last March Admiral Anderson paid an official visit to Angola and Mozambique. Admiral Anderson is the Ambassador of the United States of America in Lisbon. As Ambassador he officially represents the American Government in whatever he does and says. That is to say, the political line followed by him, his declarations and actions reflect the position of the Department of State, which represents the general political line of the Government of the United States.

When, therefore, Admiral Anderson, at the end of this triumphant visit to Angola and Mozambique, declared that he was 'tremendously impressed' by the development of the overseas territories of Portugal and by the progress and well-being of the populations of those territories, and that he had noted the complete absence of racial discrimination; when Admiral Anderson proclaims the unity which he said existed between Portugal and the United States of America, we of the Mozambique Liberation Front have no alternative but to conclude that this is the point of view of the United States Government.

The fundamental point to be underlined here is the following: Admiral Anderson could not have found racial equality in Portuguese colonies, for there is racism in all Portuguese colonies, especially in Mozambique. All the commissions of inquiry which were created by the United Nations to study Portuguese colonial problems were unanimous in this respect. Let us cite a few here. The Special Committee on Territories Under Portuguese Administration in its report presented to the General Assembly the following conclusions:

> ... the Committee finds with serious concern that political and civil rights have not been fully extended to all inhabitants and discrimination against them (meaning against the indigenous peoples) has not been removed. (Para. 410)

> ... the Committee is not convinced that the indigenous inhabitants are now guaranteed just treatment and equality under the law. (Para. 417)

> ... forced labour ... apparently continues to exist in actual practice even now in all territories under Portuguese administration. (Para. 418).

Similarly Ambassador Anderson could not have found progress, well-being and harmonious relations in Portuguese colonies except among the Portuguese settlers, for misery dominates the African population of these territories. That same United Nations Committee in its report declared, in paragraph 433, that, 'in the economic field there has been little significant change in levels of living of the indigenous population, whereas exports of some mineral and agricultural products have increased over the past decade'. Further on in the same report the Committee said, 'The Committee wishes to emphasize that in its view there can be no full participation of the indigenous inhabitants in the economic life of the Territories until they have full sovereignty over their natural resources through the attainment of independence'.

In view of the conclusions reached by this august Committee and our own experience as native inhabitants of these Portuguese colonies, one might ask: how could Ambassador Anderson have known the true conditions prevailing in these territories when his visit had an official character in which any direct contact with the overwhelming majority of the people was impossible? We can only conclude that Admiral Anderson's remarks at the end of his visit were politically inspired, reflecting the official policy of his Government.

The importance of Admiral Anderson's declarations has to be seen also against the fact that it represents a counter-position to the liberation movements of the peoples under Portuguese colonialism and imperialism, implying that they had no reason for being. In other words, Ambassador Anderson and through him the United States Government, seems to be saying that nothing justifies the accession of Portuguese overseas territories to independence, since the inhabitants of these territories are happy and have complete well-being and enjoy progress. This is even more grave when it is realized that his visit was undertaken 'with the complete approval of his Government, and, in special, of the Secretary of State, Mr. Dean Rusk' as Admiral Anderson himself declared to the journalists in Luanda on the 11th of March.

When it is to be recalled that even the Secretary General of the United Nations, U Thant, refused to accept an invitation to visit Portuguese colonies, the American Government's position and activities seem even more odd and incongruous.

The only conclusion which can be derived from these official visits is that the United States of America cannot identify itself with our ideals for self-determination and independence.

These activities of the United States Government are not only an obvious connivance with Portugal, but also raise suspicions of connivance with the imperialist Government of the Republic of South Africa.

Exactly two months after Admiral Anderson's official visit, there followed the official visit of the highest officer of the armed forces of South Africa, General Grobbelaar. Like Admiral Anderson, General Grobbelaar inspected lengthily all the Portuguese military bases in Mozambique. We already know that General Grobbelaar's visit was a preliminary step towards the establishment of a coordinated plan for the repression of our people, in which the South African armed forces will act conjointly with the Portuguese armed forces when our people take arms to fight for their liberation.

What meaning should we attribute to the visit of the Ambassador of the United States to the same Portuguese military bases?

We can only believe that the United States of America wishes to reassure its ally, Portugal, of its sympathy and material support in sustaining Portuguese colonialism and imperialism on the African continent.

On the basis of the facts above, we are forced to conclude that when our people finally rise to take up arms against Portuguese imperialism, the United States of America, like the Republic of South Africa, will intervene against us in support of Portugal.

In December 1963, the Salazar Government was granted a loan of 35 million dollars from banks in the United States. Besides that amount, the Portuguese received 112.5 million dollars from the IBRD (International Bank for Reconstruction and Development) (see *Diario do Governo*, 10 December, 1964). In receiving help from one of the biggest powers in the world with which to buy equipment against our undefended people, the President of Portugal, Americo Tomas, was able to announce recently, 'As far as we are concerned, the international atmosphere has evolved favourably . . .'.

In a letter signed by the United States Secretary of State, we read: 'Portugal is one ally which gave and is still giving an important contribution to our mutual security by permitting us to use a military base in the Azores. To sacrifice the interests of the Portuguese by supporting, in one way or another, the attacks levelled against her in the United Nations can only lead to a disaster' (*Fortune*, 14 May 1964).

Encouraged by all of this assistance, the Portuguese are feeling strong and are sure that they will not be deprived of their colonies. The power of the American dollar and of the American press are visibly with them.

From the end of July to August, Americo Tomas visited Mozambique. The main goal of the trip, according to official sources, was 'to show the world that peace, progress and racial harmony exist in Mozambique' (*The New York Times*, 20 August, 1964, p. 3).

Angola and the New Imperialist Strategy in Southern Africa

Hugo Menezes

> *Article by a member of the MPLA, in* Faulha *(Accra), 1, July 1965. Translated from Portuguese.*

June 1960. The year of Africa and of Patrice Lumumba. And, less than a year later, a group of nationalists launched an armed struggle for the liberation of Angola. It was in Luanda, on 4 February 1961.

In spite of all sorts of limitations and mistakes of different kinds, the Angolan nationalists were able to free, in a short period of time, a great part of the North of Angola and reached the outskirts of Luanda.

The events of the Congo were still fresh in the memory of the Portuguese. The colonists and the colonial administration panicked; the economy of the country was paralysed or destroyed in great part; colonists and capital fled. Portuguese colonialism was thus almost defeated. Not because it had been taken by surprise. In fact the colonial government had been preparing intensely for a long time, and engaged in quite spectacular military demonstrations, in the hope of intimidating and thus countering the growing threat of the Angolan underground organizations, which were becoming more active every day. Besides, the colonial government had been careful to arrest all those Angolan personalities, who were potential leaders of the rebellion. The Portuguese colonists simply found themselves outstripped by events, unable to handle a popular uprising of such a size, despite the fact that it was poorly organized, poorly led, and possessed only rudimentary armaments.

The armed struggle in Angola did not affect only Portuguese interests but it affected just as much and just as directly the interests of the other imperialist powers in Angola. It was thus essential to circumscribe the Angolan events, to avoid at all cost a chain reaction in the southern part of the continent, to put an end to the serious threat which imperialism was facing in this vital part of Africa.

The armed struggle and the success attained in such a short time by the Angolan nationalists, reverberated far beyond the borders of Angola. In fact, at the same time that it constituted an important factor of demoralization in colonial and reactionary circles, it acted as a catalysing and mobilizing element in the other Portuguese colonies, and even in liberal and progressive circles of Portugal. On the other hand, the war effort for Portugal, in Angola, due to its economic implications, was leading directly to the weakening of the Portuguese bourgeoisie and of its position in Angola and in the other Portuguese colonies, as well as in Portugal. The imperialist powers quickly understood that Portugal in trying to 'maintain' Angola would end by losing it, and mortgage itself to foreign interests.

Shortly thereafter the epic national liberation struggle of Guinea and later the liberation struggle of the people of Mozambique were to begin.

It was necessary to keep Angola, not so much because it was a territory essential to Portuguese colonialism, but mainly because it was a primary base in the economic-military strategy of imperialism.

Leaving thus to one side secondary divergences, imperialism decided to take upon itself, as a whole, the solution to the Angolan problem.

Thus entered NATO, jet aircraft and napalm bombs, military 'advisers', Spanish and South African 'volunteers', followed by loans of hundreds of millions of dollars to Portugal, and by investments of hundreds of marks in Portugal and Angola.

Imperialism stepped forward then in all its glory, decided not to make any concession, but to drown in a sea of blood the slightest cry of rebellion or the slightest demand of the Angolan nationalists.

And Portuguese colonialism, which in reality was nothing but a collective colonialism, came to be a simple subtitle.

Meanwhile, North American imperialism, which had just made its appearance in the Congo, needed to strengthen its positions, to play cleverly, to negotiate.

American imperialism thus mounted on the back of African nationalism, taking advantage of it as a vehicle of penetration in the competitive struggle with the interests of the European bloc in the Congo, so closely associated with the Portuguese interests in Angola, in the other Portuguese colonies, and in Portugal.

Via Angolan 'nationalism' it would be possible to find a supplementary door to the Congo, mainly through Katanga, by means of the Benguela railway and the port of Lobito.

The United States thus played on two levels, and with the greatest cunning. It sought, on the one hand, to support strongly Portuguese ultra-colonialism, while at the same time condemning some of its secondary aspects, in order to be able to satisfy the demands of world-wide public opinion and especially the clientele of the new African countries who defended so strongly the Angolan cause and who were used so effectively as a means of pressure against Portugal and the European group, to the undoubted advantage of the United States!

On the other hand it was essential to preserve the future. In this way, there arose the need to create a false leadership of the Angolan nationalist movement, in order to make it deviate from its real goals. This false leadership, constituted by approved 'nationalist' elements, would on the one hand permit the channelling of the aid destined to the people of Angola, and thus remove it from the real nationalists. Public world opinion would be channelled the same way.

This is thus the context in which Holden Roberto was brought forth, having been conceived in Washington, born in Leopoldville, and having Mr. Cyrille Adoula, then the Prime Minister of Congo, as a godfather.

Holden was undoubtedly a product of the contradictions of American imperialism. He would similarly become one of its victims.

Holden Roberto had two faces. In the interior, at the price of a few exchanges of fire at the border and a few small more or less fortuitous encounters with the colonial army, combined with dithyrambic war communiques, Holden played the role of an irritating fish bone, a permanent pressure point, a most effective means of persuasion, a factor of consumption, which forced Portugal to mortgage itself more and more to outside interests, especially the United States. Yet in the interior, Holden Roberto and his organization really contributed to the sabotage of the national liberation movement, by instigating divisions, by leading one group of nationalists against another, using racism, tribalism, religion, and the variety of political viewpoints.

To the outside world, Holden was presented as being the real enemy of Portuguese colonialism, as the spokesman of Angolan nationalism, while at the same time he attempted to stifle and isolate the real national liberation movement of Angola, represented by the MPLA.

Holden was thus, essentially, a means of pressure, which was used by the USA in the framework of the competition between the imperialist powers in Angola and mainly in the Congo. At the time of the secession, Holden constituted a potential weapon perpetually directed against Katanga and the interests of the European group. We must remind ourselves that Holden had received at the time all the instructions, technicians, and explosives required to sabotage the Benguela railway, which is a channel whereby much of the mineral wealth of Katanga is evacuated.

If there were, as we have seen, relative divergences among the imperialist powers in the interior, these became more apparent once they were projected on the international scene, and mainly, on the Congolese screen, of which the situation in Angola soon became a projection.

Thus, to American 'liberalism' and 'anti-colonialism' which found expression in Cyrille Adoula and Holden Roberto, there stood opposed Anglo-Belgian-Portuguese colonialism, embodied in the personality of Moise Tshombe.

The situation today has become clearer, especially since the elimination of some secondary conflicts among the imperialist powers in Congo, the USA having substantially strengthened its position in this country. Today the imperialists are trying to build a united front, from Pretoria to Leopoldville, from Lourenco Marques to Luanda, and going through Salisbury. One and only one front, one and only one ideology – ultra-colonialism. The era of Cyrille Adoula is over. It is not the best atmosphere for Holden Roberto, with his 'Revolutionary Government', his devastating war communiques, and his delirious press declarations. Today they certainly do not perturb the relations among the members of the colonial holy alliance.

But does imperialism really wish to destroy Holden Roberto? Possibly not, since no one knows what surprises the authentic Angolan nationalism will bring, nor even how long the present imperialist modus vivendi in Congo will last.

What is urgent at this moment is to decrease the flow of oxygen with which Holden has been kept alive by imperialism ever since he was born. It is necessary to put him to sleep, to make him hibernate, to put him in moth balls, waiting for a more wintry season – for imperialism. There is no doubt that the 'revolutionary' Holden Roberto is willing to accept this new role which his masters have assigned to him.

These are the reasons why Holden Roberto 'fell into disfavour', and why his colleague of Leopoldville, Prime Minister Moise Tshombe, at the Council of Ministers of the OAU in Nairobi, did not vote for him, but preferred to abstain.

The recent anti-Holden demonstrations in Leopoldville, those in which the headquarters of the Provisional Government was invaded by dozens of Angolan 'nationalists', must be placed in the same context.

This tactical change in imperialism is certainly the result of the resistance it finds in the national liberation movement in Africa. In effect, imperialism was forced to unite, in order to fight the liberation movement. Imperialism was forced to abandon its 'liberal' masks, to tighten its ranks, to take the positions called for by its most reactionary elements. Imperialism started openly to defend direct intervention, and became conscious of defending the last barricade, the last stage of colonialism.

But let us be vigilant. Those victories obtained in Leopoldville, the removal of Holden Roberto from the African and Angolan political scene, do in the last analysis constitute important victories for Angolan nationalism. But such victories are more than anything else an affirmation of ultra-colonialism.

Contradictions Within Imperialism
FRELIMO

From an article in Mozambique Revolution *(FRELIMO, Dar es Salaam), No. 40, 25 September 1969.*

In spite of the apparently brilliant nature of the Cabora Bassa scheme as one to unite Portuguese Fascism, Western Capitalism and South African Apartheid, there are certain serious problems which Portugal's ruling clique have to face. To begin with, Portugal is caught in the middle of capitalist interests from different imperialist countries which are competing among themselves. The contract to build the first stage of the Cabora Bassa dam was signed on

10 July 1968 with ZAMCO (Zambeze Consorcio Hydro-Electric), which is a consortium of German, Swedish, French and South African firms – under the control of the notorious South African company, Anglo-American. By awarding the contract to ZAMCO, Portugal satisfied German and South African capitalists in particular, but the British and the powerful US capitalists were left out of the picture. This raises contradictions for Portugal's foreign policy, since Caetano clearly hopes for more US and NATO aid to conduct his wars against FRELIMO, MPLA and PAIGC.

Another contradiction met within Portugal's colonial and foreign policy is that while it needs South Africa's support to maintain Mozambique and Angola, it is also afraid of a South African takeover of these regions, with the support of the whites already resident there. Further white immigration into Mozambique (such as the million farmers whom they would like to settle on the Zambezi) will not necessarily improve Portugal's position since the plan is to attract those settlers from European countries, and they may prefer South Africa rather than Portugal as their master. Besides, the close association with South Africa embarrasses Caetano's attempts to portray himself as a 'Liberal'. The ties with South Africa are being strengthened every day and in Angola there is another hydro-electric scheme (the Cunene dam) which involves South Africa. But the evidence is that some elements within Portugal's ruling circle do not like these developments.

In April this year, while visiting Mozambique (the areas still safe for Portugal) Marcelo Caetano announced that the agreement with ZAMCO was broken off. But that decision has been reversed in favour of ZAMCO once more. The changes and the uncertainty were probably due to fear of South African influence in Mozambique along with Portuguese hopes that United States investors would build the dam and bring the support of their government. It was widely rumoured that since the Spanish government was raising problems over the American bases in Spain, the Portuguese government was willing to allow the Yankees to transfer their bases from Spain to Portugal. This major step, along with the encouragement of American capital in Mozambique would then have been rewarded by armed American intervention in Mozambique.

It would be foolish to deny the possibility of US intervention and aggression against the people of Mozambique, knowing how far they have already gone through NATO aid to Portugal, and knowing the ferocious nature of imperialism. But at the moment, such hopes are only dreams on the part of the Portuguese. Being desperate in the face of the steady growth of FRELIMO, Caetano has decided to rely on the support which the South African Fascists are only too willing to offer. Therefore, in July it was announced that Lisbon and Pretoria had agreed on ZAMCO to build the Cabora Bassa dam.

Did Smith Defy Vorster Over *Fearless*?
ANC

An article in Mayibuye *(ANC, Lusaka), Vol. III, No. 2,*
13 January 1969.

One of the more puzzling developments in the Rhodesian imbroglio is the apparent impasse in the relations between Smith and Vorster after the *Fearless* talks. Perhaps it is too much to hope that these recent developments threaten the rather delicate foundation so carefully laid by Verwoerd thus endangering the unity of the 'unholy alliance' but the differences need to be understood. After UDI, Verwoerd adopted an equivocal attitude towards Britain and Rhodesia. This was an attitude of official neutrality but private help. He declared that South Africa would continue normal neighbourly relations, and would not join any international action to topple the Smith regime. In his view, this was a domestic issue. Privately, however, South Africa has helped prop the rebels to such an extent that without her material assistance they would not be making a mockery of the UN sanctions. Premier Balthazar Vorster has continued this policy. Thus, at the Ladysmith conference of his party, he reiterated the domestic nature of the Rhodesian problem. Using a rather clumsy analogy, he said, 'this argument between man and wife has got nothing to do with the in-laws'. Nevertheless, he stated that South Africa was interested in a settlement. Not only that. The Afrikaans press, especially *Die Burger* urged Smith to accept Wilson's *Fearless* proposals and then, after the return to legality, he could decide whether he wanted to honour them or not.

To the amazement of most observers, Smith refused to come to terms. And here is the big question: if South Africa through her aid dominates Rhodesia, why did Vorster not succeed in pressurising Smith into a settlement?

That Vorster urgently wants a settlement is beyond doubt. For South Africa, the Rhodesian affair is too close for comfort. It focuses world attention on her role, and provides ammunition for those who advocate stern action against her. Moreover, it mars his grand designs for the sabotage of independent Africa.

But why did Smith reject the *Fearless* proposals which, even more than the *Tiger*, were so favourable to him? Last year we frequently pointed out in these columns that in their efforts to deal with the outside world both Vorster and Smith run into serious domestic difficulties.

Since the unseemly dismissal of William Harper, and the resignation of Lord Graham, Smith has been facing mounting right-wing opposition at home. With a significant following from the white working class and from the landed gentry, these rightists argue that Smith is out of touch with the wishes and interests of the white electorate. By playing the British at their favourite game of negotiation and compromise, at which they are masters, he will sell out the whites. Under these circumstances, for Smith to settle would be political suicide, especially since his right-wing opponents have the support of Vorster's own right-wing foes in South Africa. In other words, there is some sort of a right-wing alliance in these two countries, an alliance which while numerically weak however is vociferous and shrewdly plays on the tender emotions of its respective electorate. In both Rhodesia and South Africa, 'the abdication of the white man' and 'softness' are sure to bring a government into disrepute. And since they play on these touchy emotional issues, Smith cannot crack down on his opponents or enter into any international settlement which can appear to be a sell-out of the white man.

For this reason, Smith is not in a position at present to accept the *Fearless* proposals; nor can Vorster pressure him into doing so. In this lies the answer to the enigma of Vorster wanting desperately a settlement and Smith, though held in bondage by South Africa, nòt being able to comply with Vorster's need.

Verkramptes and Verligtes
ANC

An article in Mayibuye *(ANC, Lusaka), II, 29, 19 July 1968.*

White politicians in South Africa carry on their public dialogues at an extraordinary level of personal abuse, backbiting, malicious gossip and political triviality. Entrenched behind an all-White franchise, protected from competition by a high wall of repressive, racial legislation, men with small minds reduce politics to a tedious farce, or a mirage that distorts reality and projects only a shadow of the real substance of things.

The reality must be looked for outside parliament, in the grim and heroic struggle of the subjugated four-fifths for political rights, common justice and human dignity. Parliamentary politicians ignore their claims, ban their organisations, jail or exile their leaders, and stifle their protests with bullets and the hangman's noose; but it is outside parliament, and not in the debating chamber, that the struggle for power is taking place. And politics, we know, has to do with power: how it is to be distributed, who is to exercise it, and by what means it is to be controlled.

Outsiders, and a great many South African Whites, often mistake the shadow for the substance. They attach an exaggerated importance to disputes between the parliamentary parties or within their ranks; and anxiously examine the differences for signs of a crack in the struggle of White supremacy. According to one such observer, a Mr. Stanley Meisler, the Africa correspondent of the Los Angeles *Times,* the 'most significant political development in South Africa in a decade' is the fight between *Verligtes* and *Verkramptes.*

The judgement is a poor one by any standard that measures the growth of South Africa's fascism, her imperialist expansion, or her preparations for armed struggle against the liberation movement. Dissensions within

Afrikanerdom are the symptoms of strain created by these political events, and should be regarded as being of secondary significance. As symptoms, however, they are important enough to receive attention in our journal.

Verkramp means cramped, compressed, therefore narrow-minded and 'reactionary', or opposed to change. *Verligte* is enlightened, therefore broad-minded, receptive to new ideas and flexible. The labels have been stuck on to the rival sects by opponents of the Nationalist Party, and do not in any way express its own views about the nature or aims of the disputing parties; but as is common in such situations, the mere act of attaching labels has served to crystallise differences of viewpoint and to widen the gap between the two sides.

Controversies have centred round South Africa's relations with independent African States (Lesotho, Botswana, Malawi), the acceptance of Malawi's African representative at Cape Town; the decision to send a 'multi-racial' team to the Olympic games, the encouragement of White immigrants who for religious, language or political reasons are said to assimilate more readily into the English than into the Afrikaner community; and the government's alleged attempts to conciliate world opinion by changing South Africa's image.

The *Verkramptes* are die-hard isolationists. They reject collaboration with African States on terms of equality. In the words of S.E.E. Brown, editor of the monthly *South African Observer* and an intellectual fascist, 'adaptations, concessions, deviations from, and negations of traditional policy will inevitably become the order of the day — and lead inevitably to integration, and to the ultimate crumbling of the entire policy of separate development'. 'Nothing short of Black majority rule will satisfy the outside world.' 'Every concession on our part is regarded as a weakness and as a gain for our enemies, who are then encouraged to press harder for further concessions' (*The S.A. Observer*, January 1968).

Brown and his associates argue that Vorster's government are the tools of an 'Afrikaans liberal establishment', which is headed by Anton Rupert, the tobacco millionaire, and supported by the government press. Their 'outward-looking' policy of coming to terms with Africa and the West suits the big capitalists who for long have wanted to make South Africa the industrial and financial hub of Africa. In effect, the isolationists fear that a growing imperialism will dilute the concentrated passion of Afrikaner nationalism and weaken its determination to maintain White supremacy.

The isolationists have failed to obtain much political support in recent by-elections; but the correspondence columns of the Afrikaans press suggest that an important section of intellectuals is sympathetic to their point of view. In any event, the government has reacted sharply. Nationalist spokesmen denounce the isolationists as 'splitters' and traitors, insist that Vorster is carrying out the policy laid down by Strijdom and Verwoerd, and emphasise the dangers that beset South Africa.

The Republic, they say, is surrounded by a sea of trouble: Freedom Fighters in the North, hostile African governments throughout the continent, the growing strength of world communism, and a degenerate Western capitalism that allows itself to be blackmailed by Afro-Asian States. South Africa can survive, it is argued, only by following the 'outward' policy of establishing friendly relations with her African neighbours and by cementing a strategic alliance with the big Western powers.

Internal policies are not in dispute. Both factions agree on the basic principle of White *baasskap*; both are determined to suppress the liberation movement by force and violence. The isolationists cannot provide evidence that the government has relaxed its system of fascist repression. They therefore fall back on the old techniques of political scandal, as in the recent unsigned circular letter posted to a number of prominent Afrikaners.

The authors of the letter pretend to praise Vorster and his lieutenants for doing the very things of which the isolationists complain; and damn them by coupling their names with persons and tendencies alleged to be liberal, such as the United States Leadership Programme, the United Party, Anton Rupert, NUSAS, and the English churches. *Die Burger's* editorial column made this comment: 'Beneath a transparent veneer of ironical support for the Prime Minister, the government's policy of securing for South Africa her rightful place in Africa and the world is distorted into nothing else than a sell-out and a betrayal' (*Die Burger*, 20th June 1968).

The police were called in. They identified the authors of the 'smear letter' as five young Afrikaners in Pretoria, among them an official of a Nationalist Party branch and a sub-editor of the isolationist newspaper *Hoofstad*, who is also a nephew of the Prime Minister. The investigations also led to the unearthing of another Afrikaner group which had earlier distributed a similar leaflet that praised the government for having 'left the laager of *Verkramptheid* to join the world with its progressive ideas'.

Liberalism, progressive, not to mention equality and communism, are smear words in the dictionary of Afrikaans nationalism. Vorster, who climbed into the premier's chair on a ladder of fascist laws and violations of human rights, dare not appear as a 'progressive' before an Afrikaner audience, no matter how much the disguise might suit his purpose on the international scene.

In White supremacy politics, the main challenge to the party in power comes always from the extreme right, and never from the side of those who demand freedom and equality for all races. But the 'right wing' protests would not be taken seriously, and might never have been made, except for the pressure of the anti-apartheid movement at home and abroad. It is this pressure that compels the government to adopt its new 'outward' look, and that sets up the internal strains of which the quarrel between *Verkramptes* and *Verligtes* is a symptom.

Let us therefore intensify our efforts to unmask the policies of White South Africa and isolate it from the rest of the world. The more successful we are in this endeavour, the greater will be the contradictions between the regime's 'good neighbourly relations' and its fascistic rule over four-fifths of the population. When thieves fall out, honest men come into their own.

Contradictions Among the Portuguese
FRELIMO

Article appearing in Mozambique Revolution *(FRELIMO, Dar es Salaam), Special Issue, 25 September 1967.*

The Portuguese position is unchanged. Portugal insists that Mozambique is an 'Overseas Province' and that we Mozambicans are 'Portuguese'. She continues to refuse to recognise our right to self determination and independence. Thus the armed struggle is still the only means which can lead us to independence.

Within the Portuguese position, however, major contradictions have begun to appear:

(a) On the one hand there is the Portuguese Government, which insists on wanting absolute control over all 'its' 'Overseas Territories' – not only political, but economic, administrative, and cultural as well. The system established in the colonies, is in fact, a system of direct rule, in which the organs of colonial government are tentacles, or extensions of the Central Government. The Governor Generals themselves are nominated by the Council of Ministers in Portugal.

(b) On the other hand there is a section of the white population of the colonies which does not willingly accept this policy. These settlers would prefer to see their profits used in the development of their businesses in the colonies instead of being absorbed by the Portuguese Government in the form of taxes. They think of Mozambique as their country, in the sense of their personal property. They want to get rid of their ties with Portugal. The ideal of these settlers would be to see in Mozambique a situation similar to Rhodesia's Unilateral Declaration of Independence. There is, however, only a very limited possibility of bringing about this situation. For, whereas in Rhodesia the white settlers could count on support from England when they declared independence and possessed all the material means (including military) to establish their independence, the settlers in Mozambique find themselves in a very different position. Portugal (unlike England) needs the colonies for her own survival. The very existence of Portugal in its present phase, depends on the colonies. Therefore Portugal will oppose any action from any quarter which would result in her losing the revenue provided by the colonies. Thus the Portuguese Government would actually use her vast army to oppose any movement for independence among the white settlers.

The existence of the national liberation struggle is another factor which acts against this tendency of the settlers. Even though, let us suppose, they obtained independence, they would be deprived of the military means of repression which Portugal provides. They would then, be forced to appeal, for example, to South Africa, who would send her troops in to occupy Mozambique. A bond of dependence would then be established between this regime and South Africa. The situation then pertaining would to all intents and purposes be the same – independence in relation to Portugal, but dependence in relation to South Africa. The settlers in Mozambique know this.

That is why they do nothing to make anything concrete come out of this tendency: it remains a matter of vague aspirations.

(c) A third body of opinion is for a neo-colonialist position, in which Portugal would grant independence to Mozambique, using a group of African puppet leaders, manipulated by the Lisbon authorities. The representatives of this movement are in Lisbon and constitute the so-called 'legal opposition' to the Salazar regime. Their leader is a Portuguese politician called Cunha Leal. But the neo-colonialist solution presupposes that the colonial power is sufficiently developed industrially to be able to make use of the raw materials which the neo-colony would provide her with. As Portugal is one of the most backward countries in Europe she needs, in order to exploit a territory, to have at the same time political and economic control. This is why the neo-colonialist tendency is also inapplicable.

The Settlers Are Our Most Dangerous Enemies
Agostinho Neto

> *Excerpt from an article 'People in Revolution' by the President of the MPLA, that appeared in* Tricontinental *(Havana), 12, May-June 1969.*

With the aim of populating Angola, the Portuguese Government encouraged a great many of its poor to migrate. Thousands of settlers arrived at our coasts, people who, in their own country, had had no jobs, were starving, and constituted the most backward, lowest class. They came because they were attracted by many inducements — among them land and domestic servants who would work without getting any salary or even clothes, for just a little food.

Today there are about 400,000 settlers in Angola. Many have been here for three generations already, and some have never been to Portugal. The original idea was to replace the native population with these new inhabitants, because it was expected that the Angolan population would decrease as the result of ill treatment and poor living conditions. The native population has in fact been reduced since the time of slavery.

It is obvious that the settlers are not planning to give up their property, not only because their holdings are vast but also because of the easy exploitation of manpower from among the Angolan people, who are forced to work for almost nothing. Some are even thinking of seceding from Portugal so as to rule the country themselves, as happened in Rhodesia, where a white minority has set itself up in control.

It is doubtful that this scheme will be realized in the near future, because it is not likely that Portugal will cut itself off from a large economic interest in Angola unless forced to do so, as a result of strong popular pressure — such as that we are exerting by means of armed struggle.

The settlers are our most dangerous enemies, because they are the most bellicose; they hate the Angolan population and are, in turn, hated by it. Moreover, they are fighting to defend their economic interests, whereas, for example, the soldiers sent over to fight for two or three years have no direct motivation in the conflict and carry out weaker actions, some of them even make statements against the colonial war and avoid confrontation with the guerrillas.

The Political Situation Inside Portugal
CONCP Member

A position paper prepared for internal distribution within CONCP, probably around 1968. This paper does not represent a final collective view of the CONCP, but rather one member's proposal.

The profound socio-economic transformations that can be seen to have occurred in the last decade in the structures of the highly industrialized societies of Europe correspond to a new strategy of European capitalism faced with the problems and inherent contradictions in the capitalist system itself, to wit:
a) The requirements imposed by the crisis of growth of European national capitalisms, brought about by the rise of the socialist camp and by the development of the liberation struggles of the peoples of Africa, Asia and Latin America, have forced them to restructure the processes of production and exploitation eliminating certain protectionist barriers (the Common Market) and creating new markets so as to increase considerably monopolistic profit;
b) The need to confront the leadership of the United States of America;
c) The need to eliminate internal contradictions so as to counter the onslaught of the economic policy of the socialist countries in the Third World.

These important transformations of structure correspond to the most recent phase of monopolistic concentration of European imperialism present particular characteristics of overrule and exploitation:
a) Migratory movements of large proletarian masses originating from underdeveloped European countries that have been subjected in highly industrialized countries to unbridled exploitation. These constitute a manipulable instrument of blackmail against the growing exigencies of nationally organized and politically conscious proletarians.
b) Through the penetration of financial capital and at the same time the corruption of the national bourgeoisies, we are seeing the transformation of the economic structures of these underdeveloped countries in schemes of economic and financial subjection to the European powers, and in open

alliance with European high finance. A large sector of the financial oligarchy is being organized in open struggle against traditional economic sectors, and this is having an increasing impact on the political circles of each one of these underdeveloped countries. This financial penetration in these latter countries in the economic mechanisms thus put into place have as a consequence a greater exploitation of the working masses, the proletarianization of an important part of the petty bourgeoisie and increasing economic difficulties for the middle bourgeoisie in facing the monopolistic tendencies of the upper bourgeois.

c) Seeking to avoid the radicalization inherent in the struggles of national liberation, this European neo-capitalist bourgeoisie has put in place new political and economic mechanisms utilizing African national elements to permit them to continue the exploitation of the riches of African countries.

Neo-colonialism constitutes, without a doubt, the principal obstacle to the realization of the aspirations of the primary needs of the large majority of African people. Portugal, despite the fact that it is a colonizing country, has an economy with the characteristics of an underdeveloped country: an agriculture essentially devoted to internal needs; an insignificant industrial sector; a consumption sector that is extremely limited and exporting largely primary manufactured products. Furthermore, in addition to being a colonizing country with the characteristics of an underdeveloped country, Portugal is also a colonized country, one colonized by the imperial powers.

England, France, West Germany, and the United States divide among them the economic domination of Portugal. Given these facts, Portugal is not able to escape in any way the impact of the offensive launched by finance in neo-capitalist countries, especially in West Germany and France, nor avoid the transformations which are occurring in Europe and in Africa.

The vast 'Portuguese' socio-economic space, represented above all by its colonies, has permitted the Portuguese bourgeoisie to close the breach of the fascist-corporatist edifice, utilizing the solution of a flight forward. The massive emigration of its working masses, the systematic pillage of the wealth of the colonies, and the unbridled exploitation of all sectors of the African population have led to the stagnation of the economy, the existence of a parasitic bourgeoisie and prevented the fulfilment of the industrial revolution in Portugal.

As for the distressing internal contradictions against which the regime is struggling, [the following factors] — the deteriorating position of Portugal in the international arena, the growing isolation of the defenders of fascism, the growing menace which the wave of liberation of the peoples of the Third World represents, and the growing pressures of international finance faced with the unleashing of the liberation wars in our countries — constitute *warning signals* for certain sectors of the Portuguese bourgeoisie, indicating the need to introduce profound transformations in Portuguese society.

But nonetheless the catalytic factors which condition the changes that may be presently seen in the Portuguese political and economic structures and which are translated politically into conflicts within the National Union and in the increased acuteness of social contradictions which are revealed by the acceleration and deepening of anti-fascist political struggles, these catalytic factors are essentially the unleashing of the national liberation struggles in Angola, Guinea, and Mozambique.

European imperialism, in agreement with the new neo-capitalist strategy, has decided to launch an economic offensive with the objective of cornering new markets in the underdeveloped countries of Europe itself. Portugal is being asked to participate in the great European economic and political combines. Certain sectors of the Portuguese bourgeoisie accept the possibility of an economic shift in the direction of Europe.

The last decade has seen a growing penetration of foreign capital which has had the consequence of an increase of modern economic activities replacing the traditional ones. Even our own colonized countries are seeing a transformation to a greater or lesser degree, of the classical modes of exploitation, which may be noticed in the upsurge of investment of foreign capital linked to Portuguese capital in the form of large enterprises for mineral and commercial exploitation which give this stratum of the Portuguese bourgeoisie access to considerable monopolistic profit.

We are seeing at the present time among the Portuguese bourgeoisie a differentiation of political and economic interests. There is no doubt that the traditionally conservative interests of the estate owner, of the textile manufacturer, as well as of small and medium-size settlers who utilize the colonial slave structure as the basis of their profits and even of their very existence is becoming increasingly *differentiated* from the interests of a segment of the Portuguese bourgeoisie, interested in large enterprises, in the modification of the structure, in large monopolistic profits, and which is ever more closely linked to European high finance.

This differentiation of interests may be seen in struggles for political supremacy, particularly within the apparatus which has until recently served as the nexus of political compromise among Portuguese interests as well as of the competitors of the Portuguese fascist bourgeoisie, that is the National Union. The launching of liberation struggles in our countries has weakened the fragile Portuguese economic structure and sown panic among the bourgeoisie, thereby giving new weapons to the reformist current of the bourgeoisie.

This current of the Portuguese bourgeoisie, whose political exponents are long-time collaborators of the fascist regime, strongly assisted by European finance, while they see the lessening possibility of Portugal maintaining its colonies militarily, needs a *period of transition* to strengthen itself in the political and military fields, to conquer political power, to remold the fragile economic and financial structures in a European direction, and to impose eventually neo-colonialist agencies in our countries.

The massive penetration of foreign capital in Portugal and in its colonies, especially since 1961, which will either permit Portugal to avoid momentarily the disaster which is coming and to promulgate new organic laws whose demagogic meaning will not escape the peoples of our countries or will try to constitute new African elites through the granting of study scholarships and through political and social promotion of higher African technicians, are both *symptoms* which of course represent attempts to mystify the peoples of our countries and African and international public opinion. Nonetheless, it is necessary to take into account that these means and many others were instituted only after certain political exponents of this current Portuguese bourgeoisie occupied ministerial posts. These facts may mean that real efforts to apply a policy of decolonization will begin. This policy of decolonization, announced by its ideologues in a more or less open form, in order to be applied by this current of the reformist bourgeoisie after its coming to political power, must necessarily be cautious in its application in each one of our countries. This application will therefore be a function of the existing *rapport de forces* between the revolutionary nationalist forces and the levels of mobilization of all sectors of the people in the struggle for liberation and, on the other hand, the situation of the repressive forces of the Portuguese occupier.

The African social instruments to apply such a policy of decolonization could come to be constituted by sectors of the petty bourgeoisie, the bureaucracy, and the traditional chiefs, who, although mobilized by the liberation movements, hope to come to occupy the place of the colonialists in the exploitation of the masses in close collusion with the former occupier and with international finance.

Nonetheless, Salazarism, the expression of the ultra-conservative and ultra-colonialist current of the bourgeoisie, seeks in the short run to postpone the total disaster that would result from the loss of the colonies for the Portuguese bourgeoisie (even for the reformist bourgeoisie) and avoid the outbreak of growing conflict between the two segments of the bourgeoisie. It will try to put off satisfying the legitimate aspirations of our peoples by increasing repression through a repressive machinery that is unparalleled and on the other hand by appealing to foreign capital. These constitute the two poles of the unstable policy of the Portuguese bourgeoisie.

The financial costs which maintaining the repressive military machinery on three battlefronts involves also include the costs of the large political apparatus in Portugal, itself a factor which reduces the possibilities of economic development in an underdeveloped country such as Portugal. To cover the expenses of war and of Portuguese and colonial government, they intensify the exploitation of workers, increase taxes, and provoke considerable increases of prices, thereby affecting the cost of living. Certain sectors of the bourgeoisie which up to now have been privileged are one by one beginning to suffer while the superexploited masses of the population can obtain very little more. Portuguese youth is thrown into a monstrous repression and pays with its life and spiritual perversion for useless sacrifice. Discontent is growing among the masses of the people, the youth, the middle sectors of the bourgeoisie, and even large sectors of the Church. . . .

The historic role of the national liberation struggles of our people led by the vanguard parties — PAIGC, MPLA, FRELIMO, CLSTP — is not limited to the conquest of total independence and to conferring the dignity of national and international personality on the Guinean, the Angolan, or the Mozambican.

These liberation movements have a further role. They transform the profoundly contradictory structures of the colonizing society, accelerating within the society the destruction of anachronistic structures, they prepare the conditions for the resurgence of a new and progressive society, and consequently for a new Portuguese human being oriented to justice, fraternity, and progress.

The Portuguese Opposition and the Movements of National Liberation

For many years Portuguese democratic forces have been organizing and struggling against the dictatorial and fascist power that was installed in Portugal more than 38 years ago. The resistance of the Portuguese people, accomplished through many different political actions which have been undertaken by the Portuguese opposition, against the political and social order which is in place in Portugal has been concretized by means of strikes of workers, peasants, and intellectuals; by political struggle on the occasion of presidential elections and at other times; military coups, which did not succeed, as in the case of the Beja barracks or the ship, *Santa Maria*; the denunciation of the bourgeois and fascist regime done by revolutionary militants in the clandestine press; and demonstrations against the colonial war. All these struggles are among the many actions of the Portuguese people which constituted appreciable gestures of solidarity and aid to our national liberation struggle. This is true to the degree that these struggles contribute to the creation of conditions favourable to the achievement of the objective of our liberation struggle, which are destroying gradually the colonial structures of our countries.

On the other hand, the launching and development of the liberation struggle of our countries has further catalyzed this revolutionary process of the Portuguese opposition, which has been headed by the Portuguese Communist Party (because it is the only organization with a true implantation in the exploited and oppressed masses), and is tending to create conditions favourable to the appearance of new factions and political currents which will enlarge the scope of the Portuguese opposition — organizations such as the Movement of Revolutionary Action (MAR) and the Front of Popular Action (FAP), which are in the process of being built. In effect, the fact of being today in the vanguard of the struggle which is bringing about the destruction of one basis of the Portuguese colonialist fascist edifice, provides an incentive for a greater mobilization of democratic anti-fascist forces in Portugal, renovating and increasing the energies of anti-colonialist struggle inside our unyielding enemy's camp itself. This has brought about, as a consequence, profound political economic and social changes in the life of the Portuguese people. We can thus say that the launching of liberation struggles in our countries has come to have a historic projection inside the struggle of the Portuguese people to liberate itself from the fascist dictatorship. It is thus that we find today in the programmes of the PCP, the MAR, the FAP, and the FPLN statements about decolonization and national independence in our countries one indispensable condition for the re-establishment of democracy in Portugal.

Within the Portuguese opposition we find today the following currents which are incarnated either in a faction or in a federation of groups: the FPLN (Patriotic Front of National Liberation), encompassing the PCP, the MAR (Republican Resistance), progressive Catholics, and constitutional monarchists, which was created at the end of 1962. The member organizations retain their autonomy and internal structure, it being a front, merely having a platform of minimum demands in the struggle against the fascist camarilla in power. There can be serious doubts about the attitude of the anti-fascist bourgeoisie, largely represented within the Front, towards the interests of the estate owners and the Portuguese monopolists and colonialist upper bourgeoisie linked with international imperialism.

The Front cannot be anything other than a simple platform, to the degree that we find within it, for example, alongside the PCP, Republican Resistance, which is far from accepting the ultimate consequences of a programme of struggle against the interests and privileges of the middle and monopolistic bourgeoisie and the estate owners. Confirmation of this idea can be found in the recent public statement of Popular Democratic Action (ADP) which openly rejected collaboration with the Communists in the struggle for overthrowing the Salazarist dictatorship. Now it appears that this anti-fascist movement is part of the Republic current which is represented by the FPLN.

Outside the FPLN, we find the Front of Popular Action (FAP), whose leadership is formed essentially by dissidents of the PCP, which broke with it due to divergences of an ideological and strategic character. It has some base in the working class and the peasantry but is primarily an organization of students . . . . The differences of orientation between the PCP and the FAP can be seen in different responses to the following questions: (a) What should be the basic criterion to achieve national revolutionary unity? (b) How will the armed insurrection against the fascist colonial apparatus be prepared? Should violence be used in the short run, forging a fighting organization in the fire of a struggle or only in the long run after meticulous and careful preparation of a politico-military organization which could fight almost at a level of equality with the fascist army? (c) In what way should they give concrete support to the liberation struggle of the people of the Portuguese colonies? Should it be through a democratic and national revolution, peaceful and directed in large part by an anti-fascist bourgeoisie, or should it be through armed struggle which will undermine the essential pillars of oppression of the peoples of the colonies directed by the popular and working masses and by revolutionary intellectuals? While it is not our objective here to analyse the quarrels of the revolutionary rather than of the Portuguese opposition, it is nonetheless necessary to characterize minimally the currents and political factions that are found there. Without that, it will not be possible to define the political options of the political opposition in its totality, faced with the liberation struggles of our peoples, since this opposition is far from being a homogeneous reality, both within the FPLN and outside it, in respect to its theoretical objectives and the translation of these objectives into practice. Because, while we had to have a valid interlocutor, it had to be made up in practice of all those forces and armed groups which are opposing the fascist and ultra-colonialist Portuguese regime. But if on the other hand we find that the Portuguese opposition has a heterogeneous nature in the matter of options, then we have to reserve to ourselves the legitimate right to know if and when we will collaborate with it. For our armed struggle is directed against the military and economic basis of the Portuguese colonial presence in our countries; it is the only weapon capable of defeating Portuguese ultra-colonialism and the only weapon also capable of stopping imperialist investments, which are the germ of the neo-colonization of our countries, if we do not cut these forces out, by means of our liberation war . . . .

Conclusions

(1)   The impact on the socio-economic structure of Portugal created by the European neo-capitalist offensive has contributed to the differentiation of economic interests of the Portuguese fascist bourgeoisie which expresses itself in the National Union through the struggle for conquest and political power.

(2)   This differentiation of interests and the increased acuteness of the contradictions within Portuguese social strata were furthermore essentially provoked by the launching of the struggles of national liberation in our countries.

(3)   Motives of an economic, political, and psychological order explain why the stratum of the Portuguese bourgeoisie that is in power now requires the maintenance of the political and economic status quo and therefore the continuation of the colonial wars, for this is its necessary condition for survival. In spite of the fact that new legislation has been adopted, legislation that is of a logomachy adapted artificially to the historical circumstances and to the international conjuncture, there has been a fundamental continuity in colonial ideology. The effort to move away the notion of the colonial situation as it is understood today by political sociologists may be seen in the backward juridical concepts which have been defined and concretized in the abolition of the Native Statute, in the alterations of the Organic Law, and in the form of the Code of Labour. In the last analysis, the integration [between Portugal and the colonies], of which there has been so much talk, is in fact an integration in the realm of Portugal's constitutional and economic structures. In other words, the type of economic exploitation that permeates our countries under Portuguese domination finds its consecration in the political and juridical framework that has been constitutionally established.

(4)   Starting with the present-day internal and international *rapport de forces* there may be, in the more or less immediate future, changes in the Portuguese political structure. In this case the Portuguese reformist bourgeoisie will come to play a decisive role on the basis of a compromise with international high finance.

(5)   This new current of the Portuguese bourgeoisie argues that the only way it is possible to safeguard its fundamental interests is a neo-colonialist solution in our countries. It follows that the solutions which are envisaged

will be different from territory to territory, according to the configuration of forces that are present in each territory and the existing political context.

a) The existence in Angola of a considerable petty bourgeoisie, of a bureaucracy, and of a traditional chieftaincy might offer neo-colonialist sectors a real basis for the consummation of a solution approximating the present political situation in Congo-Leopoldville, which is the solution which would guarantee the necessary time to put into place the neo-colonial structures in Angola, a solution that would have the support of a large part of the European colonial bourgeoisie in Angola and of the international neo-colonial bourgeoisie.

b) The small numbers of the African petty bourgeoisie in Mozambique, the stratum which would normally play a large role in neo-colonial solutions, would lead the Portuguese reformist bourgeoisie to envisage the solution of a Rhodesian type there. The ideas proposed by the neo-colonialist bourgeoisie in Portugal find a wide echo among many sectors of the European colonial bourgeoisie in Mozambique.

c) Guinea constitutes for this sector of the Portuguese bourgeoisie a very embarrassing case. The excellent military and political positions conquered by the PAIGC places the Portuguese colonial army in the position of possible military defeat. For this reason the preferred solution is the creation of puppet Guinean movements, which will play the game of neo-colonialism, supported by world imperialism, which is interested in arranging the creation in this part of Africa of centres of so-called subversion. However, this attempt at a neo-colonialist solution in the case of Guinea is, on the contrary, going to accelerate the radicalization of the struggle due to the already achieved implantation of the forces of the PAIGC.

(6)   While there are serious divergences of orientation among the various sectors of the Portuguese opposition in their struggle against Salazarist fascism and colonialism practised in our countries, it should be considered that this struggle is overall a beneficial political factor in our struggle for national liberation. In the meantime, the parties of the liberation movements of our countries must not base their struggle on the elaboration and carrying out of a strategy or tactics that will depend on the aid which the action of the Portuguese democratic forces might represent for our struggle for national liberation. We must count on our own forces for the destruction of Portuguese colonialism.

(7)   If we recommend a reinforcement of contacts, on the basis of mutual and equal benefit, between the Portuguese opposition and the parties and movements of liberation of our countries which are grouped together in the CONCP, it must equally be borne in mind that there exist great divergencies of interests between those of the Portuguese opposition which sees as its next step in the struggle the democratic and social revolution in Portugal, which would include in power large segments of the anti-fascist bourgeoisie, and that which we see as our next step of the struggle, national independence without the risks of neo-colonization.

(8)   Nonetheless, bearing in mind the importance for our struggle of a real

reinforcement of the struggles of the Portuguese opposition against the infra-structure which feeds the colonial machine of war and which is implanted in Portugal there, the CONCP must orient its Portuguese policy in the direction of aiding the Portuguese opposition to overcome its immobilism and internal differences, thus contributing to the effective enhancement of its struggle for the downfall of fascism.

This would be the only way possible for sabotaging the war machine which is being imposed on our peoples and, therefore, the only way at present which the Portuguese democratic forces would have to demonstrate their solidarity towards our armed struggle for national liberation.

3. Responses to Reformism

Editors' Introduction

The national liberation movements were revolutionary movements. As such, they were perpetually faced with how to respond to proposals made sometimes by their enemies, sometimes by their well-wishers, occasionally by members within their ranks, that they try some route which they would term 'reformist'. The general attitude of the movements is well reflected in the ANC statement on the 'fraud of reform'.

But a general position was insufficient. They had to face up to specific proposals. For example, when the white settlers of Rhodesia illegally made their Unilateral Declaration of Independence, the Zimbabwe movements called upon Britain to use force to suppress it. Britain refused. Instead, the British supported 'sanctions'. The ZAPU paper argued that sanctions would 'never work'. But sanctions were all the Zimbabweans ever obtained from the international community. When, in 1972, the United States reneged on even this reformist measure, ZANU denounced this step as backward.

A second recurring reformist proposal was to recommend contact rather than isolation as the way to reform in southern Africa, especially South Africa. This took many forms. One form was the visits of artists. We reproduce ANC's denunciation. A second form was 'dialogue' as advocated by such leaders as President Houphouet-Boigny of the Ivory Coast. To Tennyson Makiwane, dialogue was an 'imperialist mask'. A third form was that in which the UN itself sought to serve as an 'intermediary'. SWAPO denounced this role of the Secretariat in relation to Namibia. A fourth form was the one supported even by the 'militant' independent states in Africa, the Lusaka Manifesto of 1969. Hailed in the Western world as a manifesto for 'peaceful revolution', it was received in anguished silence by the movements. Why they were anguished but silent was revealed by Nathan Shamuyarira. Rather than all these reformist steps, Marcellino Dos Santos asked the independent African states to make active sacrifices to combat imperialism instead of mere passive denunciations.

There was also a sophisticated version of the 'contact' hypothesis. The pseudo-materialist argument is regularly put forth that as the South African economy expands, structural pressures would force 'liberalization'. This delusion has been exposed even by a white South African liberal such as Jean

Sinclair. And finally there was the extra twist on this argument which asserts that 'raising African wages' was an urgent necessity. ZANU's editorial calls this 'a carefully orchestrated gimmick to keep the Black worker in his place'.

The Fraud of Reform
ANC

Excerpt from the document 'Development of the South African Revolution' adopted by the Consultative Conference of the ANC held in Morogoro, Tanzania in May 1969.

There is no possibility of securing changes in our country except through revolution. Faced with temporary difficulties, some people especially outside our own movement, are beginning to toy with all manner of reformist theories. These find currency in the realm of Bantustan politics. Some intellectuals have decided to participate in politics as supporters of 'separate development'. In the Transkei and elsewhere some people, for selfish reasons, are endeavouring to justify government policy. The Bantustans have now been established in the Northern Transvaal, Western Transvaal, Ciskei and Transkei. We have just had elections for the Coloured Representative Council. The Indian Council has also been set up. Does all this suggest that we are now in a period of retreat in which reform comes to the fore as a tactic?

The reformist experiments are a cruel farce. The whole of Africa is virtually free from foreign rule. Independent states have sprung up on the borders of and within the Republic of South Africa. In the still colonial territories the people are waging heroic guerilla struggles for their freedom. South Africa is no exception to the developments taking place in the rest of Africa. Reformism in our country historically failed in a very long period to lead our people to freedom. On the contrary the most sustained reformist policies led to the Fascism and terror we experience today. There is not one single factor to justify any expectation that reform could even lead to any amelioration of our conditions. Our history and experience have taught us very harsh lessons. One of the most vital is that without building an army, arming our people and conducting revolutionary struggle we will remain an oppressed and exploited people. The only correct path for the oppressed national groups and their democratic supporters among the whites is armed revolutionary struggle. This is not altered by the problems and difficulties that confront us in developing the revolution.

The Sanctions That Will Never Work
ZAPU

Article in Zimbabwe Review *(ZAPU, Lusaka), I, 2, June 1969.*

On 11 November, 1965, the minority Rhodesian British settlers declared 'independence' unilaterally. Following this, the British Prime Minister, Mr. Harold Wilson, reacted against Rhodesia by banning the sale of arms and spare parts to her, terminating UK aid, removing her from the sterling area, imposing exchange controls, banning exports of British capital to her and denying her access to the London capital market, refusing to grant export credit guarantees, suspending the Ottawa Agreement of 1932, governing her trade relations with the UK, and barring purchases of her tobacco and sugar.

But today these sanctions have not brought the 'racist' regime in Zimbabwe (Rhodesia) to even anything like its undermining in spite of Prime Minister Wilson's bragging on 12 January, 1966, that they 'might well bring the rebellion to an end within a matter of weeks rather than months'.

The reality is they have not, are not, and will not achieve anything in any length of time because they were never meant to accomplish anything, but were intended to serve as an umbrella to cover and facilitate the establishment, on a permanent basis, of a racialist-fascist settler minority rule in Zimbabwe.

After more than three years of British style economic sanctions, one cannot fail to reflect on the extent to which British involvement in sanctions against Rhodesia has developed and the policies of other countries, dig out the issues raised by the sanctions and what their practice has been and try to show the impact of these measures and the degree to which they are useless.

It cannot be denied that the British people in the United Kingdom have involved themselves in sanctions against Rhodesia without losing sight of kith and kinnery. Again and again the Labour government has made it abundantly clear that it has no intention of giving a humiliating blow to the British community of under 250,000 people in Zimbabwe.

This position is, of course, characteristic of the British imperialists. To them the distinction between Black and White as well as Anglo-Saxon and non-Anglo-Saxon is the supreme criterion of judgement where problems engender moral considerations. But while the blood-brother philosophy is of significance in the UK's Rhodesia policy, it should be borne in mind that it is British economic and business interests in Zimbabwe that form its roots and stem.

Britain has about £200 million invested in the country, of which about £150 million is operating in mines, farms and property. Today British monopolies with subsidiary and/or affiliated companies in Zimbabwe, either directly or through South African companies, amount to between 200 and 300.

It is also interesting to note that quite a good number of prominent British politicians are or have been directors of companies with interests in

Zimbabwe or have interests somewhere in there. Among these gentlemen one can mention Mr. R. Maudling, deputy leader of the British Opposition and former Chancellor of the Exchequer, Mr. A. Barber, Chairman of the Conservative Party, Mr. J. Boyd Carpenter, a former Cabinet Minister, Mr. N. Birch, Mr. Quintin Hogg, Mr. C. Gresham Cooke, Sir G. Nabarro, Sir C. Osborne, the Rt. Hon. C. Rippon, Mr. Julian Amery, Sir C. Black, the Rt. Hon. H. Fraser, Sir J. Eden, Sir A. Vere Harvey, Lord Salisbury, Viscounts Amery, Watkinson and Chandos and Lord Caradon.

With this, it is clear why British involvement in economic sanctions against the Rhodesian 'rebels' has not developed in favour of the preached goal. Britain cannot be expected to implement, observe and enforce sanctions against herself.

Another point of interest is the sanction policies of other countries throughout the world. Here it is well known that Britain has very influential allies and that the latter have stuck all along to their friend's way of seeing things. After all, what could one ever expect? The Americans continue to be mad in their blind anti-communism and imperialist adventures, the West Germans are racialist and fascist-imperialist revenge-seekers, France lives by ruthless narrow-minded egoism and profit-seeking internationalist meddling, the South African Boers are fascist-racialist slavers and Portugal's colonialist mentality is a neurasthenic case.

The honest fighters in the sanctions war, one must point out are the Afro-Asian and Socialist countries. But as their share of the influence in the economy of Zimbabwe is nothing relative to that of the Western Alliance, their direct efforts cannot be expected easily and rapidly to give rise to economically pertinent effects.

A lot has been said about the advantages and disadvantages of economic sanctions against Rhodesia but for the most part they have been advanced for the sake of British human and economic resources. It is just unfortunate for everybody that the real issues raised by British-prescribed sanctions have, even if pointed out, been smoked up and brushed aside. Anyway, it is not futile to bring them out for consideration.

First of all, it may be asked whether economic sanctions are necessary in the effort to bump off the Smith 'racist' regime. The answer is no, because there are other means, better and more efficient, for that matter. If military force had been used in 1965 everybody would have forgotten about everything by now.

To be serious, the blood-bath evasion theory in as far as the Rhodesian question is concerned is from all points of view and in the long run a short-sighted naive view. On this point it is instructive to look at what is taking place now. There is freedom-fighter armed struggle in Zimbabwe. So, blood is flowing anyway and there is to be more for people of all skin colours to bathe in, whether they like it or not.

In the second place, the question is on whether economic sanctions are a sufficient measure to bring down the 'racist' thugs in Zimbabwe. Here again the answer is: they are not, for those hooligan fascist-racialist settlers prefer to become destitute countryside soil scratchers.

And if this were to happen those engaged in freedom-fighting would have no choice but to put on more smiles. But in view of kith and kinnery Britain and her allies would not tolerate such a state of affairs. This is exactly what they are doing now: breaking the sanctions that they themselves have prescribed.

Finally, even if these sanctions were to ultimately tame Smith and his cronies, what is there to make one think that there would be a just settlement of the Rhodesian problem and not an enslaving sellout of the people of Zimbabwe? The *Fearless* proposals have shown clearly that the British government has no fears about exchanging an African for less than a farthing.

It is universally recognised that the use of economic sanctions against Rhodesia has encountered insurmountable difficulties. To this day, the Rhodesian 'racists' have managed to import and export goods. This has been due mainly to commercial and financial facilities offered to them by their South African and Portuguese friends.

However, it would be a show of naivety to consider South Africa and Portugal as the only sanction-busters. Although capable of doing away altogether with Rhodesian trade ties, other countries have maintained dealings with the 'racists', either directly or through South Africa, Portugal and Malawi. This is shown to some extent by the following table:

Rhodesian Exports to Some Countries (£ '000)

	1966	1967	1968
Britain	2,200	305.5	–
West Germany	3,960	2,980	3,990
Portugal	110	425	–
France	469	444.5	–
Japan	2,390	1,390	–

As for South Africa, it is to be remembered that although her data are not available, their magnitude is substantial and has definitely been on the increase during the post-UDI period.

While they might have created certain discomforts the sanctions imposed against Rhodesia have not produced the desired effect. This is because, apart from a few important items, they have been hitting on non-essentials.

Rhodesian minerals and manufactured products remain exportable to a very considerable degree and all Rhodesian banks continue to operate very much in a normal way. The situation has become so promising that the British companies, Ford and BMC have found no point in not resuming their car assembly operations in the country. This explains the striking resilience of the Rhodesian economy since 1965. Here it may be remarked that there is no reason why this should not go on.

Of course, the country is at the moment threatened by inflation due to its excess liquidity position, increasing public expenditure and no prospects of corresponding increase in production.

In addition, there is the looming menace of a 500,000 unemployed position within five years' time if there is no favourable change in present trends. But once again it has to be pointed out that in view of the great degree of uncertainty facing the Rhodesian economy any forecast is bound to have very little utility.

So far, however, all the economy's sectors have not done badly, in spite of the sanctions. In agriculture only tobacco has been a big headache. Production of the crop is running at one third that of 1964 while the total cost of maintaining the industry to date works out at some £63 million and may stand at £75 million in 1970. In any case, it should not be forgotten that the crop is being sold. It's not stock-piling only that is going on.

As for the sector as a whole, it has been benefiting a lot from diversification and import substitution and it might be interesting to point out that its contribution on the country's Gross Domestic Product in 1967 was £72.7 million as compared with £67.8 million in 1966.

Manufacturing has on its side registered good performance except perhaps in 1966. The index of manufacturing production for 1968 stood at a level of 3.5 per cent higher than that for 1965 and 25 per cent higher than that for 1966.

The mining sector has never had it terribly bad since the year 1965. In 1967, mineral exports were valued at £32 million in contrast to about £33 million in 1965.

It is external trade that has been described as the crux of Rhodesia's problem of economic development. Well, it is true that the country has a growing balance of payments problem and is being forced into import allocation reduced to cut back imports. This, of course, is definitely going to have negative effects on overall economic performance. On the other hand, one needn't get surprised if one of these days Rhodesia pops up with a new bag of tricks to overcome this problem.

Apart from economic considerations as regards the impact of the economic sanctions being levelled against Rhodesia, it must be pointed out that there also is the political and moral side of the question to be taken into account.

The sanctions have put Rhodesia at the mercy of South African control. Smith is no more enjoying those days when he could conduct his local and international politics without consulting the Boers in Pretoria. As for the moral effects of the shadow sanctions, it can only be said that there has been a cumulative spiritual toughening up within the settler community with the result that a real feeling of independence is emerging, a development Britain is no doubt observing without regret.

It is quite clear that Britain has never been serious in her Rhodesia policy. In fact, she has been playing the world's family of nations into gradually rehabilitating her illegitimate child. In drawing up the so-called economic sanctions, the United Kingdom made sure that they would not be effective.

Moreover, she seduced everybody to the economic sanctions idea because she knew very well that the measure is not sufficient by itself alone to bring down the Rhodesian 'rebels'.

The USA – Champion of Oppression
Ndabaningi Sithole

> *Letter written by the President of ZANU, to US Secretary of*
> *State William Rogers. It was smuggled out of the Salisbury*
> *jail and published in ZANU's* Zimbabwe News, *VI, 10,*
> *October 1972.*

Dear Mr. Rogers,
 Greetings to you.
 I wish to express to you, on behalf of the people of Zimbabwe, our deep concern over the actions of your government in relation to the present economic sanctions being imposed against Rhodesia subsequent to the white minority here unilaterally assuming independence in 1965 at the expense of the African majority of this country.
 The USA has constantly stressed that she does not support violence as a means of solving the problem facing Black and White in southern Africa. She has come out on the side of non-violence as a matter of her policy in southern Africa although she is pouring more forces of violence in Vietnam. At the UN and elsewhere you have reiterated this policy, and the USA, one of the founding members of the UN, and one of the five great nations with the veto in the Security Council, is a party to the UN resolution imposing economic and diplomatic sanctions on Rhodesia as a means of solving the problem here through non-violence. What is most disturbing is that while the UN is trying to make non-violence work in southern Africa, your own country is now deliberately undermining the forces of non-violence and indirectly but effectively promoting those of violence. The action of the USA to resume chrome imports from Rhodesia under the present circumstances only goes to show that she cares more for metals than for justice and peace in southern Africa. If this deplorable behaviour was shown by a small and insignificant nation, perhaps it would be easy to overlook it, but not when it is shown by a great leader nation! From the great we expect and even demand better behaviour and a much higher level of rationality than your country is presently showing.
 The action of the USA to import Rhodesian·chrome in spite of international sanctions to solve the Rhodesian problem through non-violence has serious implications not only for the 5½ million people of Zimbabwe but also for those countries which honestly believe that the problem in southern Africa can be solved through non-violence if the various nations can fully co-operate to make them work.

The USA has often stated that it supports self-determination, representative government and genuine nationalism. At present the people of Zimbabwe are engaged in a grim struggle to realize these in the land of their birth, and one of the chief means the UN had decided on to help us realize these goals is economic sanctions against the illegal regime which denies us our full rights and full freedoms in our own country, but now the USA has decided to work against these sanctions by continuing to import chrome from this country. In doing this she has set herself against the self-determination to which the people of Zimbabwe aspire. She has in fact declared herself opposed to the establishment of representative government in Zimbabwe. In other words, she undermines altogether the possibility of non-violence, self-determination, representative government and legitimate Zimbabwe nationalism. Her recent action strengthens the hand of the oppressor and weakens that of the oppressed. Indeed, the USA has become a champion of oppression and all that this means and implies. I cannot see how the USA can rationally and honestly disclaim this role she has voluntarily assumed.

Although the USA claims to be a champion of democracy, her recent action belies that claim. In an important democratic exercise, the people of Zimbabwe have massively rejected the Anglo-Rhodesian proposals aiming to lift sanctions and to legalise white minority rule, racialism, white supremacy and paternalism, and thereby subjecting the African people here to indefinite oppression and injustice, but your country has seen it fit to act against the democratic voice of the people of Zimbabwe and also that of the UN which imposed sanctions in order to establish a democratic regime in this country. It is strange, absurd, irrational to the point of immorality that your country should take the lead in undermining the democratic verdict of the people of this country, and the democratic resolution of the UN. One would have thought that the USA would have been the first to abide by democratic decisions! The African majority has rejected the Anglo-Rhodesian proposals so that sanctions may stay on as an important bargaining lever in their struggle for freedom and independence, but your country has chosen to weaken at a very critical stage their negotiating position. By helping the illegal regime here to erode the sanctions, the USA could never have been more treacherous to the cause of the people of Zimbabwe and to the cause of democracy.

Your country's violation of the UN resolution imposing sanctions has the effect of giving the green light to other nations to get cracking with the disrupting of the whole exercise of sanctions. She has legalized the contravention of the UN resolution against Rhodesia! It now remains for other nations to follow suit. If the USA erodes sanctions in the interest of chrome, why should Britain not do so in the interest of tobacco or asbestos? Why should not France do so in the interest of beef or peanuts? Why should not the Soviet Union do so in the interest of nickel or some other mineral? Why should not the People's Republic of China do so in the interest of mealies or pork? It is most regrettable that your country as a superpower has seen it fit to declare war on sanctions against Rhodesia. Her move is as soulless as it is metallic. It is difficult for us to think of your country's act in any other terms than those of naked, unashamed bullyism engendered by arrogance of plain, brutal power deaf and blind to the interests of the majority of the people of Zimbabwe. But this is not what we expect from a leader superpower like your nation. We expect world leadership and not world bullyism. Your country's daylight defiance of the UN resolution intended to benefit the oppressed 5½ million people of Zimbabwe is an act of a world bully rather than a world leader.

In conclusion, I must repeat to you, Mr. Rogers, that your country's shameless disregard of the UN resolution does not only undermine the struggle of the people of Zimbabwe for freedom and independence but non-violence, democracy, international morality and the very conception and reality of the United Nations. It is a callous act that shakes international confidence in the leadership of the USA.

Yours sincerely,
Ndabaningi Sithole.

Dear Eartha Kitt
ANC

Article in Sechaba *(ANC), VI, 9, September 1972.*

An Open Letter to Jeremy Thorpe and Eartha Kitt – With Friends Like These, Who Needs Enemies?
There are a lot of people in the world these days wanting to reform South Africa. We are grateful for that, for South Africa can certainly do with reform, not to mention revolution. And the knowledge that their struggle enjoys the whole-hearted support of millions of freedom-loving people throughout the world has been a tremendous help and encouragement to the liberation movement.

But there are some people offering 'solutions' to the South African problem which they have thought up on their own, not so much to assist our movement as to sidetrack it. Since they have been getting a lot of publicity in both the South African and overseas press lately, we think it is about time to tell them where they get off.

Let us take as an example Mr. Jeremy Thorpe, Liberal Party leader, who returned from a short lecture tour of South Africa last June with his own plan for dealing with the problem of British investment in South Africa.

Having visited Soweto, Mr. Thorpe said he was appalled by the 'slave conditions' of the African workers, whose living conditions he found 'as bad as anywhere in the world'. 'No British firm', he opined, 'should tolerate a situation in which employees are paid wages barely of subsistence level, where trade unions are not recognised and where people are allowed to live in hovels'.

His plan is for MPs to buy one or two shares in the companies with subsidiaries in South Africa, and to press for reform from the inside, either by direct approaches to the directors or by raising the issue at general meetings. 'Those who call for the withdrawal of British investment in South Africa will achieve nothing', he said. Why? Mr. Thorpe supplies the answer: Britain holds 60 per cent of the foreign investment in South Africa. 'Many of the British firms accept the situation there and are prepared to pay the low wages offered by the South African firms.' But, says Mr. Thorpe, 'I am sure the British directors and shareholders are not aware of the treatment the African workers are receiving. If the facts are brought to their attention I feel certain improvements can be made.'

Mr. Thorpe perhaps does not realise what a condemnation his words are of all capitalist investment, not only in South Africa, but everywhere in the world. Are any investors aware of the treatment received by the workers whose labours create the profits for them? Those men who frantically buy and sell shares on the floors of the workers' conditions? Do they even know what products are made by the companies whose shares they buy and sell? No, Mr. Thorpe, the British investor puts his money into South Africa because he gets a bigger profit there than he can get anywhere else in the world. It is cheap black labour that makes his profit so big. If you take away his cheap labour and his huge profit, why, he will simply transfer his investment elsewhere, and the devil take the South African workers, black or white, who will lose their jobs.

Anti-apartheid demonstrators have been putting the facts before meetings of shareholders in the biggest British companies with investments in South Africa. They have found on the whole that the British shareholders not only know what is happening in South Africa, but condone it. Oh yes, your company chairman will of course say he disapproves of apartheid, but he will go on making use of apartheid cheap labour because, he claims, he is doing good by providing work. He even boasts he is paying as good wages as the next man. He will argue that you can't expect him to make radical reforms on his own because he would price himself out of business. He will then order his company thugs to eject the demonstrators.

The *Guardian*, in an editorial on June 5, 1972, came down four-square on Mr. Thorpe's side. 'Mr. Thorpe's approach is the right one', it opined. 'It will be much easier to persuade conservative directors of the validity of progressive policies if they have been put forward by a committee of reasonable MPs, rather than by disruptive demonstrators.'

Well, well, this is what British liberalism has sunk to! *The Guardian* does not, apparently, question the policy put forward by the demonstrators, but merely their social standing. Well, if reasonable MPs are more effective than disruptive demonstrators, perhaps the MPs could use their persuasive powers to get the British business world to implement the decisions of the United Nations General Assembly, the Organisation of African Unity and the African National Congress, all of which have called for the severing of all relations with South Africa as the best means of rendering support to the liberation movement. We would remind Mr. Thorpe that it was the late Chief Lutuli, President-General of the African National Congress and a Nobel Peace Prize-winner, who issued the call for a total boycott of South Africa in every sphere. Would Mr. Thorpe include him — and the many other men and women of great stature who head the liberation movement in South Africa — in the ranks of disruptive demonstrators who can be ignored?

What right has Mr. Thorpe to advance his own private solutions to South Africa's problems? We would not presume to tell the British people what to do about Ulster, or inflation or unemployment, or containers or the Common Market. We leave it to the good sense of the British people to solve their problems. We might even come to the conclusion that the policies of Mr. Thorpe's Liberal Party were the correct ones, and if the situation was one of sufficient gravity to warrant our intervention, or that of the United Nations, we might feel justified in declaring our support for Mr. Thorpe's cause.

But we would not, under any circumstances, launch our own campaign for the reform of Britain, as Mr. Thorpe proposes to do for South Africa. What a cheek! Imagine the African National Congress telling the British people where they get off in their own domestic politics! For that is precisely what Mr. Thorpe and those who think like him are doing to South Africa. Mr. Thorpe may say he is only telling British investors what they should do. But he is doing more than that. He is saying the ANC policy is wrong, the OAU and the UN are wrong, the freedom fighters are wrong in calling for the withdrawal of investment from South Africa. He is saying the way we have chosen is the wrong way; only his way is the right way.

And please, Mr. Thorpe, don't quote to us the examples of the US firms Polaroid, Pepsi Cola and the rest which are claiming to have increased African wages in their South African subsidiaries, and to have given so many thousands of pounds to some or other educational or charitable cause in South Africa. This is merely testimony of the enormous profits these firms are able still to extract from cheap labour in South Africa, otherwise they would not remain there. Despite their propaganda, Polaroid, Pepsi Cola, General Motors and the rest are not in South Africa for the sunshine, nor out of concern for the condition of the South African workers. They are out for profit, and they are getting it. Announcing its decision to stay in South Africa last December, the Polaroid Corporation went out of its way to stress that 'the South African Government allowed the experiment to proceed without interference or opposition of any kind'. Precisely. Nothing Polaroid, Pepsi Cola or Mr. Thorpe can do in terms of their present policies is of much concern to the South African Government because it does nothing to alter the basis of apartheid. If it did it would not be permitted by Vorster or anyone who might take his place.

Is this merely the voice of the disruptive demonstrators again? Let us then quote for the benefit of Mr. Thorpe, Pepsi Cola, General Motors and all others who are trying to excuse their blatant collaboration with apartheid the words of an American church team which spent three weeks in South Africa last October and November investigating precisely this issue: 'Most of us believe that American corporations should totally disengage from Southern Africa', said their report. 'The presence of American corporations in which we are shareholders undergirds the system of racialism, colonialism and apartheid which prevails in southern Africa.' Discussing the argument (listen to this Mr. Thorpe) that US firms would do more good for Blacks in South Africa by staying than quitting, the report said: 'Even progressive employment policies on the part of the American companies will not bring the basic changes in society that we support.'

And in case Mr. Thorpe would like to check the credentials of the commission, the statement was read by the Right Rev. John E. Hines, presiding bishop of the Episcopal (Anglican) Church on behalf of the other churches involved in the Church Project on US Investments in Southern Africa at a press conference held in New York last February and reported in the Johannesburg *Star* on February 16, 1972.

What we have said about Mr. Thorpe, Polaroid and Pepsi Cola goes as well for people like Eartha Kitt, Margot Fonteyn, Evonne Goolagong and all the others who have chosen off their own bat to break the boycott of South Africa. They all go for the profits they make in South Africa, and they all find reasons to justify their betrayal of our freedom fight. A reporter of the Johannesburg *Star* reported on May 27: 'Singing sex-kitten Eartha Kitt told me before flying to Rhodesia at the end of her South African tour this week that she believed her visit had "knocked a significant dent in apartheid"'. She hopes to come again, and to pave the way has also worked out a plan to salve the consciences of artists who want the pickings they can get in South Africa so badly they are even prepared to perform before segregated audiences.

In conjunction with OK Bazaars, Eartha has started an organisation called SPEED (Stage Performers' Endowment for Educational Development) to raise money for African education. SPEED will ask every entertainer who comes to South Africa to give 2 per cent of his or her earnings towards African education. (Only 2 per cent, Eartha? Do you think you can buy us with 2 per cent?)

She said her visit had pricked White consciences, and claimed to have done more for the benefit of the Coloured people than the Coloured Labour Party which criticised her for coming. Well, Miss Kitt, all we can say is Mr. Vorster doesn't think so. He bans leaders of the Coloured Labour Party, but he hasn't done a thing to stop you, because he welcomes your help in breaking the international boycott of South Africa. He is prepared to dine with Dr. Banda, to allow you to sing to segregated audiences, and to let in any other person who is willing to perform on his conditions, because he knows what you do hurts us. Yes, Miss Kitt, hurts us, both physically and morally. You not only break the boycott we want imposed, but you hurt us, as a Black woman who has suffered the indignities of apartheid, by taking the side of our enemies in this struggle. You do what Vorster wants you to do; you don't do what we, the oppressed, want you to do. Whose side are you on? Are you just a good girl?

Moreover, Eartha, you encourage other people to overcome their doubts and follow in your footsteps. Two days after you spoke, Margot Fonteyn said in the *New York Times*: 'What pleased me most, and made me feel justified in going was that Eartha Kitt was in Cape Town at the time I was there, and she was totally sympathetic and understanding and thought I had done the right thing. That made me very happy'. Margot Fonteyn is a principled person. She even told Coloured demonstrators in Cape Town who objected to her performing before segregated audiences, that she was glad they had come. 'I understand why you're here. I am happy to see you here with your posters. For 15 years I have refused many invitations to perform here, and nobody knew about that. At least my coming here has given you this opportunity to demonstrate.' Please Dame Margot. We've got Vorster and his gang here already to demonstrate against. We have no lack of opportunities to get hit over the head with police batons. We don't need this sort of assistance from you or anybody else.

The time has come to say firmly to those who claim to be our friends that they must make their choice. South Africa is our country. We have chosen to fight and suffer to free it. If you are not in our camp you are in the camp of the enemy. There is no room in between. Please don't try to take the weapons out of our hands. If you can't join us, then at least leave us alone. We don't tell you how to dance or sing. What makes you think you know better than we do what must be done to 'dent' or smash apartheid?

Above all, please don't sell us out for 40 pieces of silver and then pretend it is all for our own good.

Dialogue — South Africa's Imperialist Mask
Tennyson Makiwane

> *Article by the then Deputy Director of External Affairs, ANC in* Sechaba *(ANC), V, 8, August 1971.*

Just when the sun is setting — when empires all over have crumbled or are on their last legs — is precisely the moment South Africa has chosen to embark on a new imperialist adventure on the continent of Africa. Quite clearly, the Pretoria strategists have learnt little or nothing about the lamentable demise of imperialism. They would have done well for instance, to scrutinise the recent history of North American imperialism in Latin America and in South East Asia — that at least is a spectacular drama happening under everyone's nose.

There are interesting similarities between the stage of development which the United States reached at the end of World War II and South Africa's present day position. The United States emerged from the war right on top. She was bubbling over with confidence, ready to assume 'world leadership'. She was rich, and above all armed to the teeth being the sole country in possession of the atomic bomb. Pretoria considers that she meets both requirements and she beats her chest as she contemplates her economic and military might. But the similarity between the United States and South Africa ends just there — i.e. at the possession of monetary wealth and military hardware.

True, the United States embarked on the imperialist road in the post World War II period on a big wave of anti-Communism. And the Vorster regime also seeks a common front with Black African States in order to 'combat Chinese Communism' which he claims has set-up a bridgehead in Tanzania. But how different the times are — then, at the height of the cold war and McCarthyism, and today when young people in the United States march the streets waving the flag of the National Liberation Front of South Vietnam. And why should Zambia and Tanzania not accept the interest-free loan from China in order to build a railway line linking the two countries? After all, they first approached the World Bank which turned down their requests for a loan.

Normally, imperialism dons the mask of 'democracy' at home and there whips up demagogic or chauvinistic nationalism, proclaiming its 'sacred duty' to embark on a civilising mission abroad or to come to the defence of religion against infidelism etc. etc. More recently as we have seen, it proclaims itself as 'Saviour' against the inhumanity of communism.

And what is the record of the Pretoria regime? At home, the vast African majority and other non-Whites continue to be denied basic human rights in their daily lives. Their economic situation is desperate. The country boasts the world's largest per capita hangings. The jails are crowded with political prisoners including Nelson Mandela, Walter Sisulu, Govan Mbeki, Bram Fischer, Ahmed Kathrada and others. And beyond her borders, the Pretoria regime has pursued a policy of naked expansionism as evidenced by its illegal annexation of Namibia (South West Africa), its despatch of troops to aid the Rhodesian White minority regime and its aid to Portuguese colonialism. And in addition to all this, there have been constant threats of aggression by the South African racist regime against neighbouring African States such as Zambia and Tanzania. One recalls the now notorious 1967 speech which Vorster made in the East Rand threatening to 'hit Zambia so hard that she would never forget it'.

From the above observation, it would seem that South Africa's new imperialist drive is headed for ignominious defeat even before it starts — lacking as it does, even the most rudimentary prerequisites which succeeded in the past to make imperialism a going concern. But it would be naive to take such a superficial view.

It is most eye-opening to read the Vorster-Kaunda correspondence which the Zambian Government have released following the so-called 'expose' of Dr. Kaunda by Vorster. In his letters Vorster reveals his grand strategy. In the letter dated May 2nd, 1968, Vorster, discussing the policy of apartheid says inter alia: '. . . In fact, to name only two, President Banda, and Prime Minister Jonathan, have both stated in public that they disagree with the policy and it certainly did not jeopardise the very friendly relations that exist between my country and theirs.'

In other words the Pretoria regime has no intentions whatsoever of abandoning its apartheid and racist policies though ready to do a deal with leaders of independent African States who 'publicly condemn apartheid'. And why then is the South African regime attempting to overthrow leaders like Dr. Kaunda of Zambia who condemn apartheid. The answer is simple enough. The Pretoria regime is not embarking on classical imperialism which would involve direct occupation of African States. But would instead set up Black puppet 'leaders' who would dance to her tune. Such a stance by South Africa presupposes that she will make it part of her policy to topple militant anti-apartheid regimes.

Point two: it is obvious that South Africa seeks to smash the Organisation of African Unity. Vorster lets the cat out of the bag when he says '. . . the problems of any country, including your own, Mr. President, will not be solved by the OAU or any other organisation . . .' (letter of May 2nd, 1968). Now if there is anything patriotic Africans have been striving for, for decades, as fervently as they have for freedom – that thing is *unity*. It was therefore most appropriate for Nigeria's General Gowon, during his recent state visit to Ethiopia, to redefine Africa's perspectives at the present moment. After pointing out that the Independence of Africa was still being threatened today by forces wishing to recolonise Africa, he said: 'In South Africa the inhuman policies of apartheid and racial discrimination continue unabated. Those brothers of ours in agony cry out for our assistance.'

But most unhappily, Gowon's voice is not the unanimous voice of Africa. Daily, evidence is mounting that the forces behind the new anti-Africa conspiracy have gone quite far.

If the much heralded Houphouet-Boigny press conference of April 28th, is the tip of the iceberg, then we want to examine carefully his main thesis. President Houphouet-Boigny of the Ivory Coast stated at the press conference that dialogues take place either after a battle or among equals. There should be no battle, he argues because 'Africa must be spared' such wars 'if it is to be able to free its people from poverty through development'. And should Africa therefore negotiate from a position of equality? *No*, because, argues Houphouet-Boigny, Africa is so militarily weak that 'the war would be over in five days before the first Ivory Coast soldier had buckled his belt'.

What, therefore, are we to make of exhortations that Africa must talk with the Pretoria racists from a position of weakness? We get further clues when we examine the significance of Vorster's scandalous personal attack on President Kaunda of Zambia. And we must not be taken in by the propaganda that aimed at causing Zambian voters to oust the President. Anybody who knows Zambia, would realise that such an attack from the South African racists would only have the opposite effect.

Vorster was only confirming that far-reaching decisions have already been taken in high and powerful places. The sharp editorials from some western newspapers scolding Vorster for 'forfeiting secret diplomacy' were rather a reflection of the imperialists concern that Vorster's big mouth was prematurely giving the game away.

The intervention in the South African situation of Dr. Houphouet-Boigny, an old horse of the imperialist camp, a man who as a member of the French Government not only failed to denounce the dirty colonial war of French imperialism against Algeria, but permitted African soldiers from the Ivory Coast to fight on the French side, against their Algerian brothers, shows that the stakes are high. New and dangerous treasonable activities are being hatched by international imperialism against Africa!

The Luxury of Drawing Room Diplomacy
Putuse Appolus

> *Excerpt from a statement by Mrs. Putuse Appolus of SWAPO*
> *(Namibia) to the United Nations Committee on Decolonization*
> *in New York in June, 1973, and printed in* Namibia News, *VI,*
> *Nos. 7-8, July/August 1973.*

SWAPO has witnessed the attempts to maintain dialogue between South Africa and the Representative of the Secretary General, Dr. Escher, with a considerable degree of disapproval. From our intimate knowledge based on a long history of exploitation, SWAPO was sure that the South African regime was not amenable to negotiation. The stark reality is that we have been proved to be right — that the dialogue between Vorster and Dr. Escher would be fruitless. Vorster has used the opportunity to buy time in consolidating his hold over Namibia by the continued implementation of the bantustan policy, and to attempt to fool international opinion by fostering the image that he is willing to negotiate.

The niceties of drawing room diplomacy are a luxury that SWAPO cannot afford. The International Court of Justice has clearly established that my country is the subject of an illegal occupation and has affirmed the reality of the termination of the Mandate by the United Nations.

To encourage talks with Vorster, therefore, is to attack the rightness of the decision of the International Court of Justice. The decision means — and you will pardon me, Mr. President, if I express myself in concrete terms — that South Africa must get out of Namibia. There is nothing to treat about, or to argue about, or to discuss about. Vorster must go and with him all the repressive machinery which he has used to keep Namibia in chains.

The Council for Namibia must be allowed to undertake the obligations entrusted to it by the General Assembly. SWAPO, therefore, takes the stand that there must be an end to all dialogue with South Africa and an immediate withdrawal from Namibia. In the meantime, until this decision is reached, based as it is on the norms of international law, SWAPO will increase and intensify its efforts to implement the Court's decision by all means at its disposal.

The Dangers of the Lusaka Manifesto
Nathan Shamuyarira

*Excerpt from a commentary on the Manifesto (Proceedings of
the Fifth Summit Conference of East and Central African
States, held in Lusaka, 14-16 April 1969) written by a ZANU
leader and published in* The African Review *(Dar es Salaam),
I, 1, March 1971.*

The Lusaka Manifesto on liberation and human rights in Southern Africa
which was signed by thirteen Heads of States in East and Central Africa in
April, 1969 (Malawi alone refused to sign) is the most prestigious document
produced in Africa since the drafting of the Charter of the Organization of
African Unity in 1963. It has since been endorsed by the Organization of
African Unity and accepted almost unanimously by the General Assembly of
the United Nations. Its acceptance by the General Assembly was regarded by
African States as a substantial achievement of the twenty-fifth session of that
august body.

This document has been well-received in the West because of its concilia-
tory tone. Senator Edward Kennedy of the United States said, 'perhaps the
greatest importance of the Lusaka document is its tone as a manifesto for
peaceful revolution not violent revolution in Southern Africa' (*The Nationalist*, Dar es Salaam, 11 June 1969). Newspaper editors and policy-makers in
Britain, France and West Germany have drawn attention to its moderate
tone; others have seen it as a retreat by African States from the position of
total support for liberation movements taken at the founding conference of
the OAU in 1963. Even the South African Government has found itself in
agreement with certain parts of the Manifesto. Dr. Hilgard Muller, Minister of
Foreign Affairs and the chief architect of the policy to seek friendship with
African States, saw the document as a sign of growing realism on the part of
African States and a realization that they have to co-exist with South Africa.
He stated confidently that African States were changing their attitude towards
the Republic.

However, the ten liberation movements organizing an armed insurrection
in Southern Africa are opposed to the document. They view any suggestion
of achieving independence by discussion as prejudicial to the present state the
struggle has reached, and, at best, an attempt to seek for a neo-colonial solution that will create even more acute problems. However, without exception,
the liberation movements have refrained from campaigning against the document. There is hardly any reference to it in their propaganda pamphlets.
Their attitude has been influenced largely by the support given to the document by States supporting the liberation struggle, especially Zambia and
Tanzania which presented the original draft to the fourteen States.

An analysis of the Lusaka Manifesto must begin with the audience the
signatories had in mind. Although it is addressed to 'members of the human
race' (para. 4) in fact it is directed at Western nations whose economic and

military support props up the White regimes of Southern Africa. The signatories appeared anxious to secure the withdrawal of that vital Western support. As one supporter of the Manifesto put it in a letter to me:

> The Lusaka Manifesto is using the language of the West because it is speaking to the West as much as to anyone. They, as you yourself say, are the ones who are in practice helping the regimes of Southern Africa, and my belief is that the signatories wanted the West to be aware of what it was doing and what the implications were. For this purpose you have to speak the language they listen to and understand — you have to argue, not shout.

But Western nations cannot be persuaded by peaceful means alone because their security and prosperity is inextricably interlocked with that of the White regimes in question . . . .

There are some positive aspects in the Manifesto. The most important is the desire to find common ground on which African States can approach the question of Southern Africa. It is an open secret that the majority of African States do not give financial or material support to the Liberation Committee of the Organization of African Unity, or to the liberation movements. Of the thirteen signatories only three States — Tanzania, Zambia, and Congo (Kinshasa) — have given active support to the Committee and/or liberation movements. The remaining States have been passive, neutral or plainly uninterested. There is a danger that some of them may be attracted by the abortive course of collaborating with the White regimes followed by the Republic of Malawi. It was necessary, therefore, to commit the majority of African States to the realistic course of liberation through the armed struggle by means of a moderate document that threw out an olive branch of conciliation and negotiation. The unanimous support given to the document by African States at the OAU meeting last September and at the United Nations last November would indicate that this objective has been achieved.

The Manifesto has given the African States a new and valuable diplomatic instrument. The burden of guilt has been shifted clearly onto the shoulders of Vorster, Smith and Caetano where it belongs. Even if Western nations will not take any positive steps against these regimes for reasons that have been stated above, they can have no doubts about the moral bankruptcy of the case advanced by White settlers and supported both directly and indirectly by their own Governments.

It should also be stressed that the common ground struck by the Manifesto, and the favourable diplomatic posture have not been achieved at the expense of the basic principles of the struggle. There is no compromise on self-government or on the use of violence to achieve this objective when all peaceful means have failed. While the Heads of States prefer to 'talk rather than kill', they conclude on the firm note that 'Africa cannot acquiesce in the maintenance of the present policies against people of African descent' (para. 22) in South Africa. At paragraph 12, they say that on the objective of liberation 'we can neither surrender nor compromise'. This important paragraph throws out the olive branch but at the same time retains the commitment to the main principles of the struggle for liberation.

The most serious and negative repercussion of the Lusaka Manifesto is the effect it is likely to have on the freedom-fighters in the liberation movements themselves. They are likely to feel that African States are abandoning the struggle. Although the commitment to the principles of the struggle remains as stated above, the main thrust of the document is towards peaceful negotiations rather than violence. African States have retreated many steps from the position they took at the founding conference of the OAU in 1963. On that occasion they resolved to boycott South African and Portuguese goods, contribute one per cent of their national budgets into a special fund for liberation, and even provide volunteer corps as freedom-fighters. These brave words and resolutions were never fulfilled. The failure of the majority of States even to withdraw diplomatic representatives from Britain over the Rhodesia case exposed the weakness of the OAU and the bankruptcy of its moral prescriptions. The freedom-fighters who were encouraged by the 1963 position to organise liberation forces are bound to feel disheartened by the complacency that permeates the 1969 Manifesto.

The silver-lining in this cloud is that the committed States have not slackened or reduced their financial and material support for the liberation movements in the first year of the life of the Manifesto. The uncommitted have remained uncommitted. Therefore, the Manifesto has become an instrument for pan-African diplomacy outside the continuing work of liberation.

The Manifesto has revealed as never before the moderate nature of African Governments today. Many of them are products of peaceful change by negotiations with their former masters, although that change was one of personnel rather than of social systems. Naturally, they would like to apply the same procedure to a region that has totally different circumstances and conditions of oppression. Many African Governments fear the consequences of violence and revolution in any part of Africa on their own domestic societies. The OAU Charter confirms the *status quo* and conforms to the traditional concepts of sovereignty and independence. The nine States that withdrew diplomatic representatives from Britain over Rhodesia, the eight that have continually supported the Liberation Committee since 1963 and especially Zambia and Tanzania that have borne the main burden of the work of liberation, are notable exceptions. The majority are *status quo* states that would happily and willingly embrace a neo-colonial situation in Southern Africa that would change the personnel running the Governments but not the system of exploiting the masses of the people.

A Certain Sacrifice

Marcellino Dos Santos

Interview with the Vice-President of FRELIMO by Aquino Braganca in Afrique-Asie, 20 August 1973. Translated from French.

It is notorious that the military supplies of NATO, the investments, the loans and donations (such as the 436 million dollars given to the Portuguese government as compensation for the bases in Azores by the Nixon administration) allow Portugal to pursue its wars of genocide freely, and constitute the major obstacle to our independence.

Thus, it is obvious that one of the preoccupations of the African countries must be an attempt to find ways of changing this situation. In order to do so, they must exert pressure upon the Western countries and bring them to withdraw completely all support from Portugal.

Braganca: But do the African countries have the means to exert such pressure?

Dos Santos: Why not? For instance, the African delegates at the UN and the OAU have adopted annually certain resolutions which correctly state that 'Western investments in the African territories occupied by Portugal block decolonization'. But all these resolutions are dead letters, since their implementation would imply certain sacrifices for the countries in the process of development, that is, the African countries.

Zambia and Tanzania, for instance, have refused to allow multi-colonial enterprises to participate in the development of their country, in spite of competitive prices, since these firms are involved in the construction of the Cabora Bassa Dam in Mozambique. We are not attempting to impose an investment code upon the independent countries of Africa, but we ask ourselves why they do not follow the example of Zambia and Tanzania.

Improvement Within the System – A Delusion

Jean Sinclair

Extracts from a reply by the National President, The Black Sash (South Africa) to an article in the Financial Mail *of Johannesburg on 11 September 1970 that one should 'do what one can as a businessman to improve conditions of life within the system', rather than refuse investment as suggested by Neil Wates, a British businessman.*

This hackneyed argument is the standard reply given to those who criticise the lack of positive action in the face of the myriad laws, controls and restrictions which inhibit the growth of a free enterprise economy and hold workers in virtual serfdom. It is an argument which stills the conscience of the businessman in the belief that he is alleviating the deprivations and hardships suffered by the African people.

Who Is Benefiting

With respect and in all sincerity I ask who is benefiting by the opening up of new industry and the investment of new capital in South Africa? First, the Government, which takes 41 per cent of the profits in tax; second, the industrialist and his shareholders, who make a fair return on their investment; and last the African worker, who has a 'better job and 30 rand in his pocket at the end of the month'.

Poverty Rates

Thirty rands a month is an average poverty wage, is 29 rand below the poverty datum line and is the level at which the African becomes liable for income tax. Those who believe that economics will bring about change and who believe that half a loaf is better than no bread should at least ensure that every worker receives a living wage.

According to Mr. Donald Woods, two-thirds of all South Africans are suffering from malnutrition. In Soweto alone approximately 70 per cent of the population live below the breadline. Mr. W. Langschmidt (Market Research Africa) estimates that 25 per cent of all urban households had monthly incomes as low as between 1 rand and 19 rand a month; 40 per cent between 20 rand and 49 rand; 20 per cent between 50 rand and 79 rand, and only the remaining 15 per cent are earning more than 80 rand a month.

Africans constitute 68 per cent of the population and their share of the nation's income is 19 per cent. In contrast, the whites, who comprise 19 per cent of the population, receive 73 per cent of the income.

Profiting from Exploitation

The provisions of the Physical Planning Act, the recent statements of the Prime Minister and the Ministers of Labour and Bantu Administration with regard to the utilization of labour, and the insistence of moving more industry to the border areas, where wages are even lower than in the metropolitan areas, the terms of the Industrial Conciliation Act having been withdrawn from these areas, are surely indicative of the Government's determination to carry out its policy without regard to the needs of the economy and without concern for the needs of the African workers.

These facts make Mr. Wates' statement all the more pertinent. The crux of what he had to say is contained in the following paragraph of his report:

> We could not be true to the basic principles on which we run our business and we should lose our integrity in the process. We should have to

operate within a social climate where the colour of a man's skin is his most important attribute and where there is virtually no communication between the races; we should be locked into this system, we should have to operate within an economic climate which is designed deliberately to demoralise and to maintain an industrial helotry; we should, in turn, profit from such exploitation and ultimately end up with a vested interest in its maintenance.

If Mr. Wates were to adopt [the] rather presumptuous suggestion that he could use his profits for the benefit of African education, health and welfare, he would be doing the very thing which he finds so repugnant. He would be helping to bolster up the whole rotten system of *apartheid* and would 'have a vested interest in its maintenance'.

Businessmen Silent on the Inhumanity of Apartheid

For far too long, commerce and industry have sought to negotiate with the Government to obtain minor concessions and exemptions for themselves, from certain prohibitions and restrictions contained in legislation. But the public has never heard their voices raised in protest against: poverty wages which are often paid to African workers; lack of bargaining power for Africans; suffering caused by influx and efflux control and the migrant labour system; the serious shortage of housing; lack of security of tenure; broken families; the long distances they have to travel to and from work; the restrictions on the type of work they may do.

All the protest and the discussion has been with reference to the effect of the manpower shortage on the economy, but very little is heard about the effects of the policy on the African people who are being pushed around and denied the right to work.

Mr. Wates' decision, instead of invoking criticism, should cause South Africans in general and businessmen in particular to stop and think why the whole world abhors South African policy. And to question whether they are using their considerable power to bring pressure to bear on authority to alter its uncivilized and inhumane policies before the country is completely isolated and before its economy is ruined.

Black Wages and Righteous Indignation
ZANU

> *Editorial in* Zimbabwe News *(ZANU, Lusaka), VII, 4 April 1973.*

The righteous indignation raging in Europe and America over revelations of starvation wages which foreign companies in South Africa pay Black workers should not deceive supporters of armed struggle in that country and elsewhere. In reality, the revelations are not revelations at all. They are merely a restatement of the grizzly old story of exploitation and degradation of the Black worker since the advent of White minority rule in South Africa. That story applies equally to Zimbabwe, Guinea-Bissau, Angola and Mozambique.

All involved in this modern slavery, in South Africa and abroad, knew of these inhuman wages long before they hit the headlines. Indeed, the companies concerned set up shop in South Africa in preference to other countries because they knew beforehand that forced, cheap, Black labour would ensure extraordinarily high returns on investment. That is why exploiting companies are concentrated in the republic. A capitalist, whether individual or corporate, is in business to make profit — and the bigger the better.

Why the indignation then? It is an attempt to put a human face to exploitation. This is all there is to it. Those expressing 'shock and disgust' are apologists for apartheid and racism, out to protect their investment and the racist establishment guaranteeing them exceptionally high profits.

How do we know this? From the solution they propose: increase Black wages. To what point? To the so-called poverty datum line — a line arbitrarily handed down by the very establishment that has been exploiting Black labour for 300 years and more! Proponents of this 'solution' have not yet begun even to think of asking the Black worker for the solution to the problem of starvation wages to the Black worker!

Clearly, this 'indignation' is a carefully orchestrated gimmick to keep the Black worker in his place. In the meantime the White worker will go on earning wages far, far above his productivity and 10 to 15 times the wages of his Black counterpart; and the international bourgeois his excessive profits. The status quo stays put.

What is the solution? Certainly not to fight to increase wages within the framework of apartheid but definitely to struggle to overhaul the rule of the White minority — *not* just apartheid — and to place political power in the hands of the majority. The solution is political, not economic. And it can come about by no other means except by armed struggle. He who opposes armed struggle opposes adequate wages for Blacks but he who supports armed struggle supports human wages for Blacks.

4. What To Do About Bantustans

Editors' Introduction

The tactic of the South African government in launching the Bantustans was obvious. It hoped to reinforce 'tribal' consciousness among the African population, defuse political demands by creating showpiece regimes with no real power, reduce the number of Blacks in the urban areas, and create reservoirs of cheap semi-skilled labour for so-called 'border industries'. And in addition there was perhaps the motive of preparing a 'fall-back' scheme of ultimate territorial partition.

All this was clear to the movements within South Africa, and Namibia, and for this reason they denounced the idea from the very beginning. ANC's article on the Transkei reflects this view. What was less clear was whether there was any advantage whatsoever, in terms of national liberation, to working within the structure. At first, the movements were sure there was not. Later however, when Gatsha Buthelezi became the Chief Executive Councillor of KwaZulu, the movements took a moment to reflect. For Buthelezi asserted that he was working via Bantustans to destroy apartheid. Did this make any sense?

We start with a paper presented by Buthelezi in Sweden. The ANC's *Sechaba* reprinted it with the following preface:

> Although the African National Congress is convinced that the so-called Homelands Policy of the South African government is a gigantic fraud we, nevertheless, present this paper which formed the basis of Chief Gatsha Buthelezi's address to the Scandinavian Institute of African Studies recently, so that readers may see the dilemma in some of those who are forced to serve on these institutions because of their position as chief of their people, are placed.

The militant Black university students of the South African Student's Organization (SASO) were less gentle in their description of Buthulezi, also reproduced in *Sechaba*. The ANC's justification for its mitigated description of those 'who have no choice' was made briefly. How the ANC responded to specific proposals put forth by Buthelezi is illustrated in a 1971 statement on a proposed 'national convention'.

The PAC by contrast avoided distinctions and denounced Buthelezi. The

South African Communist Party was equally sceptical. As for SWAPO, there being no 'Buthelezi' in Namibia, they simply saw Bantustans as 'an exercise in eyewash and blatant hypocrisy'.

Five Years of Bantustans
ANC

Article in Mayibuye *(ANC, Lusaka), III, 1, 3 January 1969.*

In the last issue of *Mayibuye* we analysed the political developments in the Transkei over the last five years. It should be clear to the reader that the Transkei is as far from genuine political independence today as it was five years ago, that the fascist-racist regime has neither had nor intends ever to grant such independence. In fact, developmenrs reveal the real purpose of the racists which is to develop a class of middle men between the African majority and the minority White oppressors.

They hoped that the chiefs, the African civil servants, the traders, etc. can be used to bludgeon the African masses more effectively as well as to act as a cushion against revolt.

In this article we shall deal with the economic aspects of Bantustans which should make clear even to the most prejudiced observer that Bantustans are and were fraudulently conceived and undertaken. To quote from Govan Mbeki's *The Peasants' Revolt*:

> . . . but even more important is the economic aspect of Bantustan policy. For the Bantustans are the most densely populated African rural areas in South Africa, the homes of millions of peasants who live in grinding poverty, and so the traditional reservoirs of labour for the entire country. Can they exist in 'independence'? Would any government pledge to White supremacy to allow and assist them to develop their resources on the scale necessary to make self-government possible?

Govan Mbeki asks these questions rhetorically knowing the answer to be a 'no'. And every action of the racist regime before and since independence confirms this.

Aside from the stark poverty of the peasantry the Transkei started off with an apology of an infra-structure. In 1963 there were very poor railway facilities and their chief function was to take labourers from the reserve to the White farms, mines and factories. The roads were poorly developed and were to serve the same function as the railways. There was hardly any power to speak of, virtually no industries. Hundreds of years of White rule had resulted in the Transkei becoming increasingly more poverty stricken. Five years after Bantustans the position is little different. The Tomlinson Commission recommended in 1956 that at least £10 million had to be expended on the Bantustans *annually* to lay the basis for development. It also recommended improvement in agricultural methods which would displace thousands of peasants from the land. To provide employment for these peasants, secondary and tertiary industries would need to be created. According to the Commission at least 50,000 opportunities of employment would have to be created *annually*. It should be remembered that the Tomlinson Commission pointed out that even with the fullest and most extensive development the Bantustans would be able to accommodate only 10 million Africans by 1987 still leaving another 15 million in the so-called White areas. In other words on the basis of land allocation and distribution the Bantustan scheme was already a non-starter in 1956!!

But in terms of the past five years the Tomlinson recommendations appear other-worldly, something from cloud-cuckoo land. The *Financial Mail* (1/11/68) described any talk of 'development' in the Transkei as 'wishful thinking'. The government has no intention of providing the money for development in the Transkei for this would undermine the whole system of migrant labour.

However, in keeping with the pretence that Bantustans were to be independent African States the government announced originally that all Whites would have to leave the Transkei and that all commercial and industrial enterprises would be undertaken by Africans only assisted by the Bantu Investment Corporation. Needless to say this was all very well in theory but in practice Africans have not the capital to create industries. As a result the racist regime's economic policy with regard to the Bantustans has gone through several changes.

(1)   The *Africans only* policy failed for reasons given above.

(2)   *Border Industries:* This was a policy whereby White industry would be allowed to site itself on the borders of Bantustans.

While this did nothing for the development of the Bantustans the government explained that it would provide employment for residents of the Bantustans. Various incentives were given to White industries such as cheap power, cheap transport on the railways, freedom from wage board regulations, and labour legislation, etc. What this amounted to in practice was intensified exploitation of the Africans and opportunities for Afrikaner business. White enterprise was, however, reluctant to go to border areas except where existing industrial areas already bordered on the Transkei.

(3)   Allowing *White Capital*: Early this year the government finally departed from its pretence that Whites would be totally excluded from the reserves. It announced that henceforth White capital would be allowed into the Transkei but had to be controlled and channelled through Africans or through government corporations. White industrialists were taken on a lavish, all-expenses-paid tour of the Transkei but their unanimous verdict was that there were no investment opportunities in the Transkei. This scheme having failed the government has recently embarked on.

(4)   *Allowing White Industries* into the Transkei as 'agents' for the Bantu

Investment Corporation. What this means is that the industries will be allowed to operate for a certain number of years and then would have to sell out to the Corporation at a 'fair' price. One doubts if even this will be very successful. To quote *News/Check* (25/10/68): 'It may still not be an attractive enough business prospect to attract much White capital into homelands. But having gone so far, the wheel of policy is bound to go the full distance.'

In other words, the racists will shortly be compelled to allow White capital and industry to enter the Bantustans without restriction thus totally exposing their fraudulent policy. Fraudulent, that is, in terms of the racist public pronouncements. But in terms of White baasskap and Black subjection there is, of course, no fraud. For it has never been the intention of the fascists ever to grant the Bantustans complete political freedom or to enable them to attain economic viability. The reserves have always been and (so long as the fascists rule our country) will continue to be reservoirs of labour for the Whites — their continued existence as poverty stricken areas is vital to the maintenance of White privilege and profit.

After five years of Bantustans even the most short-sighted observer can see that talk of independent African States within South Africa is a hollow sham. No amount of double-talk, no number of stooges and Uncle Toms can disguise the fact that the Bantustans are as underdeveloped and poor as ever and that real power continues to be wielded by the Pretoria regime.

Another aspect of the racists' Bantustan policy was that eventually all Africans would have to leave what are arrogantly termed 'White' areas and go back to their respective Bantustans. But what is, in fact, happening is that the number of Africans in the urban areas has been steadily increasing every year. If the increase has not been even more phenomenal it is because the fascists have used the Bantustan bluff to apply influx control more stringently and harshly than ever before — the weak, the sick, the old, the women are being sent back to the reserves in thousands.

Bantustans cannot bring freedom for our people. Their only effect is intensified economic exploitation, greater political oppression, social degradation and humiliation. Bantustans (and, in fact, the whole apartheid system) are opposed to all laws of political and economic development. And for this reason they will give way to a non-racial democratic South. The People's Liberation Army, led and guided by the ANC, are engaged in bringing that date closer.

Working From Within

Gatsha Buthelezi

*From a paper by Chief Gatsha Buthelezi, Chief Executive
Councillor of KwaZulu, delivered to the Scandinavian Institute
of African Studies and reprinted in* Sechaba *(ANC), VII,
3 March 1973.*

I have chosen the above title for my talk today as I assume that most people are curious to know what Separate Development looks like through the eyes of one like myself who is participating in the implementation of this policy. It is probably one of the most controversial policies pursued by a country in our time. Because of the mass media many people know of South Africa and her policy of Apartheid, although that word now tends to be substituted with Separate Development, particularly within South Africa.

I have great reservations about the philosophy of Apartheid which is behind the policies in whose implementation I am participating. This I am not saying because I am in Sweden, it is something I made quite clear from the moment I was elected by my people to lead them. Some of you may know that this was embodied in my inaugural address delivered in the presence of the Minister of Bantu Administration and Development, Mr. M.C. Botha, on 11 June 1970 at Nongoma, KwaZulu. I have since then repeated this, not only in front of the Prime Minister of South Africa, Mr. B.J. Vorster, but at every possible occasion.

This policy is not a policy of options and to pretend that the question of accepting or not accepting this policy ever arises at all, is grossly misleading. What is worse, such pretence gives the South African White minority who rule us undue credit by giving the impression that we have any latitude in this matter at all. In my opinion, to say that we have 'accepted' Apartheid, by serving our people within the framework of the South African Government policy would be as nonsensical as to say that when great African leaders like the late Chief Albert Lutuli, Dr. Z.K. Mathews and others, served their people within the framework of the United Party Government policy of segregation as members of the Native Representative Council, that they did so because they 'accepted' the segregationist policies of the United Party Government. Nothing could be further from the truth.

It is also a well-known fact that when African political organisations like the banned African National Congress and the Pan-African Congress got militant in the early sixties they were clamped on for the very reason that the authorities in South Africa could not tolerate the militant way in which they articulated the wishes and aspirations of their people, despite the fact that they were leading an unarmed people.

There was a void which lasted for almost ten years on the African political scene as no politics are allowed except within the framework of the policy of Separate Development.

Operating as I do with my reservations clearly spelled out, I therefore do not believe that, like Dr. Faust, I have in any way sold my soul to the devil, if I may use the expression.

On the occasion of the inauguration of the Zulu Assembly I also defined what I considered to be the implications of this policy, if its propounders intend to carry it out with any degree of honesty. Foremost it is a crude joke that anyone can consider them to be countries in the making with any degree of seriousness. They all need to be consolidated if this is a serious experiment and this is the only point on which all Homeland leaders agree. I further made it clear at my inauguration that I expected us to have full human dignity and to have freedom. This leaves the ball in the Republican Government's court which is where it is as far as I am concerned.

I also wish to place on record that these so-called 'Homelands' are areas into which we were pushed after conflicts and wars with the antecedents of the present Whites. It is nonsense to call them our traditional homes. They have not been set up by the Nationalist Party Government alone. All that they have done is to romanticise the old reserves by giving them a new Christmas wrapping of 'Homelands'.

When my people asked me despite my well-known views to lead them I felt that I just could not dare to refuse. It was one of those moments in history where I felt caught between the Devil and the Deep Blue Sea. It is therefore one of those events where I think history will be the best judge of my actions in agreeing when I was called in to serve. I did so because no other chance of serving my people in politics is allowed. I did so also because I felt that when there is as much suffering as exists in that situation, it is a moral obligation to alleviate the suffering of human beings in however small a degree one does it. For the moment I have scope for articulating the wishes and aspirations of my people for the first time since the time of Sharpeville. I think this is important even at the risk of these instruments ending up as 'talking shops' in the same way in which the Native Representative Council was ultimately looked at by its members.

At present we find that the challenge is to do the utmost one can do towards the development of our people. This is the only machinery through which one can legally make this attempt in South Africa. It might rightly be said that the most we can achieve in this direction would be to nibble at the edges. This I consider much better than folding arms and crying about it.

At present we are drawing the attention of White South Africa to the cruelty of stinging us for our share of the wealth which we help to produce. More than seventy per cent of our people receive wages below the poverty-datum line. We are at present engaged in warning South Africa about the dangers of the kind of polarisation of wealth and poverty which exists. At the moment the ratio of black to white wages is 1:14. The dangers entailed in the perpetuation of this situation are too obvious if one takes the history of the human race as any guide. We feel that it is our duty at this time for our people to see themselves as Black workers instead of on an ethnic basis. Once this solidarity becomes a reality we have enough faith to know that our voice will be heard. We do not underestimate the reaction of the powerful should this moment be reached.

We are also concerned about disparities in White and Black educational opportunities. Whites have a free and compulsory education with all the wealth they command. No such facilities are anywhere in sight for Blacks. In 1968 R14.48 was spent per head on Black children. In the same year expenditure per head for white children in the four Provinces of the Republic of South Africa was as follows: R191 per white child in the Transvaal, R244 per white child in the Orange Free State. R266 per white child in the

Cape and R288 per white child in Natal. According to a February 1970 issue of Hansard this represents R228 per white child, if we take the number of white pupils in each Province into account. Or in simple terms it means that fifteen times more is spent per white child than on an African child.

When we look at the health of the people we also see a grim picture. There is a doctor for every 44,400 Africans, one Coloured doctor for every 5,200 Coloureds, one Indian doctor for every 900 Indians and one White doctor for every 400 Whites. Less than 12 African doctors a year are trained for a population of 15 Millions. I have been approached by a number of Black doctors with a request that we should launch a fund to establish a private school with a science bias in order to get as many candidates for the medical school as possible. According to an editorial in the latest edition of *The Bantu Education Journal*, a sum of R500 million is estimated as the sum required to eliminate the numerous inequalities and evils we suffer under Bantu Education. We are trying to impose taxes on ourselves to do as much as we can. But this will certainly not go very far. There is a group of white South Africans who are getting concerned about the situation and have launched funds known as the Teach Fund in Cape Town, the Learn Fund in Durban and the Rand Bursary Fund in Johannesburg. This will not solve the problem. But we feel that there is scope for friends within South Africa and also all the countries that have diplomatic relations with South Africa to help us to relieve the situation. It is of no use to be over-righteous about Apartheid if we get no concrete assistance while Apartheid lasts. In other words we feel it is not enough to condemn Apartheid as it will not crumble like the walls of Jericho merely by people shouting only without doing something concrete to alleviate our plight. While the problems of South Africa remain unresolved we feel we should be helped as Blacks to help ourselves. The ritual of resolution after resolution at the United Nations condemning Apartheid has not the same euphoric effects such as it had on Blacks say twenty years ago. We realise that we must like the Afrikaners also attempt to uplift ourselves by our own bootstraps, the difference with us is that we do not even have the bootstraps, which they had after the Anglo-Boer war.

Statute of Westminster

While many people are surprised, for instance, about the Rhodesian situation, we in the South are not. After all it was by the Statute of Westminster, a British Parliamentary Act, that South Africa was granted autonomy without any regard as to whether Blacks were represented or not. The African National Congress sent delegations to make protestations in Europe with no effect.

Friends, we have learnt the hard way that any amount of sympathy for us which is not expressed in concrete terms is like an empty echo of a mountain valley.

Those of us who have qualms of conscience about Apartheid and yet are working within the framework of the policy do so only because it gives us the only opportunity of awakening our people to help themselves. We can only judge as to who are our friends not by any torrents of crocodile tears that are shed, but by concrete contributions towards our campaign as Blacks to try and stand on our own feet despite the situation in which we find ourselves. There is a lame excuse which has become threadbare in our eyes: that is the excuse that if we are helped those who do so are strengthening Apartheid. We are living within Apartheid not out of choice and anyone interested in us will help us where we are. We will sink deeper into the Apartheid seas if we are to look at the situation from that angle, unless we are helped right where we are to keep our heads above water. Many people say South Africa is rich and can do these things for us. What a specious argument! After all there is both a White and a Black South Africa and people should know who is wallowing in wealth as much as who is wallowing in poverty.

There is also the argument that the situation should be allowed to deteriorate and this will bring about a revolution soon. Some of us are not committed to a violent confrontation. I belong to this group. We do not pretend that this might not overtake us if we do not make a serious effort to solve our problems in South Africa. We find it rather strange for anyone outside South Africa to prescribe this for us. It seems to us that in the final analysis that the South African problems will be solved whether peacefully or violently, may God forbid, within South Africa by those within the country. The question of whether it will be a peaceful denouement or a violent confrontation can be dictated by the extent to which we are or are not assisted right now to stand on our own feet as Blacks.

We have not given up the concept of Blacks as an entity. That is why although we are the so-called Homeland leaders Chief Minister Matanzima and myself have pledged ourselves to work towards a federation of the Transkei and KwaZulu and with whoever wishes to join us. It must be mere definition of such a goal however remote it might be in the opinions of others, particularly our critics, within South Africa that keeps the concept of Black unity alive as something we must strive for. The Xhosa-speaking Blacks and the Zulu-speaking Blacks are the two largest ethnic groups in South Africa. We have other things in common such as *Noski Sikeleli Afrika* as our National Anthem. This is also the National Anthem of Zambia and Tanzania. We have also Sotho-speaking communities in both the Transkei and KwaZulu which has made us keep *Morena Boloka* as an additional Anthem in both KwaZulu and the Transkei. Last month I launched the Lutuli Memorial Trust Fund in South Africa with the financial assistance from the Lutuli Memorial Foundation. I appointed the Bishop of Zululand, the Right Reverend A.H. Zulu, as Chairman of the Fund and a Committee was set up. This fund is for the educational needs of all African children who can be helped. It is in keeping with Chief Lutuli's ideas not an ethnic venture.

I mention these things to show that we have not abandoned everything which was precious to patriots who have passed on the African political scene before us. It must always be remembered that there is no situation in any country where politics cannot be defined as the art of the possible. Also in a situation like ours, even more so it remains the art of the possible. We are

What To Do About Bantustans

doing what is possible no more and no less. This I venture to say is what politics is about anywhere and in any situation.

Fragmentation of the Black Resistance
SASO

Article by a leader of the South African Students' Organization published in the SASO *Newsletter and reprinted in* Sechaba *(ANC), VII, January 1973.*

Just who can be regarded as representative of black opinion in South Africa? This question often crosses my mind in many conversations with people throughout the country and on reading various newspaper reports on what blacks have to say on topical matters. Once more the issue was highlighted during the debate on whether or not to celebrate the Anniversary of the 'Republic' of South Africa. On the one hand Mr. Pat Poovalingam in Durban was urging the Indian people to celebrate whilst, on the other, people like Mr. Mewa Ramgobin and the Labour Party argued the case against celebration. In Zululand Chief Gatsha Buthelezi stated that the Zulu people would celebrate whilst elsewhere pamphlets were distributed from various black sources reminding the people that they would be celebrating the countless sins of the Nationalist government. The interesting thing of course was the conspicuous silence of the urban African people except for the hushed objections of Soweto's Urban Bantu Council (UBC). Not at any stage did anybody state a representative opinion.

Anyone staying in South Africa will not be completely surprised by this. Political opinion is probably very clear-cut on issues of this nature amongst the African people especially. However, since the banning and harassment of black political parties – a dangerous vacuum has been created. The African National Congress and later the Pan-African Congress were banned in 1960; the Indian Congress was routed out of existence by the banning of all its leaders and ever since there has been no coordinated opinion emanating from the black ranks. Perhaps the Kliptown Charter was the last attempt ever made to instill some amount of positiveness in stating categorically what blacks felt on political questions in the land of their forefathers.

After the banning of the black political parties in South Africa, people's hearts were gripped by some kind of foreboding fear for anything political. Not only were politics a closed book, but at every corner one was greeted by a slave-like apathy that often bordered on timidity. To anyone living in the black world, the hidden anger and turmoil could always be seen shining through the faces and actions of these voiceless masses but it was never verbalised. Even the active phase, thuggery and vandalism, was directed to one's kind – a clear manifestation of frustration. To make it worse, no real hope

103

was offered by the output from the recently created black universities. Sons and fathers alike were concerned about cutting themselves a niche in a situation from which they saw no hope of escaping.

After this brief spell of silence during which political activity was mainly taken up by liberals, blacks started dabbling with the dangerous theory — that of working within the system. This attitude was exploited to the full by the Nationalist Party. Thus the respectability of Matanzima's Transkei was greatly boosted by Ndamse's decision to join hands with him. Clearly Ndamse, being a one-time banned man, convinced many people by his decision that there was something to be gained out of these apartheid institutions. Soon thereafter the Coloured Labour Party, operating on an anti-apartheid ticket, was formed to oppose the pro-apartheid Federal Party within the all-Coloured Coloured Representative Council. People's logic became strangely twisted. Said a member of the Transkei's opposition Democratic Party: 'We know that the Transkeian parliament is a stooge body. We ask you to elect us to that stooge body!'

But it seems that nothing influenced people more to 'accept' the 'working within the system' theory than the decision by Chief Gatsha Buthelezi to join in and lead the Zulu Territorial Authority. Chief Gatsha Buthelezi had for a long time been regarded as the bastion of resistance to the institution of a territorial authority in Zululand. Then one morning a newspaper intimated that he might just agree to take it up and within weeks Chief Gatsha Buthelezi was indeed the Chief Executive Officer of the Zululand Territorial Authority.

Following the capitulation of Chief Gatsha Buthelezi, a burst of activity manifested itself in these apartheid institutions. On the one hand the Labour Party was making full use of the sanctified platform — the CRC — to air their grievances against the government, on the other Chief Gatsha was fast becoming an embarrassment to the government with the kind of things he was saying.

I believe it is just here that the confusion over who are the leaders of the black world began to arise. Because of the increased verbalisation of black man's complaints, the people — especially the white world — began to take these various voices as speaking on behalf of and as leaders of the Black world. This kind of picture was particularly built up by the English press, who followed in detail everything people like Chief Gatsha Buthelezi did and said. Of course in the absence of any organized opinion it began to sound even to some black people themselves as if this were the case. The fact that Matanzima also joined on the band-wagon of militant demands has made everyone sit back and clap. People argue that the Nationalists have been caught in their own game. The black lion is beginning to raise its voice. This is a gross oversimplification.

What is, in fact, happening is that the black world is beginning to be completely fragmented and that people are beginning to talk sectional politics. I would rather like to believe that this was foreseen long ago by the Nationalist Party and that it is in fact a part of the programme. After the kind of noises made by Buthelezi, the Labour Party and of late Matanzima, who can argue that black opinion is being stifled in South Africa? Moreover, any visitor is made to see that these people are fighting for more concessions in their own area (13% of the land). They accept that the rest of South Africa is for Whites. Also none of them sees himself as fighting the battle for all black people. Xhosas want their Transkei, the Zulus their Zululand, etc. Coloured people harbour secret hopes of being classified as 'bruin Afrikaners' and therefore meriting admittance into the White laager while Indian people might be given a vote to swell the buffer zone between Whites and Africans. Of course these promises will never be fulfilled – at least not in a hurry – and in the meantime the enemy bestrides South Africa like a colossus laughing aloud at the fragmented attempts by the powerless masses making appeals to his deaf ears.

'The Transkei is the Achilles heel of the Nationalists' claim intellectual politicians who are always quick to see a loophole even in a two-foot thick iron wall. This is false logic. The Transkei, the CRC, Zululand and all these other apartheid institutions are modern-type laagers behind which the whites in this country are going to hide themselves for a long time to come. Slowly the ground is being swept off from under our feet and soon we as blacks will believe completely that our political rights are in fact in our 'own' areas. Thereafter we shall find that we have no leg to stand on in making demands for any rights in 'mainland White South Africa' which incidentally will comprise more than three-quarters of the land of our fathers.

This is the major danger that I see facing the black community at the present moment – to be so conditioned by the system as to make even our most well-considered resistance to fit within the system both in terms of the means and of the goals. Witness the new swing amongst leaders of the Indian community in Durban. (I must admit I say this with pain in my heart.) Ever since word was let loose that the Indian Council will at some near future be elected, a number of intelligent people are thinking of reviving the Indian Congress and letting it form some kind of opposition within the system. This is dangerous retrogressive thinking which should be given no breathing space. These apartheid institutions are swallowing too many good people who would be useful in a meaningful programme of emancipation of the black people.

Who are the leaders of the black world then if they are not to be found in the apartheid institutions? Clearly, black people know that their leaders are those people who are now either in Robben Island or in banishment or in exile – voluntary or otherwise. People like Mandela, Sobukwe, Kathrada, M.D. Naidoo and many others will always have a place of honour in our minds as the true leaders of the people. They may have been branded communists, saboteurs, or similar names – in fact they may have been convicted of similar offences in law courts but this does not subtract from the real essence of their worth. These were people who acted with a dedication unparalleled in modern times. Their concern with our plight as black people made them gain the natural support of the mass of black people. We may disagree with some things they did but know that they spoke the language of the people.

Does this necessarily mean that I see absolutely no advantage in the present set-up? Unless the political astuteness of the black people involved in these various apartheid institutions is further sharpened, I am afraid we are fast approaching an impasse. The new generation may be right in accusing us of collaboration in our own destruction. In Germany the petty officials who decided on which Jews were to be taken away were also Jews. Ultimately Hitler's gangs also came for them. As soon as the dissident factors outside the apartheid institutions are completely silenced, they will come for those who make noise inside the system. Once that happens the boundaries of our world will forever be the circumference of the 13% 'black spots'.

Perhaps one should be a little positive at this stage. I completely discourage the movement of people from the left to join the institutions of apartheid. In laying out a strategy we often have to take cognisance of the enemy's strength and as far as I can assess all of us who want to fight within the system are completely underestimating the influence the system has on us. What seems to me to be logical at this stage, is for the left to continually pressurise the various apartheid institutions to move in the direction of testing the limits of possibility within the system, to prove the whole game a sham and to break off the system. I will take the example of the Labour Party because it sounds the most well-organised dissident group in the system.

The Coloured Labour Party stood for elections on an anti-apartheid ticket and won most of the elected seats. Further, the Labour Party wasted no time in spelling out its anti-apartheid stance and revived political activity to a great extent within the Coloured community. In fact the growing consciousness of the possibility of political action amongst the Coloured people is due to the Labour Party. Pretty soon the Labour Party will find that it is singing the same tune and whatever they say will cease to be of news value. In the mean-- time Tom Swartz will start making demands for the Coloured people and will probably gain a few concessions. The Coloured people will then realise that in fact a positive stand like that of Tom Swartz's is more welcome than a negative attitude like that of the Labour Party who keep on saying the same things. Then the Labour Party will start falling into disfavour.

This is not just theoretical. It has happened in the past with Matanzima and Guzana in the Transkei. Guzana's party — once the pride of dissident Transkeians who wanted to demonstrate their rejection of the system — has now been relegated to the background, operating even on the right of Matanzima's Party whose militant demands are being seen as a more meaningful opposition to the system than a rehashed debate on the protection of white interests in the Transkei.

Therefore I see the real value of the Labour Party being in galvanising its forces now, organising them and pulling out of the Coloured Representative Council together with the support of all the Coloured people. The longer they stay in the CRC, the more they risk being irrelevant. 'Pull out and do what?' This is the next question. There is a lot of community work that needs to be done in promoting a spirit of self-reliance and black consciousness among all black people in South Africa.

This is what the Labour Party should resort to doing. By now, they have sufficiently demonstrated that the CRC is rejected by the Coloured people. Further operation within the system may only lead to political castration and a creation of an 'I-am-a-Coloured' attitude which will prove a set-back to the black man's programme of emancipation and will create major obstacles in the establishment of a non-racial society once our problems are settled. This to me sounds the only way of turning a disadvantage into an advantage. It is true of not only the Labour Party but also of all black people of conscience who are now operating within the system.

Thus in an effort to maintain our solidarity and relevance to the situation we must resist all attempts at the fragmentation of our resistance. Black people must recognise the various institutions of apartheid for what they are — gas, intended to get black people fighting separately for certain 'freedoms' and 'gains' which were prescribed for them long ago. We must refuse to accept it as inevitable that the only political action the blacks may take is through these institutions.

Granted that it may be more attractive and even safer to join the system, we must still recognize that in doing so we are well on our way towards selling our souls.

Collaborators in Oppression
ANC

Statement in Sechaba *(ANC), VI, 4, April 1972.*

It will not be easy to reach the stage of armed confrontation for the enemy, too, is preparing. They hope to forestall it with such measures as the creation of the Bantustans. And some of our people, sick and tired of being ruled, have thought of taking and organising the Bantustans for use against the enemy at a later date. This line of thinking is dangerous and the ANC will not allow it. For the people must always remember that the land belongs to the majority and that is the African people. They cannot allow themselves to be fobbed off with a tiny piece of the land. Furthermore, the carving up of these Bantustans will endanger all the countries in Southern Africa including Zambia, for they will all become part of a large economic unit with South Africa as the master. Eventually just as Zululand is a Bantustan so will Lesotho, Swaziland and other Southern African countries become a kind of Bantustan. The Bantustans are dangerous to the extent that they seek to break up a nation born in 1912, and those who work the system in conscious support of the South African government are collaborators in oppression.

We must exclude from this attack those who have no choice but to work within the Bantustan framework and those who use the Bantustan platform to attack apartheid and supplement our demands.

On the Convocation of a National Convention
ANC

*Statement made on 4 October 1971 on the proposal of Chief
Buthelezi that there be convened a national convention.*

Recently, Chief Gatsha Buthelezi, head of the Zulu Tribal Territorial Authority, issued a call for a national convention of all races in South Africa. This
idea is being supported by the United Party, the Progressive Party, the Trade
Union Council of South Africa, and other organizations. However, even this
very tentative move has been firmly rejected by the ruling, fascist, all-white
Nationalist Government.

A national convention has always been necessary in South Africa, where a
white minority group illegally monopolizes power to defend and advance its
interests of oppression and exploitation.

During its long history of relentless struggle, the African National Congress . . . has continually demanded the convocation of a genuine national
convention, representative of all the people, to discuss and draw up a truly
democratic constitution in which political and economic power would be
controlled by and vested in the overwhelming majority, the African people.
There could be no other meaningful, realistic convention or political dialogue.

Yet the fascist Nationalist Government rejected a national convention on
any basis . . .

In 1961, when for the last time, the oppressed people, led by the ANC,
made a call for a national convention in place of a whites-only Republic, the
fascist regime replied with the most unprecedented mobilization of the
oppressor army in an attempt to crush the national stoppage of work which
we called in reply to the enemy's refusal to summon a national convention.

Our call was answered with the ruthless forms of legalized, police and military terrorism. Political organizations were banned; the leaders of the people
were arrested, tortured and restricted. The white minority regime declared open
war against an unarmed people. This marked the close of a chapter in the history
of our struggle for freedom and justice. The peaceful avenues of struggle were
closed, and severe penalties, up to the death sentence, were imposed. In these
circumstances, the African National Congress was compelled to lead the
oppressed people in a violent offensive against a violent repression. Armed
repression could only be met by armed revolt . . .

Yet, white organizations and individuals that have supported and continue
to support the perpetuation of white rule — the United Party, the Progressive
Party and the Trade Union Council of South Africa — now want a national
convention. Why?

These white, anti-Black groups see with the greatest fear that the liberation
of the Black man is approaching. They see by the actions of the Black people
of our country that their hatred of the white oppressor and their determination to seize political power, relying on their own strength, have doubled,
despite and because of the iron heel of mass arrests, torture, indefinite detention and murder of patriots. They see that the ANC, the oppressed and

exploited people, are not shaken in their resolve to prosecute the armed struggle up to victory.

They see that the progressive peoples the world over are more than ever determined to isolate apartheid South Africa, politically, economically, culturally, in all spheres of life, and are prepared to grab at anything to save themselves from total isolation.

They realize that the South African economy itself is threatened with collapse as a result of the apartheid policy of the super-exploitation of the Black workers.

They recognize all this and they realize that they have to devise new methods of continuing the system of white rule and Black exploitation and for deceiving the international community . . .

The African National Congress declares that the only genuine national convention that can be held in South Africa would:

(1)   be vested with sovereign and unlimited authority to change South African society in all its aspects;

(2)   be attended by representatives of all the national groups in proportions that reflect the composition of the South African population.

Moreover, for such a convention to be genuinely sovereign and democratic, the African National Congress declares that the following pre-conditions would have to be met:

(1)   The suspension of the racist constitution;

(2)   The lifting of the ban on the vanguard organization, the ANC, and all other popular organizations;

(3)   The release of all political prisoners and banned, banished and restricted patriots and the full participation of the people's leaders like Nelson Mandela and others, in the preparations for and actual work of the convention;

(4)   The immediate and unconditional return of all political leaders abroad;

(5)   The immediate, complete and unconditional compliance with the Universal Declaration of Human Rights;

(6)   The immediate and unequivocal repeal of the Land Act;

(7)   The immediate repeal of all repressive legislation such as the Native Urban Areas Act, the Suppression of Communism Act, the Terrorism Act, Proclamation 400 in the Transkei, and all other such legislation;

(8)   The disarming of the police and army and disbanding the existing machinery of police and military terrorism.

The African people, other racial groups and the world must compel Vorster and his racist clique to agree to the national convention. The racist minority still believes that it is invincible and can command and herd history according to its will. It is only from a position of strength, when the Black people's war of liberation seriously threatens the white minority regime that the National Government will be obliged and ready to talk.

The main direction towards change, the content of the political struggle of the indigenous and oppressed masses in our country is through the armed struggle which the ANC has already launched and will continue to prosecute with increasing vigour . . .

Chief Gatsha 'If' Buthelezi
PAC

From an article by the editor in Azania News *(PAC, Dar es Salaam), VIII, 8, August 1973.*

Like the 'Dialogue Movement', the Bantustan Movement is a subtle creation of the imperialists and is completely in their service. It needs 'leaders of status' — what the late Malcolm X called 'celebrities with top hats, coat-tails, bowties, striped pants and all'. The same is happening in racist South Africa. The tribal leaders are completely aware of their role. The US magazine, *Newsweek*, asked Chief Gatsha 'If' Buthelezi of KwaZulu if apartheid had positive aspects. He replied:

> If separate development is carried out logically and with sincerity, there are certainly positive aspects, but if you give people hope and nothing else results, then it is a cruel sham. We are unlikely to get all the land KwaZulu needs to become a nation. When they come to realise that nothing has really changed, the Zulus will think that I have misled them.

Chief Kaizer Matanzima wa MaXhosa said much the same thing. 'We are playing a game,' he said, 'and nobody knows when (if?) we shall score.' Buthelezi makes their role even more obvious. He was asked whether as a Bantustan leader, he accepts apartheid or not. 'I am opposed to apartheid,' he said, 'I accept that the South African government is strong and calls the tune. There is no peaceful alternative and I will not embark on any course that might lead to the destruction of my people . . .' In his desperate helplessness, Buthelezi says he will make apartheid the platform from which to demand and 'fight' for all that is due to his people. What he expects to get out of it is possible 'only if the whites are prepared to make vast financial sacrifices, abolishing racial discrimination, making reasonable grants of land to the Bantustans and allowing them to have seaports to function as viable nations. I do not know yet if the whites will want to make the sacrifices. I have only my doubts.'

Clearly, the Bantustan scheme is, according to the tribal leaders, a blank cheque. So is their role, by their own testimony. But we think it is a valuable experiment by negative example. It is probably from that point of view an essential historical phase that will leave no one in doubt about what Sobukwe has called 'a feudal conception of authority'. However, our interest in the Bantustan movement lies in its material impact in the conditions of life of the African people. The problem of our people in the country and continent is not what to do, as we continue to emphasise, but only of how to do it. The tribal leaders feel the same way, but they prefer to play hide-and-seek in the meantime. They also enjoy the pay, power, privilege that the game affords them. The Bantustan movement comprises the ruins upon which our revolutionary movement is being built.

A Game He Can Never Win
SACP

From an editorial in African Communist *(SACP), 54, Third Quarter, 1973.*

In trying to liberate our people from the stranglehold of national and international capitalism we are waging a life and death struggle, not playing games. It is time to ask some of those who now claim to speak in the name of the African people which side they are on. When freedom fighters are fighting and dying to liberate South Africa, what right have Chief Lucas Mangope and some of his colleagues to print advertisements in glossy business magazines inviting the capitalists to invest in their Bantustans, and specifically mentioning the availability of cheap labour as one of the attractions? What right have chiefs Buthelezi and Matanzima to oppose the call for the removal of foreign capital from South Africa, thus undermining the work of the international solidarity movement in every corner of the world?

Some of these Bantustan leaders, like Chief Buthelezi, openly to acknowledge that they are prisoners in the Bantustan set-up, but claim to be doing what they can from within the system to achieve the emancipation and advancement of their people. We surely do not need to remind Chief Buthelezi that he was not freely elected to his present post, but like all the other Bantustan leaders was placed there by the Nationalist Government for a purpose.

If Chief Buthelezi or any of his supporters have any doubts about this, let them read the article from Washington by Ken Owen published in the *Star* on February 8, 1973. 'Under the umbrella of "communications", the US Government has brought a parade of African and Coloured leaders to the United States', writes Owen. 'What ensues is quite amusing.'

> The African American Institute, whose leading members are at pains to endorse the legitimacy of violence while questioning its efficiency, snaps up the task of organising their tours . . . Having captured the latest Black South African, the AAI steers him into the company of Black nationalists, professional South African exiles like Mrs. Jennifer Davis and Mr. Joel Carson, and here and there a fading member of the ANC or the PAC.

At public or private meetings, hostile questions are thrown at these men who are 'working within the system' to bring about change, as they claim. 'None has been so skilful at dealing with the pressures as Chief Buthelezi . . .' Questions are framed to trap him but:

> Chief Buthelezi spots every trap. He refuses to condemn Black African countries for lukewarm support, he rejects the notion that moderate American Blacks like Roy Wilkins should be condemned for visiting

111

South Africa. He suggests a modification of the campaign to force US businesses to withdraw summarily from South Africa. When Mrs. Butcher asks pointblank what American Negroes can do to help him, he does not pander to romanticism or appeal to violence. At the top of his list he puts not bombs but education. When he is challenged for rejecting violence, he is sharp and impatient . . .

At the end, the professional diplomat is awed with the sheer skill of the performance. Even the radicals, having got nothing for their cause, are admiring. The official custodians of President Nixon's policies on South Africa at the State Department could ask for no more.

Chief Buthelezi is the most effective weapon they have yet found against their critics on the left who are trying to steer the United States in the wake of the United Nations on Southern African questions . . .

And, considering the service Chief Buthelezi has rendered in undercutting the bombs-and-boycott School, perhaps South Africans should be at least as pleased with him.

Chief Buthelezi may, as he claims, be trying to outplay the Government at the game of diplomacy and brinkmanship which they call Bantustan, but he must appreciate that because he is not the banker, this is a game he can never win. Ken Owen finds it all 'amusing' — the spectacle of a Black leader allowing himself to be used to further the aims of Vorster and Nixon. We find it tragic — as tragic as the spectacle of Black policemen with guns in their hands fighting (and some of them dying) in Caprivi and Rhodesia to 'save' Southern Africa for White Supremacy.

The independence of many Black states in Africa has been threatened by the activities of White mercenaries. Let us make it quite plain here and now that we will not allow the freedom of South Africa for which we are struggling to be removed from our grasp through the actions of Black mercenaries.

An Exercise in Eyewash
SWAPO

Memorandum issued by the London office of SWAPO on 11 October 1968, concerning the implementation of 'The Self-Government for Native Nations in South West Africa Act' in Ovamboland.

The 'Self-government for Native Nations in South West Africa Act' was enacted at the end of last session in the South African Parliament. According to this act, Namibia (South West Africa) is going to be divided up into six so-called 'Native Nations', each 'Nation' as an autonomous unit. On the 17th October, the first of these 'Native Nations' will come into being. The Legislative

Council for Ovamboland will be opened in Oshakati by the Minister of Bantu Administration and Development and Bantu Education, Mr. M.C. Botha. According to the *Windhoeck Advertiser* of 3rd October,

> The Legislative Council will be representative of all the seven regions of Ovamboland. Each of the seven regional Tribal Authorities is entitled to designate not more than six members . . . As was the case when the Transkei was granted self-government, the Government of the Republic will second a number of civil servants to assist in the administration of the various departments of Ovamboland under self-government. These officials will be designated Directors. One of the Directors, Mr. F.A.J. du Preez of the Department of Bantu Administration and Development, will act as co-ordinating officer for the Departments of Finance, Economic Affairs, Justice, Community Affairs, Agriculture and Works and Education.

In other words, the same personnel, representatives of the South African regime, will continue to rule, it is only their positions which are changing names.

The South African Bantustan policy — of which this is an example — is based on the fallacy that cultural and linguistic differences between population groups prevent co-operation and communal feelings. On the basis of this idea, South Africa regards herself justified in dividing up the areas where the indigenous population live, into small, autonomous 'Bantustans' which have minimal contact with each other. SWAPO has all along strongly opposed the South African Bantustan policy. We argue that in Namibia, where the various population groups live scattered this policy is undoubtedly a deliberate move to destroy the unity of our people. We also regard it as an exercise in eyewash and blatant hypocrisy, intended to fool the outside world.

The implementation of the 'Self-government for Native Nations in South West Africa Act' has many implications. One can see that the exercise is bound to lead to great suffering on the part of the people of Namibia: all the Bantustans will be situated in poor areas without any natural resources worth developing. This, in turn, means that the Bantustans will continue to be utterly dependent upon South Africa for economic assistance. Furthermore, the areas which are left to the white minority are rich in natural resources; consequently the exploitation of these areas will directly benefit the white population, and only go to the inhabitants of the Bantustans as 'economic assistance' which, one can envisage, will be given with a patronising hand by the South African regime. As each Bantustan is going to contain people belonging to one population group only, one can foresee extensive forced moves of people from one area to the next. Many families will have to pull up their roots from the place where they may have lived for generations, and go to an area to which they have no ties whatsoever. Many families may also face financial difficulties, difficulties in adjusting to the new situation in which they find themselves; in short, they face stresses and strains which may easily lead to a break-up of the family unit.

Another facet to the South African Bantustan policy is that it keeps people without contact with the outside world. Their educational system purports this isolation, as it emphasizes the uniqueness of customs and traditions of particular population groups, and ignores the general development of modern society. Thus, people in a 'Native Nation' will end up as backwards, ignorant and unable to tackle the problems of modern society — exactly what is intended by the South African regime. The regime thus gets its justification for continued overlordship — 'these people are not ready for independence' — a phrase too often heard from representatives for the white supremacists in Southern Africa.

The Bantustan policy is a violation of human rights, of international law, of any ultra-national charters functioning today. We want to draw your attention to this and ask you to do your utmost to counteract and condemn this pernicious policy practiced in our country. We also ask you to urge your Government to support an urgent debate in the United Nations General Assembly, and to back any resolution leading to practical action. South Africa must be forced to give up her illegal administration of Namibia by all means at the disposal of the United Nations, including the use of force.

5. How to Collaborate with Other National Movements

Editors' Introduction

In addition to the problem of unity within countries, there was the question of unity across boundaries. If the oppressors in Portuguese and southern Africa had a joint strategy, should not those struggling for liberation have had a common front? Easier said than done.

Within the Portuguese colonies the movements of the CONCP – principally PAIGC, MPLA, and FRELIMO – had a long-standing and effective alliance. At various points in time, these three movements joined the ANC (South Africa), ZAPU (Zimbabwe), and SWAPO (Namibia) in common activities, most notably at the Khartoum Conference of 1968. But the level of struggle in Portuguese Africa was different from that in the other three countries and this led to some problems. One would not call these problems conflicts, nor even strains, but there were surely misunderstandings that required clarification.

We start with an internal document of the CONCP which was circulated in 1968 and which outlines how it saw an alliance based on 'mutual recognition'. Despite this, there was frequent discussion of a so-called 'domino theory' attributed by others to the CONCP movements despite disclaimers from these movements. The presumed 'domino theory' was that as one country is liberated, it would strengthen the struggle in the next, and therefore one should concentrate on one at a time. How sensitive this theory was can be seen in the reactions of a SWAPO leader in 1972 and in two statements of the ANC, one made in 1964 and one in 1972.

And yet one can see other ways in which movements asserted the primacy of their own struggles. A joint statement of ANC and ZAPU in 1968 called Rhodesia the 'essential imperialist link', and Oliver Tambo of the ANC argued in 1969 the strategy that the movements must 'capture the citadel', that is, South Africa.

The movements worked towards clarification of the issue. We end with a statement of Dr. Neto in which he specifically denounced the 'domino theory', a statement reproduced in ANC's *Sechaba*.

Collaboration Between the Movements: Towards Operational Unity
CONCP

Internal document distributed in 1968. Translated from French.

The countries which form the massive triangle of southern Africa have historically displayed a certain number of common characteristics. All of them, with the exception of Angola and Mozambique, have fought, at some time or other, British domination. The two oldest colonizers of Africa – the Portuguese and the Afrikaners – are established there. They experience, in different ways, the racial tensions resulting from the difficult 'coexistence' between autochthonous communities and human groups foreign to the continent.

Then, the sudden change of British imperialism and the outcome of the struggle in the southernmost area (and the richest one) gave South Africa economic, if not political, priority in this whole.

The countries of southern Africa have progressively become tributaries to the economic power developed by international capital invested in South Africa. Besides, one must remember that the existing modes of exploitation these countries know implies both monopoly capitalism and the apartheid system.

Southern Africa was, until the year 1963, a bloc characterised by a high degree of economic, political and military integration.

Of course, in this part of the continent dominated by white minorities, the South African companies still have control, by their financial participation, over most of the societies established in Rhodesia, Angola and Mozambique.

But there are breaches nevertheless in the fortress. Besides the dissolution of the Central African Federation, the armed struggle in Angola and Mozambique, and recently in the bastion of Rhodesia, condemns it to the universe of counter-revolution . . .

So far, how have we organized against the enemy?

Until quite recently, the various political movements of Central, Eastern and Southern Africa were grouped in a single organism – PAFMECSA – which did not survive the birth of the OAU.

In spite of the democratic principle which placed on an equal plane both the parties of the independent states and the liberation movements, PAFMECSA was not able to design a framework to orient the struggle in these countries.

At a lesser regional scale, the foundation of the CONCP in 1961 answered the pressing need to coordinate the action of the political groupings involved in a struggle for the total destruction of Portuguese colonialism. The present situation illustrates the wisdom of the principles adopted.

The efforts which were made by certain nationalist movements in 1963 at refashioning PAFMECSA, under the ambiguous form of a 'Union of Non-Independent African States' also could not lead to concrete results because the foundations were fragile, even completely false.

It was the same with both the assemblies of the 'Freedom Fighters' held in Accra in 1961 and 1962, and the All-African Peoples' Conference in its last phase, a grouping which was unable to create a programme of joint action on a long-term basis. The fundamental lack was in the fact that it included a wide variety of nationalist organizations whose degree of involvement in the struggle was not such as to permit the establishment of a coherent political platform. It lacked most of all the decision and will for ideological clarification.

However, for some years now, there have emerged a certain number of organizations confronted with the last recesses of colonialism, and possessing a political identity. The reality of warfare characterizes their main form of action and accords them an avant-garde status.

We are speaking of the authentic movements of the three countries from Africa which are involved in direct action against Portuguese colonialism (Guinea, Angola and Mozambique), as well as in Zimbabwe, South Africa and South-West Africa.

The allied offensive of the ZAPU-ANC forces appears, in this context, as the logical consequence of the ripeness of the conditions for armed struggle in Rhodesia and as the appropriate response to the export of apartheid. The enemy is already feeling the effects. In its attempt to annihilate the guerilla forces, it uses the South African military potential on a large scale and calls its allies to the defence of the 'white minorities'.

Let us stress an essential fact: we are facing a line of a single operational front in southern Africa . . . The schematic outline of the political elements which could contribute to the elaboration of a strategy is as follows:

(a)   Imperialism is the enemy of the peoples of southern Africa;

(b)   The struggle takes the form of a prolonged war;

(c)   The whole of the region constitutes a single theatre of operations directed by the power of the South African state;

(d)   The national movement and anti-imperialist movement are the same thing;

(e)   The level of cooperation among the interterritorial movements (the CONCP and ZAPU/ANC) can be strengthened, one supporting the other;

(f)   The harmonization of positions with regard to states is a prime necessity;

(g)   The practical objective is the achievement of one *operational front* throughout southern Africa.

There are contradictions and obstacles on the path which will lead us to the achievement of this operational front in southern Africa. If we wish to surmount them, we must not ignore their importance but deal with them with a spirit of positive solidarity.

Firstly, at the level of the nationalist movements themselves, the scope of cooperation should be limited only by tactical considerations. Since the effectiveness of our combat is in the end based upon the *mutual recognition* of those political organizations which alone are able to defeat imperialism. One should, consequently, start by eliminating from our analysis of strategy reservations of a political or ideological nature which hinder the founding of

117

a platform of action among the liberation movements in southern Africa.

Then, at the level of the independent African border states, the contradictions essentially stem from the economic hold which the Lisbon-Salisbury-Pretoria axis presently exerts on them.

Zambia is, in this respect, the most advanced on the path of its economic independence, while Malawi, Lesotho, and Botswana play, to different degrees, negative roles vis-a-vis the liberation movements, since their regimes and economies are subjected to the South Africa regime.

One should thus envisage the use of tactics in these latter countries that neutralize, as a first step, the support which these countries give South Africa. This can be done by determining, for example, which forces inside the countries (opposition movements) might modify the present course of events.

Financing a war on three fronts imposes increasing obligations of Portugal towards its allies. The economic bonds which already existed through the network of conventions and contracts of financial institutions, have been strengthened recently because of the need for the *common defence* of southern Africa. In this system Portugal is the weakest link, due to the mode of exploitation of its colonies.

This aspect of the question clarifies the peculiarity of the situation in Angola and Mozambique. It means that Portugal possesses two vulnerable *flanks*, one being the colonies and the other the territory of the 'metropole' itself. If on the first flank there is the combined assault of the nationalist forces, on the second there is only clandestine political activity. Thus, Portuguese Fascism has been conducting colonial wars since 1961 without suffering an active popular reaction at home which would threaten the survival of the regime in the short run. In fact, even the most advanced opposition elements have not been able to create in the 'metropole' those groups which could make the pursuit of colonial expeditions fail. In brief, Portugal is not threatened with encirclement in its 'European rectangle'.

At the present stage, we cannot rely solely on a hypothesis of the unleashing of armed action in Portugal by political groups who are awaiting the moment of the ideal convergence of the objective and subjective conditions required to do so.

We must therefore explore other possibilities, in an internationalist kind of spirit, aiming at the destruction, within the Portuguese state apparatus itself, of the basis and the material means which feed the colonial war.

Let us emphasize, nonetheless, the strong points of the framework of the total strategy of imperialism: the racist minority regimes in southern Africa have the two-fold function of blocking the development of the liberation struggle and of serving as a basis for the expansion of financial capitalism. Both complementary aspects are translated as military aggressiveness against the liberation movements and the independent African countries simultaneously.

Our enemies know how to adjust their actions to the changes which occur at the level of international relations. Integrated into the world-wide system of imperialism, apartheid Africa deploys its forces within this context.

One must thus give priority to achieving a joint front in southern Africa, based on a strategy decided upon by the liberation movements. Let us add, however, without useless rhetoric, that this war concerns the whole of Africa and the whole of the anti-imperialist forces.

Priority of support to the movements involved in the armed struggle for the liberation of South Africa – this should be the demand to be pursued henceforth within the OAU.

We are once again faced with the task of mobilizing for our objectives all those who are led by the common hope of seeing Africa bloom in the sunshine of independence and freedom.

An Incorrect Position
Andreas Shipanga

> *From an interview with Andreas Shipanga, then of SWAPO,*
> *published in* Liberation Afrique *(Paris), 4, November-December*
> *1972. Retranslated from French.*

Liberation Afrique: What do you think of the 'domino theory', expressed in Rabat at the time of the last OAU summit?

Shipanga: If we say: 'We must first free Mozambique, then Angola or Zimbabwe, concentrating all our men and equipment on one country at a time', South Africa will concentrate its forces against this same country, and meanwhile nothing will happen in the other countries.

We do not think that this is a correct position. We must always take into consideration other people's experiences. In Indochina, the Vietnamese have spread the torch of war far from their own territory. No-one says: 'Let us concentrate on Vietnam!' but rather 'Let us support the peoples of Indochina!' Thus, the enemy, US imperialism, is harassed in Vietnam, Cambodia, Laos, and is forced to fight on each of these fronts. This is the only logical policy. We must give all the peoples who want to struggle against colonialist and fascist regimes the means required to conduct such struggles.

No Waiting in South Africa
ANC

> *From the memorandum presented to the meeting of the Heads*
> *of State of the Organization of African Unity in Cairo, July*
> *1964, reprinted in the ANC's* South African Freedom News *(Dar*
> *es Salaam), 26, 31 July 1964.*

This is a school of thought that argues that the strategy for the liberation of Southern Africa should first be to liberate Angola, Mozambique and Southern Rhodesia before the South African White minority regime can be fully engaged in a decisive battle for liberation. We are opposed to this theory.

We are convinced that it is not for nothing that the Ian Smith White minority government in Southern Rhodesia has stepped up its military preparations. Nor is it for love of show that the Portuguese have been pouring more and more troops into Angola and Mozambique.

We have pointed out before that these military activities are part of a grand strategy intended not only to suppress the national liberation movement throughout this entire area but also to confront the independent African States.

Ian Smith has just concluded a visit to South Africa the purposes of which can be clearly surmised from his bellicose and aggressive speeches and from his threats to declare unilateral independence for Southern Rhodesia.

Similarly, the South African Commander-in-Chief Grobbelaar has recently paid a visit to Mozambique where he inspected various military camps and installations.

What emerges therefore from all these comings and goings of belligerent elements in Southern Africa is that:

(a)   Verwoerd will be available to Southern Rhodesia with military and financial aid as well as political support;

(b)   He will equally render full aid to Salazar in Angola and Mozambique while trying to bribe African chiefs in the neighbouring British Protectorate with the intention of surrounding himself with friendly territories and destroying hostile elements.

These tactics of the South African White minority government further confirm the fact we have insisted on, namely, that a peaceful, prosperous, powerful Verwoerd free of involvements in a struggle for survival in South Africa will delay the liberation of the territories now under White or foreign domination in Southern Africa. For these reasons, we are opposed to the strategic theory that the intensification of the struggle in South Africa must await the liberation of Southern Rhodesia and Mozambique and Angola. Indeed, to starve the South African liberation movement of assistance pending the liberation of other territories is, in our view, to play into the hands of the unholy alliance of Verwoerd, Smith and Salazar.

In our considered opinion it is on the cards that the Verwoerd regime will intervene in one way or other in the arena of battle in Southern Rhodesia and Mozambique. Verwoerd will find this easy if he does not have a greatly intensified struggle to contend with in South Africa itself. In any event as far as the African National Congress is concerned, we shall make sure in the interests of our struggle and in solidarity with our brothers in the neighbouring territories that Verwoerd is kept very busy whether we get increased aid or not.

Realities and Illusions
Sobizana Mnqikana

Article in the ANC's Sechaba, *VI, 6, June 1972.*

Two trends are meeting in collision in Southern Africa; the northward thrust of South Africa's diplomatic and military expansionism and the southward thrust of the African guerrilla liberation movements. (Stanley Uys, *Survival*, Vol. X, No. 5, May 1968).

The above excerpt characterises the most salient features of the Southern African system; collision between the forces of reaction and progress; South Africa's expansionism (economic, military and political) and hegemonial role in the system: military, economic and political consolidation of the racist Unholy Alliance of Portugal, South Africa and Rhodesia.

Meanwhile, various theories and strategies have been advocated in an attempt to resolve the Southern Africa conflict. Some of these endorse the legitimacy of armed struggle by the oppressed Black majorities against the racist White minority regimes. However, a rather disturbing theory – the so-called progressive domino theory with all its implications – as a strategic tactic, has been advanced. The theory assumes a stage by stage victory of liberation movements; a stage by stage falling of 'dominos' – Guinea Bissau, Mozambique, Angola, Rhodesia, *then* South Africa. Where Namibia fits into the domino framework is not clear. Since the purpose of this paper is to prove the bankruptcy and the illusory nature of this theory – its lack of analytical perspective – we need a rigorous analysis of the Southern Africa system, and in particular South Africa's imperialist role in the system, with the view to drawing relevant conclusions and strategies.

System here connotes a set of relationships and interactions within a given region (Southern Africa, in this case). In our definition, Southern Africa subsumes the geographic areas of Tanzania, Malawi, Zambia, Angola, Mozambique, Zimbabwe, Namibia, Botswana, Lesotho, Swaziland and South Africa.

Viewing the Southern Africa situation in system terms gives the region a wide perspective that leads to an enquiry into the processes, interactions, motivations, and the reason why governments and institutions act the way they do. Government and institutions are creations designed to serve the purposes of people: in the long term, they must reflect the motivations, drives, fears and ambitions of people.

Previous analysts have viewed events in Southern Africa in a discrete manner, with little consideration given to interaction of the countries concerned. The analysis of Southern African politics has always been fragmentary because of differing histories of the various countries and the wide variety of constitutional and legal forms under which they have been and are governed. Seldom has the significance of the links between South Africa, Rhodesia and the Portuguese colonies been properly and thoroughly assessed.

The descriptive legal and historico-constitutional approach has blurred the

121

motivations, and interactions, (social, political and economic links) of the Unholy Alliance. Formulae and expectations, completely out of touch with the realities of the situation, made by the domino theorists who naively assume some 'rational' chronologically southward progression of victories by the respective liberation movements against their respective opponents, are propounded.

The primary feature of Southern Africa is the clash between the white minority regimes determined to cling to power and continue the exploitation of the African masses, and the liberation movements which are equally determined to wrest power from the racists and eliminate colonialism, racism and exploitation and establish peoples democracies based on freedom, equality and justice. These white racist regimes share common ideological orientations: maintenance of colonialism, racism and fascism; the defence of so-called western civilisation and anticommunist hysteria; the economic objective of exploiting the indigenous peoples and the resources of their countries; the politico-military objective of stemming the tide of the African revolution, and to subvert it where it has been successful. Perceived common threats have helped to consolidate this white alliance. As the Portuguese Foreign Minister on 30.8.1967 put it, Portugal and South Africa 'not only had many interests and problems in common, but also shared the same system of values and were both equally determined to defend those values'.

One of the strategically important 'textural features' of the system is the high level of intensity of communications between the Unholy Alliance partners which has drawn them together for the common defence of racism. Structurally, South Africa by virtue of her economic wealth and needs, including military capability, is the strongest and senior partner in the racist system. A closer examination of South Africa's foreign policy vis-a-vis Africa, and Southern Africa in particular, will give us not only an insight into the dynamics of the Southern Africa system, but also expose the political opportunism and naivete of the protagonists of the domino theory. Such an examination will help illuminate the problems that beset *not only* the liberation movement in South Africa but also the liberation movements in all white-occupied Southern Africa.

The domino theory postulates that the Portuguese colonies are the 'weakest link' in a chain of dominos which have to be liberated first — the so-called 'priority' areas. South Africa is the last domino, since she is 'the hardest nut to crack' and therefore 'the last to be tackled'. In its seductive simplicity, it has evoked far-fetched hopes of quick victories. Firm and explicit proposals are put forward by the protagonists of the theory that all focus (material and otherwise) should be on the Portuguese colonies. What is deemed to be the 'impotence' of the other liberation movements in Southern Africa, in particular the absence of visible military confrontation, is deceptively used to substantiate the validity of the domino theory. There is also a tinge of arrogance in the suggestion that the development of military struggle and future battles in the rest of Southern Africa, especially in South Africa, are dependent on the outcome of the struggle in the Portuguese colonies. Wait until the Portuguese colonies are freed! The 'priority' areas argument portrays Portugal as the only actor in the scene.

No serious consideration is given to the psychological impact, to say the least, such developments (falling dominos) would have on the white racist Southern Africa fortress which uses race as a basis of political loyalty, and is garrisoned by South Africa. For example, a Mozambique Fighting Soldiers' Comforts Fund has been established in South Africa, one of whose posters poignantly reads: 'The future of South Africa depends very much on the outcome of the war [in Mozambique]'. Casual reference is made to the significance of South Africa's gradual, but effective, diplomatic, political and economic penetration of Africa. Above all, within the domino framework of analysis, South Africa is projected as a 'neutral actor' in the wars in Angola or in the Southern Africa conflict with complete disregard to what her security interests are and how these have determined and will continue to determine her future course of action. The effective application of the capabilities that she possesses seems to escape the eye of the domino theorists. The most important aspect of military capability is not its possession, but the willingness to use it. Rhodesia is a case in point. In our analysis, more emphasis, will be put on South Africa's strategy and tactics (economic, military, diplomatic, political etc.), and the implications therefrom, to perpetuate White racism in Southern Africa. If the proposition that self-preservation is a vital interest of all states is true, it holds equally true of South Africa. The survival of the White state dictates that policies should be pursued, internally and externally, to protect itself. Her role as a carrier of an ideology imposes commitments and obligations to be fulfilled. The expectations of her racist partners become important components in the formulation and execution of her foreign policy objectives. The ever-increasing danger posed by the liberation movements demands her serious attention.

Security, internally and externally, has assumed top priority in South Africa's policy. Cognisant of the impending outbreak of guerilla warfare inside her territory, and alarmed by the concerted attacks by the liberation movements in Mozambique, Angola, Namibia etc. the establishment of favourable frontiers has become an objective to which the Republic is willing to commit great resources — ranging from economic and military aid to intervention and combat operations as blatantly shown in Rhodesia, Mozambique and Angola from 1967 onwards.

Driven by economic greed and security interests, the Republic has bandied economic aid to independent African states with the view to creating client states — Malawi, Lesotho, Swaziland etc. — who have been either neutralised or have turned hostile to liberation movements. These states are proving more of an obstacle than the political wedge that some of us had expected once they had achieved independence. The aid granted to these states is not a unilateral relationship where the benefits accrue only to the recipients. It serves the Republic's economic and security interests as illustrated in the following:

Yet what appears to be a burden is not necessarily so. In aiding its poorer neighbours, the Republic opens up new export markets for its products, finds new outlets for its citizens' enterprise. In this way, South Africa will share in a real way in its neighbours' advance. Besides, South Africa's economy has reached that stage where the country needs to look farther afield for business opportunities. And meanwhile inflationary tendencies at home force it to look across its borders.

Sitting on a pile of gold and foreign exchange reserves in excess of a billion dollars, the Republic must do something to employ them profitably somewhere.

AND:

In moving out to aid Africa, South Africa furthermore, quite frankly, gains a benefit in security. (*News/Check*, pro-Government South African monthly).

One of the principles guiding the conduct of counterinsurgency is to assist threatened governments. South Africa has, therefore, placed great value on controlling or defending neighbouring territories because she perceives that a major threat to her territorial integrity might arise from the adjacent areas. 'We are good neighbours [Rhodesia and Mozambique] and good friends do not need an agreement to combat murderers. Good friends know what their duty is when the neighbour's house is on fire.' (Vorster, 25.8.1971). Vorster has also starkly stated that, should Southern African states find it difficult to contain the African guerrillas, South Africa will step in their defence: 'We will fight terrorists wherever we are allowed to fight them', he said recently.

South Africa plays a dominant role in its economic relations with her racist partners. Post-UDI Rhodesia has seen herself almost completely dependent on South Africa. It is South Africa that supplied Rhodesia with the necessities to ensure survival, especially during the early days of the economic boycott instituted by the United Nations.

The construction of the Kunene and Cabora Bassa Schemes, of which South Africa is the main financier, once more illustrates the economic and strategic objective of entrenching white rule in Southern Africa:

We believe that the future of the Portuguese provinces and that of my country are very closely linked. For this reason, we believe that South Africa will, with the passage of time, be drawn closer to Portugal and its provinces in Southern Africa. Louwrens Muller, Deputy-Minister of Economic Affairs – *News/Check*, 5.7.68.

Military cooperation – from the formulation of a common defence strategy to combined combat operations – indicates the interdependence of the racist partners. Portugal's and Rhodesia's dependence on South Africa is becoming more than apparent: 'In spite of the assistance and collaboration which she enjoys, Portugal cannot control the situation, so that her allies have been led to consider direct military intervention, already manifested in the use of South African troops and material in Angola and Mozambique' — Basil Davidson, *Sunday Times*, London, 16.8.1970.

South Africa's concern about the secured stability of her allies has made her participate in the criminal wars in the Portuguese colonies: 'It has now been proven that South Africa is involved in the Angola struggle. We have found young South African soldiers among Portuguese troops'. (Commander Monimambu (MPLA), 21.3.1969.)

In support of the above, Russell Howe has reported in *Foreign Affairs*, October 1959:

> Pretoria has supplied two battalions to Tete . . . An area specialist of London's Institute of Strategic Studies, which keeps a close watch on South Africa's forces, says that Mozambique is used to giving combat experience to draftees led by career cadres.

South Africa's aggressive policy is also directed against the independent states, notably Zambia and Tanzania, who, it is alleged, harbour terrorists. Acts of sabotage and espionage have been committed by the Unholy Alliance states and open threats of military reprisals have also been made: 'South Africa will hit Zambia so hard that she will never forget' — Vorster, 1968.

Military actions arising from similar situations have been perpetrated by, for example, Israel against the Arab countries. And South Africa has boastfully alluded to this type of action against Zambia.

The above analysis demonstrates the hollowness of the domino theory. We have shown the inadequacy of the descriptive approach which negates the significance of the dynamic trends in Southern Africa which these idealists have fallen into. We have suggested that only by looking at the significance of the increasing interactions between the white system could we predict what policies are or will be followed. The analysis, above all, has shown that South Africa is the dominant state in the alliance and her tentacles grip the whole of Southern Africa, dependent and independent. No strategy or tactic whose implementation understates South Africa in the Southern Africa conflict could hold political, more so military validity, as long as South Africa perceives her interests to be the same as those of her allies — resistance to change in the subcontinent. The puerile assumption that the Republic will stand by and witness the dominos fall into place is not borne out by facts. Her geographic location compared to that of Portugal, for instance, presses the dangers to her security more than it does to Portugal. Portugal, a classical colonial power, is distant from the theatre of war. The importance of location here is that it serves to determine who the potential enemies or allies are and what their effects on territorial security are.

It is becoming clear that South Africa's security depends on the security of her allies, hence the high propensity to intervene, as demonstrated in the case of Rhodesia and elsewhere. There is nothing to stop her from intervening on a much more massive scale in Angola and Mozambique if she considers the victories of the liberation forces in these areas pose a threat to her own security. Stanley Uys, a South African journalist writing in *Survival*, Vol. X, No. 5, May 1968, states: 'There is not the slightest doubt that if guerrillas in either Angola or Mozambique were to show any signs of winning, the South Africans will be there like a shot.'

The question of who rules Angola, Rhodesia, Mozambique, or even some of the independent states closer to her borders, cannot be a matter of indifference to the Republic. She cannot afford to be 'neutral' with respect to her security as the domino theorists suggest.

Evidence also proves that Portuguese foreign policy is not formulated in a vacuum. Her membership of the Unholy Alliance restrains her 'independence' in policy formulation and execution. It also imposes commitments, just as the US, through its alliance commitments, participates directly or indirectly in the decision-making processes of the Saigon regime.

There can be no doubt that there is a common defence policy between the states which constitute the Unholy Alliance. There is no doubt also that South Africa will not shirk her responsibilities by abandoning her allies to guerilla onslaught. Her commitments will force her to participate more actively on the side of the other white-ruled states as the guerilla offensive gathers momentum. As Dennis Austin, *News/Check*, 30.8.68, put it: 'The continued existence of white Rhodesia, Angola, and Mozambique is not simply part of the old concept of a forward defensive line, but part also of a European dominated South African world in which South Africa is both the major power and the chief proponent of the philosophy of 'white civilisation'.'

It is inconceivable that such beliefs, which are deeply ingrained in both the Nationalist and United Parties, and the white South African population in general, will be discarded. In her own selfish interests it is unimaginable that the Republic will turn a deaf ear to calls for help from whites in the north threatened by the forces of liberation.

Whilst it might be true that Portugal is a weak link in the white alliance, as we are constantly reminded, such weakness is compensated for by South Africa's capabilities and resources, and an escalation of the guerilla offensive in the Portuguese territories will provoke a corresponding escalation of South Africa's involvement in the conflict. The level and degree of South Africa's involvement in the wars in Angola and Mozambique will be determined by the extent to which the conflict in these areas develops.

The domino theory, therefore, is based on a superficial premise, and may unwittingly be motivated by political expediency. It will undoubtedly lead to incorrect strategic conclusions with the inevitable disillusionment once its ideals do not materialise.

Having shown the domino theory to be incorrect, both politically and militarily, what then is the more plausible strategy for the liberation movements against white minority regimes?

Whilst not underestimating the achievements and the future role of the liberation movements in the Portuguese colonies in particular, it seems that the intensification of the struggle in the rest of Southern Africa, and in particular in South Africa, Rhodesia and Namibia, could bring some qualitative changes in the African sub-continent. It seems militarily sound that an extension of the war on all fronts in South Africa will force the enemy to over-extent his forces – a strategy which, historically speaking, proved effective in the Allied war effort . . . . Leo Kuper proposes that the United States could mediate to provide a basis for relatively peaceful democratic change.

The mind boggles at the proposal of a US intervention in South Africa in the name of easing human suffering. Black Americans could bring forward some interesting views on US democracy. And experience of US intervention in Vietnam is yet another story.

But how is Kuper able to even suggest that the US should mediate in South Africa? The reason is that he focuses not on the very real conflict for political power between Black and White but on the 'conflict of values'. This is his version of the 'conflict of minds' we met with in Ngubane. As long as it is merely a conflict of 'values' or 'minds' that is taking place, external mediation is possible and even desirable. Mr. Kuper says, 'as I see the position in South Africa, industrialization gives rise to tension between the political and economic systems, and this tension is resolved by an increasingly rigid emphasis on racial differentiation'. So for Mr. Kuper it is the emphasis which is significant, and not the increasing racial differentiation.

And this at a time when everyone is increasingly aware that living standards of Black and White are moving apart at a greater rate all the time. It is the real differences between Black and White that are significant, not the emphasis given to it by racialists nor the values used to give them expression.

There is much more on these lines to show that Black and White are really wholly interdependent in South Africa and that the polarization is merely artificial. Kuper suggests that those who talk of polarization are doing so in the interests of ideology. And it is not only the ruling group that does so, it is also the work of the liberation movement which uses violence as a means to polarize society thereby 'awakening an apathetic populace' and 'fostering political action'. On this count violence is an instrument not for liberation, for defeating the authority who is actually oppressing the people, but a technique used by those who want to increase conflict, spread disaffection all in the interests of revolutionary ideology. Hence, the intervention of the US becomes reasonable and even desirable.

Perhaps the two instances quoted will suffice to bring home the point of this article that it is not enough to depend upon the large fount of moral goodwill in the world for relief and support for our struggle. Anti-apartheid feeling is vast and universal, but if it is not based on a genuine understanding and respect for the struggle line of the liberation movement, this support is insufficient and may, in certain circumstances even lead us into difficulty. What has to be emphasized is that in South Africa there is a very real conflict between Black and White not merely in the realm of attitudes but for political and economic power and this conflict can only be resolved by struggle, at this stage by violent struggle. This is the issue and this is what we want support for. The form this support takes will alter with circumstances. It may be a tightening of the economic boycott, it may be in the field of sport, it may require demonstrations of some kind or another, but the forms must be clear. It must be against White power in Southern Africa. Solidarity means not mediation nor imposing conditions. It means action in support of the concrete struggle of the liberation movement.

Rhodesia — Essential Imperialist Link
ZAPU/ANC

From the joint statement 'Forward From Wankie' issued in November 1968.

The war in Zimbabwe therefore developed against a wide ranging vortex of internal and external interests determined to maintain White minority dictatorship throughout Southern Africa. *What has to be clearly understood is that Rhodesia (Zimbabwe) is not only the gateway to the citadel of fascism — South Africa — but it is now, more than ever before, the most essential link in the entire imperialist strategy of maintaining the Zambezi Frontier as the advance battle-line in defence of colonial interests in Southern Africa.* If this Line were breached it would open the floodgates of revolutionary war on a grand scale everywhere in the Whitebeleagured south.

It is not necessary in this short interview to analyse in detail the reactions of the imperialist world to the guerilla war in Zimbabwe. It is a war that is part and parcel of other such wars being waged in different parts of Southern Africa. Suffice it to say that NATO weapons have streamed into South Africa: that clandestine and overt military consultations have taken place between the Pretoria/Salisbury/Lisbon axis and now even between the Pretoria/Bonn axis of fascist rulers. The role of USA imperialism has been to announce full support for British policies on Rhodesia in return for British acquiescence in the world-condemned US policies in Vietnam.

Indeed the general imperialist strategy in Rhodesia is to maintain the status quo or prolong it by such devices as the *Tiger* proposals. UN sanctions, ship talks, until a puppet group of Africans emerges to be installed in the service of colonialism. . . .

Desmond Lardner-Burke has said in the Rhodesian Parliament: 'We are on the frontline for South Africa as well as for Rhodesia. South Africa appreciates this, and there are now South African police in Rhodesia looking for these ANC terrorists.' There are now approximately 1,700 soldiers of the South African regime in Rhodesia, and following the Smith visit there in July, more SA troops have been sent to Rhodesia. 5,000 soldiers of the racist regime backed by helicopters, French supersonic strike aircraft etc. have carried out extensive anti-guerilla warfare exercises in Sibasa on the SA border with Rhodesia in August.

Capture the Citadel
Oliver Tambo

> *A broadcast to South Africa by the Acting President of the*
> *ANC on 16 December 1969, the 8th Anniversary of the*
> *formation of* Umkhonto we Sizwe, *military wing of the ANC.*

Comrades-in-arms and fellow fighters in the struggle for freedom:
On December 16, 1961 a national army — Umkhonto we Sizwe — was born to resume the armed resistance of our fathers, this time against the modern oppressor and his allies. Already that army has won historic battles in the battlefield against armed enemy forces. Thus, the formation of Umkhonto we Sizwe joins together three periods in our history: the first, the period of wars of resistance waged by our forefathers against the white invaders of our country. This lasted for centuries. The next began with the formation of the African National Congress which meant the birth of a new united African nation in South Africa. The third is the emergence of Umkhonto we Sizwe itself. This signified the resumption of armed struggle under modern conditions for the restoration of our land to its rightful owners.

The last 8 years have seen the steady unfolding of armed guerilla struggle throughout Southern Africa. The people of Mozambique, Angola, Zimbabwe and Namibia are at war with the racists and colonialists. FRELIMO, MPLA, ZAPU, SWAPO — these are familiar names in international and revolutionary circles. In this war our own Umkhonto we Sizwe, in alliance with our ZAPU brothers has already performed great deeds in Zimbabwe where the soldiers of white supremacy were made to bite the dust. But, the supreme challenge to our nation, to the African National Congress, to all democrats in our country and to the Umkhonto we Sizwe, indeed the challenge to all Africa and all anti-imperialists still remains; this is the capture of the citadel of white supremacy, South Africa, and its conversion into a fortress of true democracy, peace and progress for all our people and for mankind.

This is the formidable challenge in the face of which many fighters will flee the ranks of revolutionary forces and join condemned platoons of counter-revolutionaries and traitors. A challenge, in the face of which governments, once counted among militant opponents of colonialism and imperialism, will abandon their positions in the anti-imperialist front, and crawl cap in hand for crumbs under the neo-colonialist table. But the oppressed and freedom-loving masses of our country are equal to that challenge. Like their counterparts in Guinea-Bissau under the leadership of PAIGC, in Palestine, in heroic Vietnam where the FLN of South Vietnam has trounced the imperialists, in Latin America, like their counterparts in the United States and elsewhere,

129

our people under the leadership of the ANC are now poised for large-scale guerilla warfare against the usurpers of the peoples' power and we too shall defeat the racists and exploiters.

Redouble Our Efforts

Our Morogoro Conference last May sought to accelerate our progress towards this armed confrontation with the enemy. It examined in detail various aspects of our struggle, it carried out a thorough review of our strategy and tactics, our programme and our policies, it called for the closing of ranks, for unity and for vigilance against splitters and wedgedrivers and against conscious or unconscious enemy agents in our midst. We are called upon to work very hard and faithfully to achieve the goals set by the Morogoro Conference. We have to redouble our efforts to eliminate flaws in our work and create and maintain an increasingly more efficient machine for the prosecution of our struggle at all levels whether we operate in South Africa or from outside its borders. Already the distribution of thousands of leaflets and the broadcasts in East London, Durban, Cape Town, Johannesburg and Port Elizabeth under the fascist noses of Vorster and his execution squad – this has already demonstrated the determination of the ANC and our people to outclass the forces of reaction in the struggle for the seizure of power and for the liberation of our country.

Umkhonto Shall Avenge

To say this is not to underestimate the strength of our enemy. The South African white minority regime has vast resources which have been mobilised against our people. It has made great efforts to corrupt our natural allies in independent African States. Already some states have fallen for the blandishments of apartheid and have succumbed to its bullying and blackmail. The enemy has powerful allies in the imperialist countries such as America, Britain, Japan, France, West Germany. In no other part of the world and at no time in history has an oppressed people been confronted by such a formidable combination of imperialist powers and fascist forces. In spite of all this, however, the enemy is headed for inevitable and ignominious defeat.

The South African Supreme Court which in the course of our political struggle has ordered the murder of so many of our people, which has sent thousands of our leaders and activists to prison, including Namibians, and which is at present sitting in farcical judgment over Winnie Mandela and others, this entirely white-skinned institution has become a notorious instrument of persecution manipulated by a clique of fascist criminals whose hands have for long been dripping with the blood of the innocent. Who shall avenge the blood and settle accounts with the murderers? Umkhonto we Sizwe, the ANC, the masses of our land, backed and supported by the united might of progressive and anti-imperialist forces.

LONG LIVE THE REVOLUTION! MAATLA KE ARONA!
AMANDLA NGAWEHTU

130

Struggle Everywhere
Agostinho Neto

From an interview with the President of the MPLA, published in Angola in Arms *(Dar es Salaam), IV, 2, and republished in the ANC's* Sechaba, *VII, 2, February 1973.*

Q: The increasing tendency to give priority to putting pressure on Portugal as the potentially weakest link in the Southern African power structure was noticeable at the recent OAU summit at Rabat. This seems to imply acceptance of a 'domino theory' — once Guinea Bissau falls, it can only be a matter of time before Mozambique, Angola, Zimbabwe, Namibia and South Africa are also liberated.

Some South African freedom fighters are known to be unhappy about this theory since it does not take into account Vorster's need to protect South African capital, and border security, and thus the probability that he will intervene militarily to stop the liberation processes in other countries. What are your views on the subject?

A: Our idea in MPLA is that it is not very good to separate the parts of the liberation struggle in Africa. There are several divisive tendencies in the Continent — trying to separate the liberation movements from the independent African States, for example, and trying to separate the Portuguese colonies from other dominated countries that are not fighting with arms. It is necessary to open different fronts in Africa; to fight in Rhodesia, South Africa and so on . . . If not we shall always be in a weak position. I don't agree that it is necessary to liberate first one country, then to go on to another. It is necessary to struggle everywhere using every means possible.

If independent African countries, mainly those with resources, like Kenya and the Ivory Coast, consider the struggles of those countries that are still dominated as their own struggle and give full support to the liberation movements, this would obviously make things a lot easier and the enemy attacked from different points, would face defeat sooner.

6. How to Wage Warfare

Editors' Introduction

In any long struggle, one of the tactical dilemmas is inevitably the choice of military modes. This was all the more true in a situation such as that of southern Africa where the level of military activity varied from country to country.

In South Africa, where there could not (in the 1960s and 1970s) yet be said to be active guerilla warfare, some of the debate seemed directed inwards, towards considerations of morale. We present three papers of the ANC: an analysis of the overall military strategy in southern Africa as one of 'spreading' warfare; Joe Slovo's presentation of the 'objective and subjective conditions' of guerrilla warfare; and Joe Matthews's warning against pessimism.

In the 1970s, South Africa began to have a number of strikes by Black workers. The ANC tended to see these strikes as signs of militant discontent following their own guidelines and hence the process of political mobilization. The PAC, on the other hand, saw these strikes as 'spontaneous' and argued that the encouragement or even approval of these strikes was 'reformist'.

In Portuguese Africa, the issue presented itself differently. The overall attitude was reflected clearly in two documents: that of MPLA on the necessity of maintaining the 'guerilla' form of the struggle to the very end; and that of FRELIMO on the necessity of a 'prolonged war'. The particular forms of warfare changed as the struggle developed. The detailed story of this evolution was recounted by FRELIMO for Mozambique. Samora Machel defines the potential role of organizations of solidarity within the framework of armed warfare.

Another fundamental question is the totality of violence, what might be called the 'humanitarian' issues of warfare. Here the movements were quite clearcut. Dr. Neto rejected terrorist bombings. FRELIMO appealed both to Portuguese settlers and to Portuguese soldiers in Mozambique, indicating its attitude to those who would refuse to participate in the oppression. And Jose Monteiro of FRELIMO stated the demands of the movements, conversely, that they be accorded the rights recognized internationally for combatants.

The Creeping War
ANC

Article in Sechaba *(ANC), I, 1, January 1967.*

For perhaps two years — since about the end of the Rivonia trial — there appears to the casual observer to have been calm on the South African scene, where previously there was turmoil, mass protest and upheaval. In Rhodesia too, as the constitutional crisis has matured and come to boiling, there has been an apparent aura of calm and quiet over the home front, in contrast with the disquiet and turmoil abroad over Rhodesian affairs.

The reasons for the seeming quiet are several. There are the obvious ones: the security laws and persecutions, which have thrown many thousands of the most articulate and conscious of the peoples of both countries into jails, frightening some of their followers and supporters into silence and blanketing their opposition. Only rarely does that opposition burst out to be heard in the world outside. There are the less obvious but yet significant reasons: the censorship which has clamped its grip on all Southern Africa, so that ever less and less that is damaging to the Smith-Vorster regimes is allowed to leak out. And the self-censorship in the press of the western world, which generally plays the 'establishment' game of preserving an appearance of calm in this most vital trade and investment area, and does nothing to shake the props from under one of the centres of international stock-exchange and financial manipulations.

But these alone cannot explain the situation. Only the most reckless optimists can claim that, were it not for censorship and self-censorship, Southern Africa would be providing a steady flow of reports of mass struggle and epic resistance. It would not. The surface calm, though more ruffled than it is made to appear, exists. There are few overt struggles, few overt demonstrations of mass resistance. Smith, Vorster and their apologists and publicists everywhere seize on this reality to claim that the people are, in reality, happy; that the governments have crushed subversion finally and forever; that Southern Africa is a stable peninsula in an unstable continent.

Those who argue thus are deceiving themselves with dangerous illusions. For the surface calm in Southern Africa is not a sign of stability. It is perhaps better likened to the calm in the centre of a tornado, a calm which marks the passing from fierce buffeting on one side of the whirlwind into an equally fierce, perhaps even fiercer, battering from a different direction.

Southern Africa's calm marks the passing from one era of struggle to another. It is the interregnum between the old struggles of mass peaceful agitation, propaganda and demonstration, to the new struggles of military character. Southern Africa is passing into the phase of civil war. And the calm is the accompaniment of the change.

There have been heralds of the new era for several years. In Rhodesia, spasmodic sabotage, usually with home-made Molotov cocktails, has occurred almost since the dawn of the 1961 Constitution. In South Africa, organized sabotage opened in December 1961, and broadened out, as the evidence of many trials has revealed, into a large-scale campaign of acquiring military equipment and building a military liberation force outside the country under African National Congress command.

The change has been piecemeal and unspectacular. It has not been particularly remarked by the world outside, even though it has been recognized by the authorities in all Southern Africa, who have placed all their territories on a virtual war footing, complete with massive military training and mobilization schemes, stock-piling, building of strategic roads, multiplying security laws and regulations, and unrestricted government-by-decree not far removed from martial law.

In South Africa and Rhodesia the change began with sabotage. But in Angola it came more dramatically, with full-fledged guerilla war. After more than three years, the war is still on; considerable sections of the country are under guerilla control; the Portuguese force required to maintain the war grows greater as the years pass. Angola is fully in the war.

Mozambique is following the pattern of Angola. For perhaps two years guerilla operations have ranged along the northern frontiers, and are developing in scale and in the spread of territory involved. More recently, in Rhodesia, there have been military clashes between liberation guerillas and the Smith regime's army on a scale not yet fully known. And last in time, but surely not least in significance, is the report in recent months that the first armed bands of political fighters have penetrated the real citadel of white Southern Africa — South Africa; and have engaged Vorster's government forces in a remote corner of South West Africa.

This is the evidence of the change in Southern Africa to a period of war, and of the fact that the old era is passing. It was an era of mass struggle, of strikes and demonstrations. When there were shootings — and there were many — they were always the shootings of unarmed men and women demonstrators by heavily armed police. It was an era when hundreds of thousands pitted their voices against the guns and truncheons of the regimes: Portuguese, Rhodesian and South African.

That is the era that is dead. It is the dying of that era that has left the deep silences, the surfaces of apparent calm, which so many supporters of the liberation movement view with such misgivings today. But the dying of that era marks the birth of the new — the era of civil war in Southern Africa.

It is not the purpose of this article to make the military struggle in Southern Africa larger than it is. The size of the actions is not the essence of the matter. The essence is that the actions have begun; that they grow; that they are coming into general operation to replace the era that passed. A beginning towards military struggle and civil war has been made. The conflict between oppressor and oppressed, between majority people and minority rulers which gave birth to those beginnings, persists, and will continue to exist until it is destroyed in struggle. Civil war will develop and broaden out. Of this there can be no doubt. We are moving into the era of war, and from here on, nothing in Southern Africa can ever be the same again.

Objective and Subjective Conditions
Joe Slovo

From an article by Joe Slovo of the ANC, entitled 'The Armed Struggle Spreads', published in Sechaba *(ANC), II, 5, May 1968.*

Of course favourable conditions for armed struggle ripen historically. But the historical process must not be approached as if it were a mystical thing outside of man which in a crude deterministic sort of way sets him tasks to which he responds. In this sense to sit back and wait for the evolvement of objective conditions which constitute a *'revolutionary situation'* amounts in some cases to a dereliction of leadership duties. What people, expressing themselves in organized activity, do or abstain from doing, hastens or retards the historical process and helps or hinders the creation of favourable conditions for armed struggle. Indeed in one sense the process of creating favourable conditions for military struggle does not end until the day of victory. Given the sort of minimum preconditions I referred to above, the actual commencement and sustaining of guerilla activity operates as an extremely important factor in creating more favourable conditions for eventual victory. But it is not the sole factor.[1] Other forms of mass activity, including those inspired by the successes of the guerilla units, also play a vital role.

Of course no political struggle (and this is what guerilla struggle essentially is) can be taken up only on condition of infallibly favourable chances.[2] It does not however follow that licence must be given for every act of adventurism, irresponsibility and 'trying your luck'.

There is not a single serious segment of the organized liberatory movement which does not believe that, in a general sense, political conditions in South Africa are favourable for the commencement and development of armed struggle. This does not necessarily imply a belief that there exists at the moment a classical-type revolutionary situation, with an all-round revolutionary insurrection as an immediate possibility.

Is there evidence that the course upon which the ANC has embarked has a political basis in the existing South African situation? There is, I believe,

1. Debray, *Revolution in the Revolution* tends to proceed from the proposition that 'the most important form of propaganda is military action', to a conclusion that in most of Latin America the creation of military skilled guerilla *foci* is sufficient to bring about favourable conditions for an eventual people's military victory. Thus he underrates the vital connection between the guerilla struggle (which in its early stages must of necessity be of a limited magnitude) and other forms of militant mass activity. He sees the *foci* (which in terms of his approach must assume overall political as well as military leadership) as having (certainly in the initial phases) to cut itself off from the local population. There are many indications, including the increasing devotion of resources to mass illegal propaganda throughout the country, that the ANC's approach on this important question is different.
2. 'World history would indeed be very easy to make if the struggle were taken up only on condition of infallibly favourable chances' – Karl Marx in a letter to L. Kugelman, 17 March 1871.

abundant evidence that it has. The Africans of South Africa have a history which is rich in resistance to alien rule not only in the initial period of colonization but also in the last few decades when it reached new heights. The people have over and over again demonstrated their capacity to act at a most sophisticated political level.

The 50s and the early 60s witnessed four impressive nationwide general strikes all called by the ANC and its allies. The significance of these strikes should not be underestimated. On each occasion, hundreds of thousands of urban workers risked their jobs and their consequent right to remain in an urban area, in quest not of reforms, not for better working conditions, but in response to a purely political call to demonstrate a demand for votes, opposition to racial laws, and so on. In the face of repression Trade Union organization was minimal — and the above responses were important pointers to the high level of political consciousness which a half-century of urbanization combined with vigorous political leadership had inculcated into the townspeople. There are many more examples to be found in the 50s and 60s which illustrate the capacity of those in the urban areas to react impressively to calls for action involving both tenacity and sacrifice: the Defiance Campaign of 1952-53, the bus boycotts of the late 50s, women's resistance against the extension of pass laws to women, the pre-Sharpeville anti-pass campaigns.

Militancy in Rural Areas

And what of the people in the countryside, which is the focal point of guerilla activity in the initial stages? Here too there is convincing evidence of a peasantry which, despite centuries of intensive repression, lacks submissiveness. In the very recent past and in many important areas it has demonstrated a capacity for action to the point of armed resistance. In Sekhukhuniland (Transvaal) in the late 50s the peasantry, partly armed, doggedly resisted the attempts by the authorities to replace the traditional leaders of the people with government-appointed servants, in the so-called Bantu Authorities. In Zululand similar resistance was encountered. The most intense point of peasant resistance and upsurge was amongst the Pondo in the Transkei. By March 1960 a vast popular movement had arisen, unofficial administrative units were set up including people's courts. From the chosen spots in the mountains where thousands of peasants assembled illegally came the name of the movement — 'Intaba' — The Mountain. Although this revolt had its origin in local grievances the aim of the resistance soon became the attainment of basic political ends and it came to adopt the full programme of the ANC.

What is also significant about many of these actions in the countryside is that despite the traditionally strict legal sanction against the possession by non-whites of any arms or ammunition they always manage on appropriate occasions to emerge with an assortment of prohibited weapons in their hands.

These then are pointers to the validity of the claim by the ANC that the African majority of the country can be expected to respond in growing numbers to a lead which holds out real prospects of destroying white supremacy, albeit in a long and protracted war. The conviction held by all African political groupings (except those sponsored by the government) that the white state can be shifted by nothing short of violence reflects what is today both an incontrovertible objective fact and a belief held by a majority of ordinary people both in town and countryside.

If then all these subjective elements in the situation tend to argue in favour of the ANC decision, what about some of the formidable objective difficulties? On the face of it the enemy of the guerilla is in stable command of a rich and varied economy which, even at the stage when it is not required to extend itself, can afford a military budget of £186 million. He has a relatively well-trained and efficient army and police force. He can draw on considerable manpower resources because he has the support of the 3.5 million privileged whites who can be expected to fight with great ferocity and conviction (albeit one that is born of economic aggrandisement).

In addition South Africa has very influential and powerful friends. In a situation of crisis these friends may well lose their existing public inhibitions to openly associate with and bolster up the racist regime.

If there is one lesson that the history of guerilla struggles has taught, it is that the material strength and resources of the enemy is by no means a decisive factor. Witness the resources at the disposal of the French in Algeria; at the height of the fighting 600,000 troops were supplied and serviced by a leading industrial nation whose economy was quite outside the reach of military operations. In terms of pure material strength and almost limitless resources, can anyone surpass the USA in Vietnam? And no amount of modern industrial backing, technical know-how or fire power appears to sway the balance in favour of the invaders. What about the spectacle of Grivas and his Cyprus group challenging the British Army with 47 rifles, 27 automatic weapons and 7 revolvers? ('It was with these arms and these alone, that I kept the fight going for almost a year without any appreciable reinforcements').

The answer lies in this. Guerilla warfare, almost by definition, posits a situation in which there is a vast imbalance of material and military resources between the opposing sides. It is designed to cope with a situation in which the enemy is infinitely superior in relation to every conventional factor of warfare. It is par excellence the weapon of the materially weak against the materially strong.

Given its popular character and given a populace which increasingly sides with and shields the guerilla whilst at the same time opposing and exposing the enemy, the survival and growth of a people's army is assured by a skilful exercise of tactics. Surprise, mobility and tactical retreat make it difficult for the enemy to bring into play its superior fire-power in any decisive battles. No individual battle is fought under circumstances unfavourable to the guerilla. Superior forces can be harassed, weakened and, in the end, destroyed. 'There is a saying: "the guerilla is the maverick of war". He practises deception, treachery, surprise and night operations. Thus, circumstances and the will to win often oblige him to forget romantic and sportsmanlike concepts. . . Some disparaging people call this "hit and run". This is exactly what it is! Hit and run, wait, stalk the enemy, hit him again and run . . . perhaps this smacks of not facing up to the enemy. Nevertheless it serves the goal of guerilla warfare: to conquer and destroy the enemy' (Introduction to *Guerilla Warfare*, Mao Tse Tung).

The absence of an orthodox front, of fighting lines; the need of the enemy to attenuate his resources and lines of communication over vast areas; his need to protect the widely scattered installations on which his economy is dependent (because the guerilla pops up now here now there). These are amongst the factors which serve in the long run to compensate in favour of the guerilla for the disparity in the starting strength of the adversaries. I stress the words '*in the long run*', because it would be idle to dispute the considerable military advantages to the enemy of his high level of industrialization, his ready-to-hand reserves of white manpower and his excellent roads, railways and air transport which facilitate swift manoeuvres and speedy concentration of personnel.

But we must also not overlook the fact that over a period of time many of these very same unfavourable factors will begin to operate in favour of the liberation force:

(a)   The ready-to-hand resources including food production depend overwhelmingly upon non-white labour which, with the growing intensity of the struggle, will not remain docile and cooperative.

(b)   The white manpower resources may seem adequate initially but must become dangerously stretched as guerilla warfare develops. Already extremely short of skilled labour — the monopoly of the whites — the mobilization of a large force for a protracted struggle would place a further burden on the workings of the economy.

(c)   In contrast to many other major guerilla struggles (Cuba is one of the exceptions) the enemy's economic and manpower resources are all situated within the theatre of war and there is no secure external pool (other than direct intervention by a foreign state) safe from sabotage, mass action and guerilla action on which the enemy can draw.

(d)   The very sophisticated character of the economy with its well developed system of communications makes it a much more vulnerable target. In an underdeveloped country the interruption of supplies to any given region may be no more than a local setback. In a highly sensitive modern economic structure of the South African type, the successful harassment of transport to any major industrial complex would inevitably inflict immense damage to the economy as a whole and to the morale of the enemy. (The South African forces would have the task of keeping intact about 30,000 miles of railway line spread over an area of over 400,000 square miles!)

One of the more popular misconceptions concerning guerilla warfare is that a physical environment which conforms to a special pattern is indispensable — thick jungle, inaccessible mountain ranges, swamps, a friendly border and so forth. The availability of this sort of terrain is, of course, of tremendous advantage to the guerillas especially in the early non-operational phase when training and other preparatory steps are undertaken and no external bases are available for this purpose. When the operations commence, the guerilla cannot survive, let alone flourish, unless he moves to areas where people live and work and where the enemy can be engaged in combat. If he is fortunate enough to have behind him a friendly border or areas of difficult access which can provide temporary refuge, it is of course advantageous, although it sometimes brings with it its own set of problems connected mainly with supplies. But guerilla warfare can, and has been, waged in every conceivable type of terrain, in deserts, in swamps, in farm fields, in built-up areas, in plains, in the bush and in countries without friendly borders.

The sole question is one of adjusting survival tactics to the sort of terrain in which operations have to be carried out. In any case in the vast expanse that is South Africa, a peoples force will find a multitude of variations in topography; deserts, mountain forests, veld, and swamps. There might not appear to be a single impregnable Sierra Maestra or impenetrable jungle, but the country abounds in terrain which in general is certainly no less favourable for guerilla operations than some of the terrain in which the Algerians or the resistance movements in occupied Europe operated. Tito, when told that a certain area was 'as level as the palm of your hand and with very little forests', retorted: 'What a first-class example it is of the relative unimportance of geographical factors in the development of a rising.'

In particular South Africa's tremendous size will make it extremely difficult, if not impossible, for the white regime to keep the whole of it under armed surveillance in strength and in depth. Hence, an early development of a relatively safe (though shifting) rear is not beyond the realm of possibility. The undetected existence of the SWAPO training camp for over a year and, more especially, the survival for years in the mountains and hills in the Transkei of the leaders of 'Intaba' during the military occupation of the area after the 1960 Pondo Revolt, are both of importance in this context.

False Theories and Pessimism
Joe Matthews

From an article by Joe Matthews, then of the ANC, commenting on the documents of the Consultative Conference at Morogoro in May 1969 and published in Sechaba *(ANC) III, 12, December 1969.*

Confronted by the inevitable difficulties of a complex struggle such as ours, some people have become infected by false theories concerning our revolution. We are on the threshold of a great advance in our struggle for freedom based on mobilization of the masses at home. The movement has scored some notable successes in the last few years. We have also sustained severe setbacks. A careful balance sheet will show that since Rivonia we have made a steady recovery of our initiative. But some people unable to see events in their totality pick on certain negative features and draw wildly generalised conclusions about the progress of our revolutionary struggle.

In the early part of this decade the ANC and the liberation movement in general had to combat the idea that the struggle in South Africa would be a short one. In those days slogans promising freedom by a particular year were shouted by some irresponsible elements. The ANC pointed out then that the struggle in South Africa would not follow the path by which many African countries achieved independence. We made it clear that negotiations and constitutional advance would not bring about our freedom. We said then that the struggle would be long and difficult. History has proved that those who thought the struggle would be brief were utterly wrong.

As is usual with petit bourgeois intellectuals, the same elements have now swung to the other extreme. Confronted by a tough and long revolutionary struggle the people who were prattling about a quick victory have become the biggest pessimists. Basing themselves on the great disparity in military strength and resources between ourselves and the enemy they conclude that there is little hope of a change in the situation. This attitude also is quite wrong. The situation in our country is not static but is rapidly developing in many different directions. The period of lull is rapidly coming to a close. The reactionary offensive that has marked the last nine years has now lost impetus.

Faced with a growing armed revolution in Southern Africa the ruling classes in our country are beginning to commit strategic mistakes with far-reaching consequences for the future. Recent divisions within the ruling group reflect differences in the strategy for preserving white supremacy. The contradictions that have always been inherent in the South African social structure are growing acute. Provided the movement gives clear leadership and puts forward correct strategic and tactical plans and directives as well as selfless organizational work, an upturn in the struggle is inevitable.

Our movement must be oriented on the perspective of a struggle that will be fairly protracted but will undoubtedly be crowned with success. The armed revolution in Algeria took about eight years before victory was achieved. In heroic Vietnam the struggle has been going on for decades first against the French and then against the United States. The revolution in Angola began eight years ago and has registered big successes. The struggle in Guinea (Bissau) and in Mozambique have similarly gone on for some time now.

Like all oppressed peoples we would naturally like to get rid of the oppressors and exploiters in the shortest possible time. Should it turn out that the revolution develops faster than expected we should be ready for that. But any serious analysis seems to suggest that our struggle will be a long one. The ruling oligarchy in our country has been entrenched in power for a long period. Everything has been done to deprive the majority of the people of any element of power. The coercive machinery of the state is virtually entirely manned by members of the privileged white minority. The enemy have at their disposal all the resources of a wealthy and fairly developed modern state. Last but by no means least the enemy has been able to count on the many-sided support of the major imperialist powers.

On the other hand the oppressed people start off the armed struggle with a number of serious disadvantages. The most important of them is the relative absence of military equipment and techniques. The people also have not acquired knowledge of the method of guerilla warfare in the mass. To correct these weaknesses will be a slow process during the course of developing our armed revolutionary struggle. Why then in spite of the factors mentioned above are we so absolutely certain of victory?

The fundamental and decisive factor to bear in mind is that the national liberation movement is historically and socially a progressive force fighting for a better life for the people. The enemy on the other hand fights under the banner of reaction to protect ill-gotten gains and privileges enjoyed by the minority at the expense of the people. The policy of imperialist and colonialist suppression of the people is retrogressive and doomed to defeat. On no account can the enemy ever gain support from the people for a policy of suppressing them. This is a fundamental and permanent feature of the situation which is often undervalued, precisely because it is so obvious. But in a prolonged armed revolution it is the factor that more and more determines the side which wins.

Very powerful social forces stand fundamentally opposed to the present regime. The national movement of the oppressed Africans, Indians and Coloureds stands opposed to the regime. The forces of social change among the workers, peasants and intellectuals stand opposed to the regime. These forces have within them tremendous power when organised. The onset of every new form of struggle has the immediate tendency to temporarily disrupt organisation. This happened in our case also at different times in our history. When the period of non-violent struggle came to an end it found the liberation movement in our country in possession of a stable leadership in command of a relatively well organised mass movement. The adoption of the decision to wage armed struggle for the overthrow of the regime involved a complete change of strategy, tactics, propaganda, organisational machinery and so on. This could not but result in some disruption of organisation to say nothing of the fact that the reaction of the enemy added further difficulties.

The Morogoro conference has laid the basis both in principle and in organisation for a complete remoulding of our movement so as to enable full utilisation of our possibilities in mobilising the masses. It should be noted that in conditions such as obtain in our police-ridden country it is not possible to organise the masses except as part of and in conjunction with the waging of armed struggle.

It is also necessary to get rid of the concept that the masses will be organised by a few people at the top. Our experience teaches that the masses of the people display great organisational initiative themselves. We must make it possible for our numerous activists and supporters to do organisational work in support of the armed struggle. Whilst we begin the struggle in a relatively weak position in so far as military technique and arms supplies are concerned, this is not inevitable or permanent. Step by step, our people must acquire both the techniques of war and the means for fighting such a war.

In the resistance war, it is now practical to achieve complete co-ordination and unity of the national liberation and progressive forces under the leadership of the ANC. This means that an authoritative organ for prosecuting the revolution is now being built with the full support of all those forces opposed to the continued existence of the present Fascist regime. No organisation outside the united Front built around the ANC and its allies exists which is capable of leading the struggle. All reformists and opportunist groupings which at one time existed in our country have disintegrated both ideologically and organisationally. This is an extremely favourable factor for conducting the revolutionary war.

We have said that the resources of the South African regimes are great relative to ours at the moment. But this must not be exaggerated. South Africa is not a world power and the privileged minority is numerically small. In the long run this weakness of the enemy will tell very much.

A vital factor making for our inevitable victory is that our struggle has the support of friends all over the world. Firstly we have direct allies in the millions who support the armed struggle in our neighbouring countries of Namibia, Angola, Zimbabwe, Mozambique. In particular the alliance with ZAPU and the people of Zimbabwe is of great importance to our prospects of victory.

As the struggle develops in our country it will reach a level which will oblige neighbouring countries to increase their support to our people. At the moment some of our neighbours who sympathise with our case are hesitating and wavering under the threats of the Fascists. A time will come when the level of the struggle in South Africa will enable our neighbours to come out in their true colours of genuine supporters of the oppressed people in our country. At that stage any government that did not support the armed struggle of our people would be overthrown by the masses in the neighbouring countries who know full well the evils of Apartheid and Fascism.

In other African countries we have to take the long view. Some countries like Malawi are taking a direction hostile to our struggle and collaborating with our enemies. Others take up political and economic positions of which we as the representatives of the South African people, disapprove. It will not be possible for these countries to take up positions which we in the ANC dislike, the moment the struggle in our country reaches what might be called the 'critical point'. Our immediate task is to work hard to achieve the requisite level of armed struggle in our country. But there is no doubt that in the long run the independent African states will form a major part of support for our struggle.

Further afield are the Afro-Asian states, the Latin American countries, the Socialist states which already play a vital role in isolating Apartheid and its allies internationally. This international support will eventually be translated into massive direct resistance to our armed struggle. Hence it is important constantly to develop our international work as an aid not only now but in the future.

To sum up then, our struggle for liberation is likely to be a prolonged one and we must base our actions and planning with that as our orientation. This does not mean we have all the time in the world. It is necessary to work hard and selflessly to achieve the overthrow of the disastrous Apartheid regime as fast as possible. But we consider that the struggle will be long and we must get our people and our friends and supporters to understand the implications of this perspective. On the other hand our victory is absolutely certain. Both historically and in practical terms the conditions now exist which were not there ten years ago for a successful revolutionary war in our country.

Strikes as Reformism
PAC

From an editorial in the PAC's Azania News *(Dar es Salaam), VIII, 4, April 1973.*

For some time now, the propaganda of the South African Liberation Movement abroad has been describing a narrow circle of economic strikes as if it were the essential part of the political struggle for the conquest of political power. Some of it has gone further and described them as being purposefully instigated by the underground activity of the liberation movement. The problem here is inability to distinguish between two distinct objectives — reform and revolution — and the issues involved in each. There can be no denial that the struggle of workers in a single factory against their employers or a single branch of industry for economic reforms in wages, working hours, working conditions and fringe benefits, can have tremendous political importance under certain conditions, for example, as a means of propaganda or organisation towards a specific political end, or when it is an initial phase in the long-term development of a working class that has become conscious of itself as an exploited class whose ultimate aim is the seizure of political power from the exploiting classes. But this does not happen automatically, and that is why such activity is scattered and isolated, rather than systematically spread out and evenly concentrated throughout the country, as revolutionary activity should be, or as the liberation movement should strive to make it.

We have also found that significant sections of the liberation movement of our country deny that the economic struggles of the workers for reforms are spontaneous. The problem here is one of dealing in dictionary meanings, rather than seeing things in historical perspective. It is argued that the action of the workers arises, in the main, from the underground activity of the liberation movement. This certainly is an insult to the intelligence of the workers who are not granted the independent capacity to desire or feel the spontaneous need for improvement in their conditions of life. This is not to deny or undermine the underground work of our resistance movement, but reforms for higher wages, shorter hours, better working conditions and social benefits are the spontaneous objectives of every working person and he does not need someone to stuff this into his allegedly empty head. Its political value emerges when underground activity develops it into the political struggle of the whole working class against the entire capitalist class for the seizure of political power in an organised way. Reforms are conscious demands for concessions from the ruling classes within the existing system, whereas revolution is designed to take power from the ruling classes, in order to establish a new order of society. This is what the racist regime fears and we must have a revolutionary approach to it.

It cannot be the task of a liberation movement to draw up plans for refashioning bourgeois society or to preach to the capitalists about improving the lot of the workers. Its task is to organise and to lead the struggle for the seizure of political power. Otherwise it can have no business to call itself a liberation movement, but must accept what it is in actual fact — a reform movement. The historical distinction between a liberation movement and a reform movement is best assessed through the manner in which each conducts struggle in terms of the vital material interests and national aspirations of its people. A revolutionary movement does not drag at the tail of the movement in order to glorify its successes and apologise for its reverses. It must be the further task of a revolutionary movement to see the spontaneous activity of those people in our country who rise in struggle in proper perspective, at best as a by-product, rather than the essential content, of revolutionary struggle and to treat it accordingly, if we have firmly grasped the essential form that revolutionary struggle should take.

Strikes as Mass Revolt
ANC

From the paper presented to the International Conference
of Experts for the Support of Victims of Colonialism and
Apartheid in Southern Africa, held in Oslo, 9–14 April 1973.

Recently in the Durban industrial complex alone, 100,000 black workers participated in strike action. The strikes have been spreading to all the parts of South Africa. They are following an organized pattern and have demonstrated very high discipline and leadership. The black working class is challenging the system that denies them political and economic rights, a system that condemns them to squalor and poverty, that dumps them into resettlement areas and barren reserves, a system that afflicts them with lethal diseases like tuberculosis and causes numerous cases of maiming accidents.

The white State of the oppressor groups and the employers was thrown into a panic by the strike wave. The political and economic fabric of the apartheid system was shaken. The various sections of the white establishment reacted in different ways but their aims were the same – to crush the militant actions by force, victimization and 'hypocritical concessions'. The South African regime, in typical reaction, amassed a huge army (some airlifted from Pretoria) to protect the interests of the 'South African way of life' (racism under the guise of the maintenance of 'law and order'). In some factories the army has been called upon to maintain production. Strikers have been teargassed, baton-charged, arrested and persecuted. The employers are making gestures to meet the workers' demands by contemptuous token offers of wage increases.

The extent of their gestures is evidenced by the fact that after the increases, the wages are still very meagre and remain a pittance. What is more, despite the increases, the average wage is still below that paid to African workers in Zambia – a country that has been independent for less than ten years and does not have South Africa's vast natural resources. The mining industry, in a blaze of publicity, increased African wages in the mining sector to less than one-quarter of those paid in Zambia . . .

The strikes in South Africa must be seen in their proper perspective as part of the mass revolt against the regime of terror. This mass revolt is taking many forms and shapes. It embraces legal and illegal forms of struggle. It embraces distribution of clandestine material and the establishment of clandestine groups. The African National Congress and its allies are part of this mass revolt and represent its advanced and properly equipped detachment.

The Generalization of the Armed Struggle
MPLA

From an article in MPLA's Angola Arms *(Dar es Salaam),*
4 February 1969.

All the conditions existed, therefore, for succeeding in the great task which Dr. Agostinho Neto, President of the MPLA, had announced to the world in his historic speech at the beginning of 1967: *the generalization of the armed struggle throughout the national territory.* A new phase in the Angolan people's struggle was about to begin.

Pursuing this strategic line, the Movement opened a new front in the North-East of Angola, the Fourth Region, which includes the districts of Lunda and Malange. The first Assembly of the Third Region, which was held in August 1968, noted that more than one-third of Angolan territory was controlled by the MPLA and that nine of the fifteen districts through which the colonial administration governed the country were in a state of war: Cabinda, Zaire, Uige, Cuanza Norte, Lunda, Moxico, Bie and Cuando Cubanga. The President of the MPLA later announced that: 'Other regions will be developed this year, so that there should no longer be a number of combat fronts, but only one enveloping the enemy in an encirclement which will paralyse him and render him inoffensive. This will be the prelude to the final blow, which will culminate in the seizure of political power by our people.' (Press Conference given by the President of the MPLA in Brazzaville on 3 January 1968).

He added that the headquarters of the organisation was no longer outside the country and was now operating in one of the regions controlled by the Movement. This fundamental statement illustrates an essential aspect of the MPLA's strategic line – *the struggle must be waged inside the country. It is therefore a question of conducting a protracted popular and revolutionary war extending throughout the national territory and encircling the towns, which are also mobilised by clandestine work and which will be taken in the final phase of the war. It is also a question of waging a guerilla war, which will be transformed into other more advanced stages, without ever totally abandoning the guerilla form. The MPLA's struggle is a politico-military one, with emphasis placed on the political aspect.* This is the reason for the great attention the MPLA pays to the work of mobilising and organising the masses of the people, both those in the liberated regions and those still under the foreign yoke. That is why the MPLA makes it its constant concern to train cadres who are good both from the political and the military point of view.

The liberation struggle of the MPLA has *a profoundly national content* so that all Angolan ethnic groups and social strata should join it. It is the consistent policy of the *national front*, without at the same time neglecting the establishment of *a party structure* within that front.

On the Necessity of a Prolonged War
FRELIMO

> *Article in FRELIMO's* A Voz da Revolucao *(Dar es Salaam), 8 May 1968. Translated from Portuguese.*

During the visit of the Secretaries of Defence and Security of FRELIMO to the Province of Tete, in the first week of April 1968, they held several meetings with the people. At one of those meetings, in Fingoe, an old man spoke about the Revolution. Speaking of the war that had started in his province, he said: 'We must not have illusions that the war will last one week and that we will then be independent. No. This war will last for some time, it will be a hard one. We must be aware of this, and be prepared to fight as much as we have to.'

This old man, who never went to school, because the Portuguese colonialists did not allow him to, this old man, without book learning, knew the truths and the fundamental principles of our Revolution. He knew that a prolonged war is necessary in order to defeat the enemy and to free our land.

But why is a prolonged war necessary? Some of our comrades think that we could win the war quickly. To do this, they think we should concentrate all our forces and throw them against the enemy.

It is clear that those comrades who believe this have not analysed the situation in Mozambique.

Our forces are far inferior to those of the enemy. We have only about one-fifth of the soldiers the enemy has. Besides the enemy has superior war supplies. He has got airplanes, tanks, bombs, cannons. If we gathered all our forces in a single battle against the enemy, he would send all his airplanes, tanks, and his 60,000 soldiers, and thus destroy all our forces. Therefore, this is something that we cannot do. It would mean sacrificing our soldiers uselessly and ending the Revolution. It would be adventurist.

What can we do then? We must conduct a prolonged war. Why? Because we can only free our homeland with a prolonged war.

In fact, we see that when we started the armed struggle in September 1964, FRELIMO only had 250 soldiers, and very few weapons. Today, there are over 12,000 soldiers equipped with modern weapons: FRELIMO has now got mortars, anti-aircraft guns, and even cannons. We can also see that the number of our troops is increasing, because each day there are more people who want to join the FRELIMO army. With further success in the struggle there will be further increases in the numbers until one day we shall outnumber the enemy. On the other hand, the weapons which we are capturing from the enemy, and those which the countries sympathetic to our liberation struggle are giving us, reinforce our military equipment.

We must also remind ourselves that Portugal is a small and under-developed country, involved in three wars simultaneously, in Mozambique, Angola and Guinea. On each one of these three fronts, Mozambique, Angola, and Guinea, there are Portuguese soldiers being killed every day by the guerrillas. Now Portugal does not have that many soldiers, that they shall be able to replace all the dead ones.

At the economic level, the cost of maintaining three armies, in lands far from Portugal, is destroying the economy. Today, Portugal is able to sustain the war thanks to the help which it gets from its NATO imperialist friends. But even such help is decreasing, because those countries — the USA, West Germany, England, France — have their own problems and cannot thus give Portugal too much.

As for us, international aid to our struggle is ever greater. It comes from African countries, socialist countries, and even from the progressive organizations of the imperialist countries themselves. At this pace, we are becoming stronger, while Portugal becomes weaker. All that has been said leads us to conclude that the final victory will be ours, if we know how to take advantage of our situation, and of the weaknesses of the enemy.

Our *advantages*, our strong points, are the following:

(a)   Our war is a just one. We are fighting the invaders, in order to reconquer our land. The fact that our war is a just one ensures the participation of all the people, and the support of all the progressive countries in the world.

(b)   All our people, seven million Mozambicans, are united in a single front against the common enemy, the Portuguese colonizers.

(c)   The morale of our people and guerrillas is high. All fight heroically in the defence of our country.

(d)   We are fighting on our own land, in the defence of the interests of our people. Thus, our guerillas have three advantages: they know the terrain well, they are used to the climate, and they are supported by the people.

(e)   We have many allies, in all parts of the world, who support our struggle.

Our *weaknesses* are the following:

(a)   We have not enough weapons.

(b)   Our troops are still inferior in number to those of the enemy.

(c)   Our propaganda is very weak.

As to the enemy, these are his weaknesses:

(a)   Their war is not a just one. Their aggression, oppression, and exploitation arouses the hatred of our people.

(b)   The enemy is divided. Even in Portugal there are many people who are against the colonial war, and against the Fascist government of Salazar.

(c)   The morale of the Portuguese troops is very low. In battle we see that the Portuguese soldiers are afraid to fight.

(d)   The enemy is not fighting on their own land. Thus they have three disadvantages: they are not used to the climate, have no knowledge of the terrain, and are not supported by the people.

(e)   The enemy has the support of only some of its allies, but these allies have their own problems and are thus not able to bear all the expenditures of the war. Even Salazar has complained of this fact, and accused America and England of abandoning him. On the whole, Portugal is isolated.

(f)   The enemy must fight in three territories at the same time, in Mozambique, Angola, and Guinea. And in each one of these countries he must fight on several fronts. In Mozambique there are three fronts — Cabo Delgado, Niassa and Tete; in Angola there are four. In Guinea he is fighting in almost all areas of the territory. This forces the enemy to scatter its already weak forces.

The enemy's strong points are the following:

(a)   He has large numbers of modern weapons.

(b)   He has many troops.

(c)   His means of propaganda are more sophisticated.

In comparing our strength and weaknesses with those of the enemy, we see that for now the enemy is still superior to us. He has more troops, more weapons, and better propaganda. *But this is only a temporary advantage*, since, as we have seen, our forces are gradually increasing, while those of the enemy are decreasing. With the development of the war thanks to the efforts of the whole people in struggle, our strong points will be consolidated and our weaknesses will disappear. On the contrary, the enemy's strong points, the advantages which he holds today, will disappear and he will become weaker every day, isolated and discouraged. And thus, we will one day be stronger than the enemy. The Portuguese colonizers will then be defeated and we will finally free our land, Mozambique. The secret of our victory lies in the participation of the whole people in the struggle. We must be aware that we must continue to fight, to develop production, to train people, to mobilize the people. We must not expect that independence will fall from the sky, or that others may come to free our land for us. It is all of us, through a day by day, constant, continuous struggle, who will build independence of Mozambique, fighting as long as we have to.

The First Steps
FRELIMO

> *Analysis in FRELIMO's* Mozambique Revolution *(Dar es Salaam), 51, April-June 1972.*

The first process which merits examination is that of the structuring of the movement. As President Mondlane said in his report to the 2nd Congress, the first task we had to face was that of constituting an executive body capable of putting into effect the programme of action drawn up at the 1st Congress. True, a Central Committee with executive duties had been created, as well as departments, each headed by a secretary, in some cases aided by an assistant.

But what remained to be determined was not only the internal structure of each department, but also the allocation of duties of the various members of the Central Executive, and the division of labour between the Presidency and the departments; the latter was a particularly crucial problem because it raised the whole question of the degree of centralisation of leadership which is necessary at certain phases of the struggle. In short, the organisational methods best suited to the concrete fulfilment of the programme drawn up inside our country remained to be determined.

There were problems which could not be solved theoretically; their solution was largely dependent on the nature and the extent of our experience. Of course, we did know that a revolutionary struggle could not be led using anti-democratic structures, without collective methods of work. We were aware that a popular programme requires a revolutionary structure. But what sort of tradition had we built up in this respect?

This calls for a keen appraisal of the organisations which had existed previously and which came together to form FRELIMO. They all displayed the same weaknesses, reflecting their similar origin and tradition.

First, both the leadership and the rank and file consisted mainly of people who had lived abroad for a long time, either as refugees or as migrant workers in adjacent countries. Thus MANU operated in Tanganyika, bringing together people from the northern provinces of Niassa and Cabo Delgado, most of whom worked on the sisal plantations of British settlers. Their principal activity was holding meetings with these workers, issuing membership cards to them and collecting funds. However, they lacked any clear perspective on concrete work inside the country, apart from the distribution of membership cards, which was done in Cabo Delgado Province.

Similar features characterised UDENAMO, though it grouped together people from the centre and the south of the country. These Mozambicans were, on the whole, rather more urbanised and they lived in Rhodesia, either as refugees from Portuguese campaigns of repression or as employees in the service sector. A substantial part of UDENAMO's activity involved recruiting militants inside the country and sending them to Tanganyika or helping political refugees to go north. As for UNAMI, it had somewhat limited activity in Nyasaland and Tete.

A second feature followed: the very fact that most of the members of these organisations had lived abroad for some time meant that they had no very deep understanding of the true conditions prevailing in the country. Not only was there a loss of direct contact with the living conditions and the feelings of the people, their information being garnered instead from reports and from the stories told by the refugees, but above all, there was scant knowledge of the true nature and dimensions of the enemy's machinery of repression.

Thirdly, and this is perhaps the most relevant point in our analysis, because they lived abroad these parties were greatly influenced by the kind of organisation typical of the British colonial tradition. Therefore, in their structural organisation and in their very concept of the work to be done, the example of the NDP in Rhodesia, the Malawi Congress Party or TANU was followed.

Carried away by the euphoria of the 'wind of change' and by the achievements of these parties in neighbouring countries, they believed in the inevitability of change. They therefore misinterpreted the political and economic nature of fascist Portuguese colonialism, ignoring the fact that it could never accept any degree of political freedom or peaceful evolution to independence. Under such conditions it is not surprising that the decisive role of bringing the three organisations together and in shaping the new organisation, came to be played by other militants coming from inside the country where they had been working clandestinely. Undoubtedly, the political consciousness and, above all, the concrete knowledge of this latter group was much surer, though it is also true to say that they lacked the tradition of organisation which the special conditions of clandestine struggle had never allowed to develop.

Such, therefore, was the sum of experience that nationalist militants from various backgrounds could draw upon in structuring a political party at the time of FRELIMO's creation.

The constituent Congress drew up a programme which can be summed up in three points:

(1)   mobilising the people and heightening national consciousness;
(2)   launching an education programme to increase combat effectiveness;
(3)   drawing up a plan for military action taking into account the nature

of Portuguese colonialism.

It was through the implementation of these programmes that FRELIMO was going to transform itself into something entirely new in relation to the organisations that preceded it.

The last point was decisive. While appeals for a peaceful solution to the problem were made from international platforms, we could not be under any illusions: war was already being waged in Angola, and in Mozambique the enemy was reinforcing his police and army apparatus.

It was under such conditions that the military programme took concrete form. We needed a sound and consistent programme, and this presupposed both a detailed study of the country, and of the control established by the enemy and, at the same time, a survey of the political and social traditions of each region. Another aspect of this task was the creation of a body which would be able to ensure the recruitment and training of a large number of solidly united and well-organised militants to spearhead the programme of armed action.

But the manner in which this organisational and operational stage was tackled was decisive. Our people had already had bitter and painful experience of mass demonstrations, strikes and peaceful protests which ended in repression and massacre. It was therefore vital to create an organ capable of undertaking consistent and effective action against the colonial military apparatus. We had learned that it was not sufficient merely to have right on one's side when confronting Portuguese colonialism!

The aims and scope of our activity having thus been defined, political organisers who were already established inside the country were entrusted with the task of mobilising and recruiting young people wishing to take up arms; there was a large and enthusiastic response to this call. From that moment political action ceased to be the prerogative of a restricted group and for the first time involved a great number of militants. In fact because they thus demonstrate the process of affirming the popular content of the movement through the growing participation of the masses, it is worth describing these first phases of the formation of the liberation army in some detail. In this process we can also see a clear example of the way in which our overall programme of activities has been put into effect ever since in the formation of the army; there the three elements of our programme — mobilisation, education and the training of cadres — were all combined in one. Finally, the whole process and the way in which it has unfolded, also explains much about the present character of our movement.

The initial steps were relatively straightforward. Militants were recruited and sent to friendly countries for military training. But on their return there was the very much more complex task of structuring all these militants into a homogeneous body imbued with the movement's political line, which they had to be able to interpret and represent among the masses.

This was an immense task, given the differing experiences, geographical backgrounds, customs and traditions. In most cases the only common denominator among the militants was the fact of their being oppressed by Portuguese colonialism and having a common desire for liberation. Although these shared feelings made it possible for people to take a stand, they were nonetheless insufficient foundation for sustained action. It therefore became necessary to go to the very roots of unity, to explain the size and complexity of our country and the logic of having people from different linguistic and tribal groups live together. Such discussions made it possible for old divisions and antagonisms exacerbated by colonialism to be collectively analysed and overcome.

It became essential for each militant to be thoroughly acquainted with the lives and customs of other groups. In this way militants came to identify aspects of the enemy's activities which differed from what was known in their own regions, and this enabled them to fight the enemy anywhere. These efforts were decisive to the consolidation of national unity, even though they required more time and more thorough work and despite the great temptation to take the easy way out and send each militant to fight in his own region.

Thus, the first task was above all to consolidate national unity within the movement itself. It was important to bring together all the separate experiences of militants — in villages, in plantations, in mines, in prisons and in towns — in order to gain an overall picture of the colonial system. This made it possible at last to define accurately the scope of the war, the many faces of the enemy and the need for unity.

But experience had already taught us that mere talk could not give rise to an effective political line. Theoretical courses and discussions, however profound, could never make up for lack of experience or efface the marks left on us by the evils of colonial society. A new social morality, a new way of life, had to be internalised and fully exemplified in our behaviour and our day-to-day activity.

This need to confront this further challenge also arose out of the very character which our struggle had come to assume. It was clear that at the start we would never be able to mobilise an army of militants capable of confronting the colonial machinery of repression with equal tactical forces. The then few dozen militants armed with light arms would have to draw their strength from the people and act on the basis of this strength in order, through the development of their potentialities, to change the existing balance of forces.

Hence, it was necessary to reinforce the popular character of the army. This was to a great extent ensured by the deep interpenetration between the movement's structures and the people out of which the army had come. But to strike deep roots among the people, it is not sufficient to have come from the people. In its behaviour, methods and structures, the army had to be a people's army. Only in this way would the rules of revolutionary conduct be observed in relations with the people and their full confidence and support ensured.

Realising this goal meant defining and establishing new relations within the army and developing a spirit of criticism which would eliminate lack of confidence and create a collective method of work. Many meetings were held for this purpose at which such methods of work, as well as military preparedness and individual comportment, were thoroughly discussed. Each militant recounted his own experience and described the traditions of his region. This served to supplement the work of our reconnaissance teams of course, but the chief importance of this kind of discussion was in helping to perfect the type of relations which would be established with the people.

In order to strengthen in the army the feeling of belonging to the people, and counter the tendency for membership of the army to become a privileged position, productive work was made a part of the army's programme of work from the very start. Later on, when the progress of the struggle led to a considerable increase in our numerical strength, this practice proved extremely valuable in that it prevented the army from being too much of a burden on the people where food was concerned.

Of course, this programme also had to do with the need to prepare for a protracted war and to mobilise ourselves for such a war. Faced with such a challenge, it was necessary to clarify the aims of our struggle in terms other than those slogans which might be useful for purposes of rapid mobilisation. For some militants, for example, the initial feeling was one of hatred for the white man as the source of all ills. This feeling had to be transformed into political awareness of the need to fight oppression and to direct our weapons against the system of oppression, not against mere skin colour.

We saw that it was only with this type of mobilisation and on the basis of this level of political awareness that it would be possible to sustain a protracted war, one which would enable us progressively to mobilise all the resources of our people and country and to liquidate, little by little, the enemy's material and human resources, their economy and their morale.

Developing national consciousness, strengthening the movement's popular character and clarifying the political line were therefore, the first tasks that our army and our movement as a whole, had to face. These are undoubtedly the first steps many nationalist movements have had to take in their political activities. But, over and above programmes and formal statements, in them we have come to find the essence of an increasingly progressive political line and the direction for the advance of our movement, our militants and our people.

Solidarity is Mutual Aid
Samora Machel

From the speech given on 25 March, 1973 by Samora Machel, President of FRELIMO to the National Conference of Solidarity for Liberty and Independence of Mozambique, Angola, and Guinea-Bissau, convened by Italian organizations in Reggio Emilia.

It is within a perspective of united action that it seems to us solidarity activities must be located. Solidarity activities must be impregnated with a political content to be able to perceive concretely their limits of action and methods.

The liberation struggle of the Mozambican people is a struggle against colonial fascist Portuguese domination, against imperialism, a struggle to install in our country a new social order that is popular and democratic.

Colonialism and Portuguese fascism are aberrations in our epoch. Colonial fascist domination is the worst form of negation and humiliation of the human person. Colonial war foments the most abject and horrible crimes which are repugnant to human conscience. We regularly hear throughout the world courageous voices who denounce and unmask the horrors of Portuguese colonialism and its colonial wars. The honest voices of priests and bishops have in recent years forced growing sectors of world public opinion to perceive the existing reality.

The struggle against colonialism and Portuguese fascism is no different in its essence from the struggle against Fascism and Nazism that took place in Europe. European people who offered up millions of lives in the holocaust to the dreams of domination by 'superior' races, will understand perfectly our struggle against this cancer of our earth. Destroying the domination of the great imperialist companies over Mozambique and diminishing the buffer zones for racist empires in Rhodesia and South Africa is of interest to all forces in the world which accept the need to fight against imperialist pillage and the policy of aggression.

This struggle is that of the Mozambican people and of all peoples. As it is also a common struggle, our struggle to install in our land a new people's social order, which will liberate man from poverty and exploitation, will introduce justice in society and liberate the creative energy of the masses.

In this context solidarity is not an act of charity but mutual aid between forces fighting for the same ends.

The liquidation of the Portuguese colonial fascist system will mean the destruction of one of the principal contemporary bastions of fascism which stimulates the growth of fascist forces elsewhere in Europe, including Italy.

In the present phase it is important that the solidarity movement decide on a certain number of objectives and methods of work.

In the first place, the struggle against Portuguese colonialism and fascism, as you know from your own experiences, is a cause which interests and mobilizes all honest men, irrespective of their social origins, party affiliations, or religion.

We believe the solidarity movement must therefore be developed as a unitary movement, encompassing numerous sectors which up to now have not been touched. To popularize the solidarity movements means to mobilize different sectors, from the factories to the schools, from the universities to the offices, from the hospitals to the churches. It means making known the horror of colonialism, but at the same time its nature and the successes of our struggle.

In this regard it seems to us it could be useful for this conference to study the ways of increasing the efficiency and speed of the distribution of information between our movements and the Italian people.

To mobilize and organize means also to fix specific objectives for the solidarity movement, to decide on specific lines of action. The necessary tasks are two: political, and material aid.

Politically our central preoccupation is to isolate Portuguese colonialism from its sources of moral, political, diplomatic, economic, and military support. At the same time it is to bring the international community to recognize the existing political reality in our country and to be aware that the Mozambican people is recovering its sovereignty and exercising it through FRELIMO which leads it and represents it.

Within this double preoccupation may be located the different lines of action. Political parties, trade unions, and other mass organizations are called upon for a persistent action of vigilance, denunciation, and pressure — vigilance to uncover and impede actions of their government and of financial consortia in favour of Portuguese colonialism; denunciation of such activities; and pressure to end them, and to lead governmental bodies to recognize contemporary Mozambican political reality.

It is obvious that this type of action must be developed at all levels, in the press and in parliament, in petitions and in popular demonstrations.

On Bombings
Agostinho Neto

Interview with the President of MPLA in the Standard
(Tanzania) on 9 October, 1971.

Certain news agencies are trying to insinuate that the bomb which exploded in the Congo Kinshasa mission to the United Nations was an act of protest against the fact that the Congo Kinshasa Government does not allow the MPLA freedom of action in its country. What is your view of this?

In the first place, it is not the custom of the MPLA to use such methods to solve problems. The problem of freedom of action for the MPLA in Congo Kinshasa has been put before the OAU and all friendly countries with a view to finding a solution.

To the Portuguese in Mozambique
FRELIMO

Appeal upon the proclamation of the War of Independence by FRELIMO on 25 May, 1964.

155

Portuguese,

The first Congress of the Mozambique Liberation Front was clear about our position concerning you.

FRELIMO will not take responsibility for the loss of human lives and material damage caused by the obstinacy of your government.

We want to destroy completely the system of oppression and exploitation of our people.

Portuguese,

Our people realise that a peaceful means of getting independence is impossible. The Salazar government does not give us any other option but for an armed struggle. And we have decided to fight until the end because independence and liberty are of supreme value and no people of any worth can renounce this. During your own history, at the times when your country was under foreign domination, you too were possessed with a feeling of liberty and thus were able to drive out your oppressors. So you must therefore understand our longing for liberty and realise that it is inevitable.

Now, when an armed struggle is about to be launched against the Portuguese regime in Mozambique, it is important that the Portuguese people in the country define their position. Our struggle is not against the Portuguese people but against the system of colonial oppression. And so the Portuguese people who refuse to take up arms against our people will not suffer. The Portuguese soldiers who lay down their arms and refuse to participate in this colonial war will be welcome among our militants.

This is FRELIMO's position.

Portuguese,

The democratic principles, which in the past inspired the Portuguese people and are now contravened by the fascist government, impose on you a clear position against a colonialist policy that for centuries has denied our people their basic rights.

FRELIMO hopes that your position will be in agreement with the aspirations of the Mozambican people.

Down with Colonialism!
Long Live Mozambique!

Message to Portuguese Soldiers
FRELIMO

A leaflet distributed in Mozambique circa 1972. Translated from Portuguese.

This message is for Portuguese soldiers, those soldiers who came from far, far away, from another continent, who have invaded our land and are killing our people, burning our fields, raping our sisters.

Portuguese soldier, we want to tell you that what you are doing is wrong, cruel, inhuman, criminal. Just think: if we left our land, Africa, and invaded yours in Europe, how would you feel? If we Mozambicans destroyed the fields that your parents and you yourselves have cultivated with such effort and love, if we burnt your home, pillaged your goods, assassinated your children, raped your mother, your bride, and your sisters, if we installed ourselves as rulers of your land, would you stay with your arms crossed as cowards? Would you allow yourselves to be humiliated, beaten, robbed, chained down, without rebelling? No, you would not react like that. You would pick up your weapons and fight the invader. Your ancestors did so. When they were invaded by the Arabs, the Spaniards, the French, they fought heroically in order to defend their independence, and they refused to submit to a foreign people. This is precisely what we are doing.

Portuguese soldier, you are fighting us because you never really thought about what you were doing. They took you from the fields where you were quietly helping your family to cultivate the land. They put you on a boat and set you down in Mozambique. They gave you a weapon and told you 'Fight the terrorists'. And you went, like robots, like instruments, without thinking whether the war they told you to make was a just one, without knowing who you were fighting for or against.

It is time that you examine your conscience. You are a man like us; you were not born a criminal. It is they who sent you to a war and made you a criminal. The Portuguese people, your people, is an honest and hard-working one; it is not a people of assassins. We know that. Why then are you killing our people? All we want is to live in peace, in our African land, as rulers of our land. We have a right to that. It is precisely because we are denied this right that we fight. We fight you, Portuguese soldier, because you are opposing peace and progress in our country. If it were not for you, if instead of being here fighting against us you were on your own land cultivating your fields, we would not be fighting. There would not be a war in our land. We would be able to build our homes peacefully, to love our wives and our children, to develop our wealth. But this will not be possible as long as you stay here, with guns pointed at us.

Why do you fight? They told you you were coming to defend your homeland, but your homeland is Portugal, not Mozambique, nor Angola, nor Guinea. Each one of these countries is a different home from yours, with a different people, with customs, traditions and a history different from yours. Have you ever seen a Mozambican, Angolan, or Guinean threaten your real home, Portugal? No, you have not. It is the PIDE, the officials who seized you, who took you from your job and brought you here, to fight against our people, who threaten you. They invented that lie that says that your country is threatened, in order to mobilize you, and to justify the war.

Actually, the only reason that leads the rulers of your country to make war against us is that they refuse to give us back the wealth which they robbed from us a long time ago. Perhaps you do not know, Portuguese soldier, but the truth is that Portugal is being governed by a minority of 27 families. Those 27 families control all the wealth, both of Portugal and of the colonies. They own the land, the factories, the mines, the commerce. The rest, almost all of the Portuguese people, live in misery. We need not tell you, you know it better than we do. Peasants work in Portugal from sunrise to sunset, and what they are paid is scarcely enough to buy bread. The family lives in huts, the children are in rags and hungry. When someone gets sick there is no money for the medicine. Meanwhile, those great capitalists live surrounded by the greatest luxury, own several cars for themselves, their wives and children, send their children to the university so they can become doctors, and later take their place as managers, ministers, bankers. They not only rob and exploit the Portuguese people. They do the same to our peoples of Mozambique, Angola, Guinea. And now that our peoples have decided to say *ENOUGH* to oppression and exploitation, they send you, Portuguese soldier, to defend the wealth of our land for them.

In effect, what do you gain from the riches of Mozambique? Absolutely nothing. Have you ever got any of our minerals, our cultivations, our oil? No, it is the great capitalists who get them. They do not go to war. They stay safely in Lisbon or Lourenco Marques, receiving the output of exploitation, going to the casinos, the banquets, the receptions, and send you to the jungle, where death lurks behind each bush, each turn, each post. Thousands of your companions have been killed in this way, in an ambush or from a mine, without glory, just so that the interests of the capitalists would be saved.

Portuguese soldier, it is time you changed your attitude. Colonialism will not last long. It has been condemned all over the world. The United Nations itself has already asserted that Portuguese colonialism is a crime against humanity. Many countries openly criticize the Portuguese government because of its colonial policy. There are many countries and organizations which are supporting us morally and materially. Thus, the success of our struggle shall proceed at an even quicker pace. And if you get caught up in the process, in this struggle, you will be killed by the FRELIMO guerillas. And you will have died for nothing. You will not even have the glory of having been killed heroically. Are you aware that your government is far more interested in conserving material than in saving human lives? Since the offensive which it led against FRELIMO last year, your commander Kaulza de Arriaga, when forced to leave said that 'the worst was the material lost, because it costs a lot of money. The dead soldiers can be easily replaced.' You can see what your superiors feel for you. It is just this: for them you are purely and simply meat for cannons, far less worthy than a G-3 or a car.

Portuguese soldier, we do not want to influence you into making a decision. You are a man, you have a conscience, and the capacity to make your own judgements. If you think you are right in making a war, in assassinating people, then go on. But if, in the light of reason and justice, you understand that the fight you are leading is unjust and immoral, and you want to put an end to it, then desert and come to our side. Several Portuguese soldiers have already deserted and sought the protection of the FRELIMO. For instance, Luis Machial, Americo Neves da Souza, Manuel de Jesus Santos, Manuel da

Silva Lopes, Eusebio Martinho da Silva, Jose Antonio Ferreira da Mata, Jose Augusto Lopes. Two others have surrendered during battle, Joao Borges Gomes and Fernando dos Santos Rosa. They were all taken care of by the International Red Cross, on behalf of FRELIMO. Most of them wished to go to France or to Algeria to work, and there they are today, away from the war, working in peace. Only one soldier who was captured by FRELIMO during an attack to the Nambude post in Cabo Delgado, Joao Borges Gomes, preferred to go back to Portugal. He was wounded and gave himself up during the attack, the guerillas took him to our zones, took care of him and when he was taken to the Red Cross said that he wanted to go back to Portugal. His wish was granted — but since he returned to Portugal we have no longer heard from him.

This is our policy: to welcome as brothers, as allies, the Portuguese soldiers who desert and who through that act, show their opposition to the colonial policy against our people.

Portuguese soldier, it is possible and natural that you have certain doubts, hesitations, before taking this step which will give you your freedom. We know what king of propaganda that Portuguese officials spread to their soldiers. They say that every soldier caught by FRELIMO is killed and tortured. They say that we are terrorists, assassins, and similar things. But be certain of this: the only ones who massacre, torture, and assassinate are the Portuguese colonialist authorities, or the soldiers under the orders of these authorities.

Never do we mistreat a soldier who deserts or gives himself up or even a prisoner. At a meeting with the people, some weeks ago, the President of FRELIMO said: 'If anyone of you were to mistreat a Portuguese soldier who has deserted or surrendered himself, it would be just as great a crime as to kill or mistreat a comrade, or a brother of yours.' Neither do we define the enemy according to his skin colour, his place of origin or his nationality. There are Whites, Portuguese people, who work and fight with us.

And there are Blacks who fight against us, on the side of the colonialists. Skin colour thus cannot be a criterion in the definition of the enemy.

This means that all the fears that you may have are totally unfounded. Our orientation is deeply humane and just. All Portuguese soldiers who may desert the colonial troops, or give themselves up, will be welcomed by FRELIMO.

On the Treatment of Captured Guerillas

Jose Oscar Monteiro

From a speech by J.O. Monteiro, representative of FRELIMO,
at a conference organized by the Algerian Red Crescent in
Algiers, 21 May, 1971. Translated from French.

Let us look at a few specific problems which arise in guerilla warfare, in the light of present humanitarian legislation.

There is one, the most important one, which concerns the applicability of one of the principles of the current code of humanitarian rights, i.e. the distinction between combatants and non-combatants. This principle, considered to be one of the keystones of this right has been, some say, seriously called into question by guerilla warfare, which cancels out any distinction between the civil population and the forces in combat. Since guerillas are supported by the population, have their cooperation to obtain supplies, and for logistical news in general, as well as to get information on the enemy's movements, and to recruit into the armed forces, it eliminates any distinction between combatants and the population at large. We can see the dangerous implications of such reasoning. One can find in it legitimacy for the repressive practices of the occupation forces in particular, of those 'free fire zones' of the American army in Vietnam, or its Portuguese version as 'death zones' where any living being is killed without appeal.

We would like to pose the problem in different terms: is the responsibility of the Portuguese civilians who directly or indirectly support the Portuguese war effort, and those who give their support to the colonial war (since there are some who do) in the National Women's Movement which stimulates the Portuguese soldiers, different to that larger group who pay taxes which finance and make the war possible, any the less?

It is not at all our intention to confuse the Portuguese people, our ally, with its government, but this parallel is a legitimate one. In other words, should we, and consequently the civilian population of the liberated areas, be penalized for the fact that we have successfully mobilized our population and involved it in agreement with its interests, in a much better way than the repressive regimes have been able to mobilize theirs?[1]

The experts have often claimed that the guerilla poses a formidable challenge to humanitarian rights. So be it. We prefer to say that the present system of humanitarian rights poses a still more formidable challenge to the guerilla. This is particularly illustrated by the problem of our combatants who have been captured.

There too, the UN has had occasion to express its emotion in the face of the inhuman treatment — at the best treatment given to common criminals — which Portugal applies to those of our captured combatants and arrested militants. The UN demanded that 'given the armed conflict which reigns in the territories and the inhuman treatment given to the prisoners, the Geneva Convention relating to the treatment of the war prisoners signed in 12/8/1949 be applied to this situation' (Res. A/2395/XXIII/par. 12).

In Teheran, the International Conference for Human Rights, held in 1968, established 'the right of freedom fighters in southern Africa and in colonial

---

1. If one wishes to be legalistic, we might suggest popular wars, as they are conducted in our countries, are assimilable to the mass risings foreseen in Art. 4, No. 6 of the 3rd Convention.

territories to be treated, if captured, as war prisoners, in virtue of the Geneva Convention'.

However, an examination of the same conventions, notably the 3rd Convention, concerning the treatment of war prisoners, which establishes its famous four conditions in Art. 4, par. 2, shows it not to be adapted to the conditions of the liberation struggle in our countries.

How can one believe in it and in the validity of the texts, when one sees the enemy let himself go, utilizing all forms of repression? Not long ago, *Der Spiegel* magazine (15/6/1970) published pictures of Portuguese soldiers decapitating a FRELIMO suspect, with an openly sadistic laugh undiminished by the quality of the print.

How can one believe in humanitarian neutrality which is silent in the face of the crimes committed in the Portuguese colonies and in southern Africa in general, in Palestine, in Indochina, and on the American continent, when a part of the international opinion specialized in humanitarianism, and so available for so many causes, openly hides in this case?

As M. Bedjaoui has said at the opening of the Conference of Arab Jurists on Palestine:

> All this, and so many disguised or unknown contradictions, are in fact simply the signs of a struggle between the iron kettle and the clay pot. It is our destiny to be part of millions of oppressed people who are the eye of Cain on our planet. But the day will come when, thanks to our work, our organization and our discipline, our faith and obstinacy, we will bring about the irresistible and victorious rebellion of those oppressed of the earth and when, in our turn, we will weave a shroud for imperialism which has long been abandoned by moral values which have taken refuge with our refugees, among us and in us.

7. The Party and the Army

Editors' Introduction

Guerilla actions led by a national liberation movement pose a fundamental political issue, the relationship between the political organization and the military cadres. Historically, national liberation and revolutionary movements throughout the world — from China to Vietnam to Algeria — had asserted the primacy of the political over the military. It was only with the Cuban Revolution and with the strong critiques of Latin American parties and movements by Che Guevara (and Regis Debray) that this truism was brought into question, and an alternative thesis put forward: that of the primacy and autonomy of the *foco*, the unit in active combat.

The movements in southern Africa all in one way or another rejected the *foco* theory and reasserted the traditional position of the primacy of the political. Amilcar Cabral did it gently and inferentially in an interview he gave to the Havana-based *Tricontinental* in 1968. But the seriousness of his position can be seen clearly from the General Directions the PAIGC issued in 1965 under his name in which the 'mania of militarism' is attacked.

As for the ANC, they were less willing to mince their words. See the direct attack on Debray in the article by Slovo reproduced in the previous section. See also the excerpt reproduced here from the 'Strategy and Tactics of the ANC'. Iko Carreira of the MPLA spelled out the role of the political commissar. And ZAPU and ZANU issued a joint statement denouncing those who would give primacy to military cadres. (In this case, the reference was to FROLIZI.)

The underlying assumption of these arguments was the theory that in a guerilla situation the party was the state, spelled out here by the PAIGC. But the party referred to is presumably the national liberation movement. The theory of the 'party-state' should be read in conjunction with the theory of the 'nation-class', which is to be found in the section 'On the Role of Various Classes and Groups in Colonial Society'. There was much discussion of the possibility of creating within the movement a 'vanguard party', as the brief excerpt of the interview with Paulo Jorge indicates. But no such 'vanguard' parties were created during the period of armed struggle. Perhaps this was related to the question of the movement's relationship to its military cadres and uncertainties about what the creation of such a party might do to this relationship.

Guerrilla Tactics and Guevara's Book
Amilcar Cabral

From an interview of Amilcar Cabral, Secretary-General of the PAIGC by Tricontinental *(Havana), 8, September-October 1968.*

Tricontinental: What is the strategic aim of the armed struggle? . . . .
Cabral: The strategic aim of our armed struggle of national liberation is, obviously, to completely free our country from the Portuguese colonial yoke. It is, after all, the strategic aim of all the national liberation movements, which, forced by circumstances, take up arms to fight against repression and the colonial presence. In our struggle, we set down our principles after having become thoroughly familiar with our country's conditions. For instance, we decided that we should begin the struggle within the country and that we should never struggle from outside the country, for which reason we never had armed forces outside our own land. And, for the same reason, in 1963 we started the armed struggle in the centre of the country, both in the south and in the north. This means that, contrary to what has been done by the peoples in Africa or other places who are fighting for national independence, we adopted a strategy that we might call centrifugal: we started in the centre and moved towards the periphery of our land. This came as the first big surprise to the Portuguese, who had stationed their troops on the Guinea and Senegal borders on the supposition that we were going to invade our own country.

But we mobilized our people secretly, in the cities and in the countryside. We prepared our own cadres, we armed those few that we could with both traditional and modern weapons, and we initiated our action from the centre of our country.

Today the struggle is spreading to all parts of the country, in Boe and Gabu and in the south; in the north, in San Domingos, in the Farim zone; in the west, near the sea, in the Mandjakos region, and we hope to be fighting within a short time on the island of Bissau, as well. Moreover, as you were able to see for yourselves in the southern part of the country and as other newsmen and film-makers have seen in the north and east, we have liberated a large part of our national territory, which forms part of the framework of our strategy. . . .

Tricontinental: Could you tell us something about the tactical principles followed by the PAIGC guerilla army?
Cabral: At present, to carry out the national liberation armed struggle it is not necessary to invent much along general lines. Already a wealth of experience has been gained in the national liberation armed struggle throughout the world. The Chinese people fought. The Vietnamese people have been fighting for more than 25 years. The Cuban people fought heroically and defeated the reactionaries and the imperialists on their island, which is today

a stronghold of progress. Other peoples have struggled and have made known to the world their experience in the struggle.

You know very well that Che Guevara, the great Che Guevara for us, wrote a book, a book on the guerilla struggle. This book, for example, like other documents on the guerilla struggle in other countries, including Europe, where there was also guerilla struggle during the last World War, served us as a basis of general experience for our own struggle.

But nobody is committing the error, in general, of blindly applying the experience of others to his own country. To determine the tactics for the struggle in our country, we had to take into account the geographical, historical, economic, and social conditions of our own land, both in Guinea and Cape Verde.

It was by basing ourselves on the concrete knowledge of the real situation in our country that we set down the tactical and strategic principles of our guerilla struggle.

We can say that our country is very different from other countries. In the first place, it is quite a small country, about 36,000 square km in Guinea and 4000 square km in Cape Verde. While Guinea is on the African continent, Cape Verde is in the middle of the sea, like an archipelago. We took all of this into consideration, but, in addition, Guinea is a flat country. It has no mountains, and everyone knows that in general the guerilla force uses the mountains as a starting point for the armed struggle. We had to convert our people themselves into the mountain needed for the fight in our country, and we had to take full advantage of the jungles and swamps of our country to create difficult conditions for the enemy in his confrontation with the victorious advance of our armed struggle.

As for our other tactics, we follow the fundamental principle of armed struggle, or, if you prefer, colonial war: the enemy, in order to control a given zone, is forced to disperse his forces; he thus becomes weakened, and we can defeat him. In order to be able to defend himself from us he needs to concentrate his forces, and when he concentrates his forces he allows us to occupy the areas that are left empty and work on them politically to prevent the enemy from returning.

This is the dilemma faced by colonialism in our land, just as has been the case in other lands, and it is that dilemma, if it is thoroughly taken advantage of by us, that will surely lead Portuguese colonialism to defeat in our country.

This is sure to happen, because our people are mobilized. They are aware of what they are doing. Also, the liberated regions of the country, where we are developing a new society, are a constant propaganda force for the liberation of other parts of our country. . . .

Tricontinental: You mentioned Che Guevara's book *Guerilla Warfare*. In this book Guevara divided the guerilla struggle into three phases. According to this, what phase do you think the struggle in so-called Portuguese Guinea is in?

Cabral: In general, we have certain reservations about the systematization of phenomena. In reality the phenomena always develop in practice according to the established schemes. We intensely admire the scheme established by Che Guevara essentially on the basis of the struggle of the Cuban people and other experiences, and we are convinced that a profound analysis of that scheme can have a certain application to our struggle. However, we are not completely certain that, in fact, the scheme is absolutely adaptable to our conditions.

Within this framework, we believe that, in the present phase of our struggle, we are already in the stage of mobile warfare. This is why we have been reorganizing our forces, creating units more powerful than those of the regular army, and surrounding the Portuguese forces; this is why we have been increasing the mobility of our forces, thus diminishing the importance of the guerilla positions in order to advance against enemy positions. But today an essential characteristic of our struggle is the systematic attacking of Portuguese fortified camps and fortresses. This in itself indicates that we are in the stage of mobile warfare. And we hope that the time is not far off when, advancing with this mobile warfare, we will at the same time have the conditions for launching a general offensive to end the Portuguese domination in our land. . . .

Tricontinental: Could you tell us briefly how the political and military leadership of the struggle is carried out?

Cabral: The political and military leadership of the struggle is one: the political leadership. In our struggle we have avoided the creation of anything military. We are political people, and our Party, a political organization, leads the struggle in the civilian, political, administrative, technical, and therefore also military spheres. Our fighters are defined as armed activists. It is the Political Bureau of the Party that directs the armed struggle and the life of both the liberated and unliberated regions where we have our activists. Within the Political Bureau is a War Council composed of members of the former who direct the armed struggle. The War Council is an instrument of the Political Bureau, of the leadership of the armed struggle.

Each front has its command. On the sector level there is a sector command, and each unit of our regular army also has its command. That is the structure of our armed struggle, and it is true that the guerillas are installed in bases and that each base has a base chief and a political commissar. In relation to organization proper, a Party congress is generally held every two years, but within the framework of the struggle it is held whenever it is possible. The Party has a Central Committee and a Political Bureau which directly lead the local bodies — that is, the northern and southern interregional committees and the sector and *tabanka* [village] committees. That is our structure.

In the cities and urban centres, the Party organization remains underground, in general under the leadership of a very small number of individuals.

Combat the Mania of Militarism
PAIGC

> *From the* Palavras de Ordem Gerais, *issued by the PAIGC and
> signed by Amilcar Cabral, Secretary-General, November 1965.
> Translated from Portuguese.*

Comrades,
In order to continue to develop our struggle victoriously . . . .

We must develop and strengthen the day by day political work with the
people, among the militants and combatants of the Party:

(1) In the liberated zones, we must take all the necessary measures to
normalize political life. The local committees (*tabankas*) of each zone and
region must be consolidated and function normally. They must hold frequent
meetings with the population, in order for them to be aware of the struggle,
the watchwords of the Party and the criminal intentions of the enemy.

(2) In the areas which are still occupied by the enemy, we must reinforce the Party's underground work, the mobilization and organization of
the peoples, and prepare the militants to act and support appropriately the
actions of our militants. In particular, in the urban zones (cities and towns)
we must establish watchwords to strengthen the work of the militants, re-
establish the bonds where they have become loose, prepare the members of
the Party, especially the workers, for action against the enemy and in defence
of our material goods.

(3) Among the armed forces (army and guerillas) wherever we are, we
must develop political work, hold frequent political meetings, demand serious
political work from the political commissariats. We must make the political
committees of the People's Army, composed of the political commissars
and the commandant of each unit function properly.

We must combat the mania of *militarism* and make each combatant an
exemplary militant of our Party.

(4) We must reinforce political work and propaganda among the enemy
forces. Make posters, leaflets, letters, write things on the streets, send mess-
ages, etc., in order to inform the enemy forces of the policy of our Party. We
must establish prudent contacts with elements of the enemy forces who want
to contact us, act with audacity and initiative in that field, bring those elements to serve the Party in favour of our struggle, and against the criminal
colonial war. We must do everything to help the enemy's soldiers to desert,
and to guarantee them, by any means necessary, their safety so as to encourage them to make the decision to desert.

(5) We must do political work among those Africans who still serve the
enemy (civilians and soldiers), bring these brothers to change their way,
either to serve the Party among the enemy or to desert with weapons and
ammunition and join our forces. But we must act strongly, destroy all those
who deliberately betray us, who continue to fight on the enemy's side, against
our Party and our people.

(6)   We must do everything to strengthen our fraternal relations with the neighbouring countries, with their people and authorities. We must not permit any member of the Party to become involved in the internal affairs of those countries. We must be vigilant towards elements of those countries who may wish to become involved in our affairs, or take advantage of our struggle. We must act firmly against those agents of the enemy who are citizens of the neighbouring countries. We must place at the frontiers only those in whom we place absolute trust, who are honest, devoted and able to carry out their duties. In particular, we must take all necessary measures in order urgently to improve our relationship with Senegal, to establish good cooperation with its authorities, in defence of our interests. . . .

On the Application of Some Principles of the Party

In the present stage of our struggle, and in order to strengthen our organization in the face of its large responsibilities, it is not enough to make every leading organism of the Party function, it is not enough to do valid political work and act efficiently, victoriously at the military level. In order for the Party to be better everyday and to meets its responsibilities, it is indispensable to apply the principles of organization and struggle which the Party has adopted as being fundamental norms of its actions at all levels of life. Such is the case of the principle of *criticism and self-criticism* for the resolution of internal problems and contradictions, of the principle of *collective leadership* in the life of the Party, the principle of *democratic centralism* and *revolutionary democracy* in the decisions to be made at all levels and in carrying out the watchwords of the Party.

(1)   We must develop the spirit of criticism among the militants and leaders. We must give each one, at each level, the opportunity of criticizing, of giving his opinion on the work and behaviour of the others or their actions. We must accept criticism, wherever it may come from, as a contribution to the betterment of the Party's work, as a demonstration of active interest for the internal life of our organization. We must remember that criticism is not to speak ill or to make intrigues. To criticize is and must be the act of expressing an honest opinion, in front of the interested parties, based on facts and in a spirit of justice. It is to evaluate the judgement and action of others with the aim of improving this thought and this action. To criticize is to build, to help to build, to give proof of sincere interest in the work of others, and in the improvement of such work. It is to combat *gossip*, the mania for intrigue, tattling, unjust and unfounded criticisms. To evaluate the thought and actions of a comrade is not necessarily to gossip. It is to praise, to encourage, to stimulate, but also to criticize. We must not spare a compliment to those who deserve it, even though we must be vigilant against personal pride and vanity. We must compliment joyfully, honestly, in front of others, all those whose thought and action serve the progress of the Party. We must also apply just criticism, honestly denounce, censure, condemn and demand the condemnation of all those who engage in acts which contradict the progress and the interests of the Party. We must combat errors and faults face to face, help

167

others to improve their work. We must learn lessons from every mistake we or others may make, in order to avoid making new mistakes, so that we do not do foolish things others have done. To criticize a comrade does not mean to be against him, to make a sacrifice of which the comrade is the victim. It is to show him that we are all interested in his work, that we are one and the same body, that his mistakes hinder all of us, and that we are aware, as friends and comrades, of the need to help him overcome his deficiencies and to contribute each day to the improvement of the Party.

We must develop the principle of criticism at each one of the Party's meetings, in all committees and in the armed forces. Both in the guerillas or in the army, after each operation against the enemy, we must evaluate the results of such action and the behaviour of each combatant. We must learn lessons from that action in order to do more and better actions. In school, in production, in commercial activity, in assistance — all levels of our life and struggle — we must be able to criticize and accept criticism.

But criticism (a proof of the others' wish to help us or of our wish to help others) must be complemented by a process of self-criticism (a proof of our wish to help ourselves in the improvement of our thought and action).

We must develop among all militants, leaders and combatants, a spirit of self-criticism, the capacity which each one has to analyse concretely his own work, to distinguish what is good or bad in it, to recognize his own mistakes and discover their causes and consequences. To criticize oneself is not to say simply 'yes, I recognize my fault, my mistake — and forgive me,' and then be ready to commit further mistakes. It is not to pretend to be sorry for one's mistake and then feel that in effect it is others who do not understand one. And least of all self-criticism is not a *ceremony* which one undergoes in order to commit further mistakes with a clean conscience. To criticize oneself is not to buy an indulgence or to do penitence. Self-criticism is an act of honesty, courage, comradeship and of awareness of our responsibilities, a proof of our will to do our duty, a demonstration of our determination to be better each day and to improve our own contribution for the progress of the Party. Sincere self-criticism does not necessarily involve acquittal. It is one's engagement with one's conscience in the aim of not committing further mistakes. It is to accept our responsibilities in front of others and to mobilize all our capacities in order to do more and better. To criticize oneself is to remake oneself in the aim of serving better.

(2) We must apply the principle of collective leadership progressively at all levels of the Party. We must do everything so that the leading organs of the Party may really function, not on the basis of one, two, or three people, but of all of its members, men and women.

Collective leadership means leadership by a group of people and not by one or more people of a group. To lead collectively, in a group, means to study problems together, so that a better solution may be found. It means to make decisions together, to take advantage of the experience and intelligence of each and everyone in order better to direct, to command. In collective leadership, each person in the executive must have specific, well-defined functions, and be responsible for the execution of the decisions taken by the group in terms of his functions. To lead collectively means to give each leader the opportunity to think and act, to demand that he be responsible, that he have initiative, that he demonstrate with determination and freedom his creative capacity, that he serve well the work of the group, which is the product of everyone's efforts and contributions. To lead collectively means to coordinate the thinking and action of those who form the group, so that there be the greatest success in carrying out the groups' tasks, within the limits of its competence and the framework of the activities and interests of the organization. But it is not and could not become, as some may think, the right to uncontrolled opinions and initiatives, the creation of anarchy (lack of government), disorder, contradiction among leaders, empty discussion, a passion for useless meetings. Nor does it mean to allow incompetence, ignorance, intellectual insolence free rein, so that one may feel that everyone is leading. If it is true that two heads are better than one, we must know how to distinguish the heads, and each head must know exactly what it has to do. In the framework of collective leadership we must respect the opinions of those who are more experienced, we must learn with their experience, and they must help the less experienced ones to learn and to improve their work. In the framework of collective leadership there is always someone who ranks higher in the Party and who therefore has greater individual responsibility, even though the responsibility of the group's tasks is shared by all the members of the group. We must give them prestige, help them to improve themselves, but not permit that they take care of all of the group's responsibilities. We must, on the other hand, fight the spirit of laziness and lack of interest, the fear of responsibilities, the tendency to agree with everything, to obey blindly, without thinking.

We must combat the spirit of the petty king, the traditional chief, the boss or the foreman among the leaders. And we must also combat the spirit of the vassal, of the subject at the service of the chief, and of the zealous worker, servant or boy, among the leaders and militants. In the framework of collective leadership, the higher ranks of the Party must demand from those below them the rigorous fulfilment of their duties in the spirit of intelligent and constructive cooperation. The lower ranks must demand from the higher ones the distribution of specific duties, clear watchwords, and the taking of decisions within their competence.

We must combat the spirit of factions or cliques, the desire for secrecy among certain people, personal quarrels and hunger for power.

Collective leadership must strengthen the capacity for leadership in the Party, and create the conditions that will allow the Party members to show their worth.

(3)   We must develop, respect, and make respectable, the correct application of democratic centralism in the practice of the Party's decisions and watchwords. We must concretely limit the functions of each leading organ, study deeply each problem or new initiative, make objective decisions and give clear watchwords for each task and for the practical fulfilment of the Party's watchwords.

Democratic centralism means that the decisional power, the establishment of tasks, of dire action, is concentrated within central organs or entities, with well-defined functions, but that those decisions and orders, etc., may be taken democratically, in terms of the interests and opinion of the mass representatives, based on the respect for the opinion and interests of the majority. It means that each decision related to a new problem must be made after a wide and free discussion by the interested parties, from the base to the summit, if it concerns a matter related to the whole life of the Party. After that discussion, and in accordance with the results of that discussion, the central organs must make a decision which must be immediately carried out at all its respective levels without further discussion.

It is *centralism*, because the power, the capacity to decide and lead is concentrated in special organs, and no other organ or individual may use that power. It is *democratic* because the utilization of such power by those organs does not depend solely on the will of those who rule, but is based upon the interests and opinion of the majority. In order to improve our practice of democratic centralism, we must be attentive to the aspirations and opinion of the masses in respect to all important problems of our life and struggle. We must make all the basic organisms of the Party and all the leading organs function well. We must develop criticism and self-criticism and accord prestige to the leaders who fulfil their duty.

Democratic centralism is a school of discipline, of respect for the opinions of others, of democracy, and of the capacity to put into practice the decisions that are taken.

(4) We must practice, at all levels of the life of the Party, the principle of revolutionary democracy. Each leader must assume his responsibilities with courage, must demand from others respect for his activity and must respect the activity of others. Nothing must be kept hidden from the masses. We must not lie and we must fight those who do. We must not disguise difficulties, mistakes and unsuccessful ideas. We should not believe in easy victories and in outward appearances.

Revolutionary democracy demands that we must combat opportunism, tolerance towards error, unfounded excuses, friendship and comradeship when these run counter to the interests of those of the Party and the people, the feeling that one is indispensable in his post. We must practice and defend truth always, in front of the militants, the leaders, the people, whatever difficulties may result from the knowledge of such truth. Revolutionary democracy demands that the militant should not fear the leader, and that the latter should not fear the militant or the masses. It demands that the leader live among the people, ahead of and behind the people, that he work for the at the people's service.

In the framework of revolutionary democracy, the power comes from the people, from the majority, and no-one must be afraid of losing power. The leader must be a loyal interpreter of the will and aspirations of the revolutionary majority and, it must not be the owner of power, the absolute ruler who takes advantage of the Party without serving it. In this framework, we must avoid demagogy, promises which we cannot keep, exploitatio. people's sentiments, and the ambitions of the opportunists. We mus agreement with reality, give each one the possibility of making progι verifying, through his actions and those of others, that the Party is everyone's doing, and that we all belong to the Party which is our tool in the conquest of the people's freedom and the achievement of progress. In the framework of revolutionary democracy and in the concrete conditions for our struggle, we must always increase the force of the people, for the radical transformation at the base of the life of our people, in preparation for a stage where the weapons and the means of defence of our revolution will be entirely in the hands of the people, once we have conquered the power. We must not be afraid of the people but must bring it to participate in all decisions which pertain to it. This is the fundamental condition for revolutionary democracy, which we must accomplish little by little, in accord with the development of our struggle and life.

Revolutionary democracy demands that the best children of our land lead our Party and our people. We must eliminate, step by step, the bad elements of our Party, those who are ambitious, opportunistic, demagogic (deceivers of the people) those who are dishonest or who do not fulfil their duties. We must make room for those who understand and live fully the life of our Party, those who wish really to serve the Party and the people, those who fulfil and wish to carry out still better their duties as militants, as leaders, and as revolutionaries. The correct application of the principles of criticism and self-criticism of collective leadership, of democratic centralism and of revolutionary democracy, are the effective means of obtaining one of the most, if not the most, important victory of our life and struggle, and that is:

To make the Party belong more every day to those who are capable of improving it.

To make of our Party an efficient instrument in the conquest of freedom, peace, progress and the happiness of our people in Guinea and Cape Verde.

The Relationship Between the Political and the Military
ANC

From 'Strategy and Tactics of the ANC' issued at its Consultative Conference in Morogoro, April 1969.

When we talk of revolutionary armed struggle, we are talking of political struggle by means which include the use of military force even though once force as a tactic is introduced it has the most far-reaching consequences on every aspect of our activities. It is important to emphasise this because our movement must reject all manifestations of militarism which separate armed people's struggle from its political context.

Reference has already been made to the danger of the thesis which regards the creation of military areas as the generator of mass resistance. But even more is involved in this concept. One of the vital problems connected with this bears on the important question of the relationship between the political and military. From the very beginning our Movement has brooked no ambiguity concerning this. The primacy of the political leadership is unchallenged and supreme and all revolutionary formations and levels (whether armed or not) are subordinate to this leadership. To say this is not just to invoke tradition. This approach is rooted in the very nature of this type of revolutionary struggle and is borne out by the experience of the overwhelming majority of revolutionary movements which have engaged in such struggles. Except in very rare instances, the people's armed challenge against a foe with formidable material strength does not achieve dramatic and swift success. The path is filled with obstacles and we harbour no illusions on this score in the case of South Africa. In the long run it can only succeed if it attracts the active support of the mass of the people. Without this lifeblood it is doomed. Even in our country with the historical background and traditions of armed resistance still within the memory of many people, and the special developments of the immediate past, the involvement of the masses is unlikely to be the result of a sudden natural and automatic consequence of military clashes. It has to be won in all-round political mobilisation which must accompany the military activities. This includes educational and agitational work throughout the country to cope with the sophisticated torrent of misleading propaganda and 'information' of the enemy which will become more intense as the struggle sharpens. When armed clashes begin they seldom involve more than a comparative handful of combatants whose very conditions of fighting-existence make them incapable of exercising the functions of all-round political leadership. The masses of the peasants, workers and youth, beleagured for a long time by the enemy's military occupation, have to be activated in a multitude of ways not only to ensure a growing stream of recruits for the fighting units but to harass the enemy politically so that his forces are dispersed and therefore weakened. This calls for the exercise of all-round political leadership.

The Role of the Political Commissar
Iko Carreira

From an interview of a member of the MPLA's 'High Command', by Tony Hall of The Standard *(Dar es Salaam), published 23 April, 1971.*

Standard: Of course in a country like Tanzania where there is a party the political commissar should be the man trusted by the party. He is the man who introduces the party's directives for implementation.

In our country the political commissar is also responsible for liaison between the mass movements. But he is also the second in command of any unit, and his decision is always of very great importance in the decision of any organ of power.

It should be something similar for independent countries who are going to organise themselves in this way. But I don't think one should make the political commissar the key man in the whole political-military organisation.

I think that the key to any organisation is a firm, clear and correct line, and good mobilisation. That is the key.

Carreira: I think in order to arm people for a struggle like this they have to have an ideology and the road ahead has to be absolutely clear. This is the prerequisite for arming the people. The worst thing is to give someone a weapon when he does not know what to use it for.

In our situation it is not difficult to make our people understand what exploitation is, and who the exploiter is. In an independent country it is rather more complicated. But in an African country which has not long emerged from colonialism there are still elements which can make this explanation easier.

Of course the image of modern towns, and African administrators enjoying privileges can hide the real truth – that most African states are still dependent.

Some leaders are afraid of announcing an ideology which will mobilise the masses. If the leaders don't find an ideological line the masses will. What is needed is a vast campaign of mobilisation and explanation, so the masses can see what has to be done to continue the struggle which the independent countries still have to wage.

There are already now in the towns a certain number of workers who can easily follow this line. They can give a firmness, a definite orientation to the general movement. This should be taken advantage of.

Against a Coup-ist Mentality
ZAPU/ZANU

Excerpt of a joint statement to the OAU's Council of Foreign Ministers held in Rabat (Morocco), June 1972.

There seems to be a calculated manoeuvre to displace the established national leadership of the Zimbabwe Liberation Movements and substitute it with direct control of the Executive Secretariat or with elements in the movements eager to get this kind of support. This kind of frustrating and dismantling approach to the Zimbabwe struggle is irreconcilable with the renowned intentions of the Liberation Committee.

The above approach is based on an open attempt to drive a wedge between what is called 'political leadership' and military cadres. The attempt to make a distinction between the military cadres of ZANU and ZAPU and the political leadership is founded on a misconception and is wrong. We would like to explain that ours is a revolutionary struggle which implies that a freedom fighter is at once trained politically and militarily for the attainment of his political objective. That is why we have a system of political Commissars. The leadership, like any other Zimbabwean joining our revolutionary struggle, is or must be equipped both politically and militarily for the liberation task. No component of the JMC, therefore, must be thought of in terms of regular or professional soldiers, for that matter, mercenaries who can be taken over by any political establishment. In short no component of the JMC will fight as mercenaries with no political mission.

It is a tragic mistake, therefore, to give currency to the false notion that unity in Zimbabwe has been hampered by political leadership and that if military cadres were left on their own they would proceed to total unity any more quickly than the political leadership. On the contrary military cadres, like any other members, respond to moves towards unity only on guarantees from the leadership that the political direction is revolutionary and certain.

It is, in our view, imperative that the OAU should not encourage a coup-ist mentality among our cadres by trying to weaken their faith in their leadership.

The Party-State
CONCP

> *Excerpt from the publication* Guinée et Cap-Vert, *published in Algiers in 1970. Translated from French.*

The PAIGC, by endowing the people of Guinea with political, social and economic institutions which are in accord with the spirit of its traditions and allow for the most progressive measures aiming at its liberation, and by ensuring control and administration over the liberated zones, has erected itself as a Party-State.

In the present stage of the national liberation struggle, the Party has taken over a number of tasks which would normally be of the competence of a State. In this respect, the structuring of the two countries (Guinea and Cape Verde) is as follows:

In Cape Verde, where armed action has not yet been developed, the whole country and the whole population are still suffering the yoke of the colonial administration.

In Guinea, on the contrary, over two-thirds of the territory has been liberated since the beginning of armed action dating from January 1963. In the other third, the Portuguese military administration sees its field of action diminishing every day, while the struggle spreads to new areas upon whose populations the Party exerts its control. The Portuguese control nothing but the cities. We are dealing with an *evolving State*. In the liberated zone of the national territory, the people is in power, it has organized itself, and exerts consolidating power effectively, through the party. It is the Party committees which administer the populations and the territories, which give the people direction, which take on such responsibilities as those concerning education, health and civic rights, which judge, repress and defend efficiently the security and the freedom conquered by the people.

A Vanguard Party?

Paulo Jorge

From an interview with Paulo Jorge (MPLA) by the Liberation Support Movement, published in 1973.

It is true that we passed such a resolution in 1968 and that since then our leaders have been studying and trying to devise the best method of providing the MPLA with a vanguard party structure. But in order to build and consolidate such a structure it is necessary to prepare a sufficient number of cadres, of militants with a strong and high level of political and ideological consciousness. And this is not an easy task, though I can tell you that over the past four years we have succeeded in preparing a fairly good number of such cadres. I think that in the next period, not too long from now, this vanguard structure will emerge more clearly. According to our analysis of the revolutionary process, we believe it will be necessary to carefully and seriously build a vanguard party in order to carry forward the legitimate aspirations of the Angolan people and the basic principles of the MPLA. I am quite confident that at the correct stage in the development of our struggle we will achieve the establishment of such a party.

8. The Struggle for Cultural Liberation

Editors' Introduction

The struggle against cultural distortion, cultural uprooting, and cultural subordination was fought on many fronts. One crucial front was that of 'high culture', and most particularly that of literature. This problem was one of the first to attract the attention of nationalist intellectuals.

In the history of the cultural awakening of Black Africa after the Second World War, there have been two main streams, one Francophone and one Anglophone. Because of linguistic and other cultural affinities, intellectuals of the Portuguese colonies were caught up in the Francophone stream, particularly since many of them passed part of their lives in Paris.

One central theme of the Francophone stream has been that of negritude. We shall not review here the long debates of this theme. We reproduce simply a critical contribution to this debate by Mario de Andrade, himself associated at an earlier period with *Présence Africaine*, the focus of much negritude literature.

When FRELIMO published a collection of 'poetry of combat', they were concerned that such poetry cease to be a 'privilege of an elite, of a class', but rather a weapon in the struggle for liberation. South Africa has the longest continuous literary tradition in southern Africa. How this tradition has been an integral part of African resistance to domination is the theme of the ANC paper.

But culture is more than poetry. It is also the daily customs of the people. Are these to be preserved as indigenous and hence valid or discarded as outdated and constraining? The movements took a very nuanced position. It is important to know and appreciate the values that are Africa's heritage. It is important, too, to know how to criticize one's own values and one's own past. It is important thus to revive and preserve culture without being held back by it. As for the daily customs of the people, sometimes they are to be accepted, sometimes rejected, as they serve or not the revolution. In this regard, the responses of Eduardo Mondlane and Amilcar Cabral to the interviewer's question on their attitude towards traditional magical beliefs expressed this duality well, as did Dr. Neto's similar answer.

There are various ways in which these attitudes became translated into a concrete programme for cultural liberation. One was the performance of

176

certain crucial symbolic acts, the renaming of countries. Where a name was identified with colonialism, as Rhodesia, all the groups rejected it in favour of Zimbabwe, a name linking the peoples of today to a kingdom and a great cultural achievement of pre-modern times. In other cases where the colonial name is more neutral such as South West Africa, there has been division. The leading movement, SWAPO, felt the name linked the country to its oppressor South Africa and offered Namibia as a substitute. Both the OAU and the UN have accepted the designation of Namibia. SWANU, perhaps because 'Namibia' was first suggested by SWAPO, protested at this acceptance. We reproduce their plea, followed by SWAPO's justification of the new name.

But more fundamental than new names was new education. The problems and the solutions are discussed in detail in the FRELIMO document which recounted their experiences in the liberated areas. The objective was very clear: to develop 'a new culture . . . based on traditional forms with a new content dictated by our new reality'. We end with a major statement by Amilcar Cabral, one which he himself thought reflected his mature views, in which he argued that 'whatever ideological or idealistic forms it takes, culture is essential to the historical process'.

Negritude in Question
Mario de Andrade

From article by de Andrade (MPLA) entitled 'Autour du Congrès Culturel de la Havane', and published in Algérie-Actualité *(Algiers), 261, 15-21 February, 1968.*

In the light of the political development of the Third World, there are many who ask themselves about the validity of a concept which, in the 1930s, became the ideology of rebellion of an important sector of the African and West Indian intelligentsia. The poet Aimé Césaire who has always had the noble care of reminding us of the historical context of the blossoming of Negritude, considers that it represents an 'irritated and impatient postulate of fraternity'.

Two authors (René Depestre from Haiti and Nene-Khaly from Guinea) proposed a revolutionary approach to the question in the Cultural Congress of Havana. For Depestre, it meant essentially to denounce the tragic mystification according to which the 'Duvalierist revolution' is a brilliant victory of Negritude. However, in anticipating the objection, he adds: 'Naturally, one must not conclude that, in throwing out the child with the bloody water of the bath, this concept would invariably lead to an annihilation of the human condition'. Nene-Khaly expressed himself in these terms:

A thesis which, from the start, had been forged to be used as a conjunctural weapon in the struggle, could not become an ideology characterizing a category of men and ending, mutatis mutandis, by placing them outside historical evolution . . .

The traits which constitute, in error, the pride and honour of the advocates of Negritude belong to the common essence of humanity and have marked the features of the civilizations of all peoples. The romanticism about nature, the communion with the telluric forces, the simplicity and the candour of the customs are all values which the memory of peoples still conserves. Homer, the Russian *bylini* [medieval folk-tales] and other ancient pieces of literature from a number of peoples in the world constitute a sufficient proof of its development in which still predominates the representations of the peasant civilizations which were all largely oral. All peoples once placed in similar historical situations give rise to cultures which share among them many similarities. The forms of expression may assume different aspects displaying particular affinities and choices, but the basis is nevertheless universal. It is what the movement of so-called Negritude has not yet been able to discern and understand.

We must thus now go beyond Negritude.

To the question asked by Jean Paul Sartre in his essay 'Black Orpheus', namely 'What would happen if the Black, once casting off his Negritude for the advantage of the revolution, would no longer wish to consider himself as a proletarian? What will happen if he will not allow himself to be defined in terms other than of his objective condition?', René Depestre is right to respond:

Look at Cuba and you will have an answer. Take a look at how Negritude is embodying itself in the socialist revolution, and how it finds itself in there beyond itself through a non-alienating historical process where the White, the Black and the Mulatto become everyday less and less antagonistic one to another, and where the tragedy of their destiny finds its denouement in one and the same brilliant human truth: the revolution. This process of real decolonization, rather than Negritude, is the only one which allows the mobilization of the patiences of the under-developed peoples on the three continents. It is this eminently revolutionary process which today allows the neo-colonized Black, White, Yellow, Indian man to cast upon the face of the Earth this ultimate postulate of reason in the Third World 'I make the revolution, therefore I am, therefore we are'.

The debate which has commenced in this fashion has a fundamental importance in the ideological re-evaluation of a concept which has ceased to reflect the living reality of Africa and the black condition in the New World, for the demands of the present time force one to insert these specific realities in the far vaster field of the anti-imperialist struggle.

Clearly, the discourse of Negritude announced the awakening of consciousness of the Black man, but is it not obvious today that revolutionary praxis replaces 'dynamic patience'?

Poetry and the Revolution
FRELIMO

Introduction to a book of poetry, Poesia de Combate, *Caderno No. 1, published by FRELIMO in Dar es Salaam in 1971. Translated from Portuguese.*

Thanks to the Revolution in Mozambique, poetry, like all other art expressions, has ceased to be the privilege of an elite, of a class. The colonialists, the capitalists, have taught us that in order to be a poet, one must have gone to school for many years, have gone to University, and be what they call 'an intellectual'. The people, the peasant, the worker — so claim the colonialists, the capitalists — is not able to feel and understand poetry, and least of all be able to express himself in poetic form. Their contempt for the people has led them to say that the people as a whole is 'rude', 'lacking sensitivity'.

The colonialists and the capitalists claim this but they are aware that it is a sheer lie. They know that in every civilization, in all times, the most beautiful art pieces were all done by the people and that they are the expression of the thinking and feeling of the people. But their attitude has a justification which is related to the society in which they live. In colonialist and capitalist societies there is a small group — the exploiters and oppressors — who own everything, the land, the homes, the factories, the banks, the work of the people, even the police and the army. Still not satisfied with this, they try by all means to establish culture itself as their own private property, and to exclude the people from it.

One of the greatest merits of the Revolution is precisely to allow the people to produce, to free the creative energy of the people, stifled as it was for so long. And when this energy is freed, it is as if it exploded, and then we see the people creating wonderful things in all areas — in politics, in art, in technology, in science.

This collection of poems is already one of the fruits of our Revolution. They are poems by the FRELIMO militants, all of them directly involved in the armed struggle for national liberation. Because this is the essential characteristic of Mozambican poetry today: there is absolute identification between revolutionary praxis and the poet's sensibility. Poetry does not speak of myths, of abstract things, but rather of our life as struggle, of our hopes and certainties, of our determination, of our love for our friends, of nature, of our country. When the poet writes 'Forward, comrades,' he goes forward. When he finds happiness in owning a gun, he is actually holding it, just as truly as he feels in his hands the warmth of the hoe and in his pained feet the long marches which he does with us.

It is for this reason that poetry is also a watchword. As a watchword, it is born out of necessity, out of reality. While, with colonialism and capitalism, both culture and poetry were the rich man's leisure, our poetry today is a necessity, a song from the heart to give us courage, to guide our will, to reinforce our determination, to widen our perspectives.

This anthology is like a sharing of experiences among our poets. It is also a stimulus for other comrades, so that in the bases, the schools, the villages, there may be created and recited new poems, thus developing our cultural wealth.

Literature and Resistance in South Africa
South African Delegation

Paper submitted by the South African delegation to the Afro-Asian Writers' Conference in Beirut and published in the ANC's Sechaba, *I, 6 (June 1967) and I, 7 (July 1967).*

South African literature is a vast subject covering not only the stylistics of literature in four major languages — Nguni, Sotho, English and Afrikaans — but also the very content of the history of nations that today make up the peoples of South Africa. To understand contemporary resistance writing in our country, one must know the background of traditional literature, whose grandeur and greatness can be understood only in the context of the historical processes that shaped the destinies of our peoples. That this very literature and history remains suppressed and almost unknown to the world is one of the tragedies of colonial occupation. But since the task of our revolution involves the rediscovery of our heritage, it is our mission to reveal the epics which have been left us as a record of a dynamic and creative people. In this sense our task is to define the soul of the African people, and simultaneously to expose colonialism's depredations.

Recorded literature dates from the late 15th century. This is of course misleading, because like everything in Africa few civilizations are 'discovered' until a day after independence. We can therefore accurately predict that the day of liberation will see the discovery of our literary tradition. Because African traditional literature is a product of a collective organized society its products became, in a few generations, a synthetic everyday description used in the very extension of the collective ethos.

The 15th century is outstanding in its pacific, almost idyllic, existence. This is clearly shown by the romantic quality of the dynastic poems of Ndaba, for instance. The primary occupation is to eulogize the beauty of physical features, the beauty of human relations, and satirical concern with greed and other anti-social habits. The impression one gets is of a people concerned with maintaining traditions and the integrity of a patriarchal structure.

This form of literature was to continue until the late 17th century, when the increase in population began to cause serious social and political upheavals. The Portuguese and British colonial incursions had begun to undermine the highly organized empires of Monomotapa and Kakongo, resulting in the shifting of populations. This period is symbolized by works whose heroic diversions surpass those of any previous or subsequent period. Most of the literary works of this period have perished with the communities that composed them. But thanks to the deep oral tradition we can piece together some of the legends and stories which form the history of the period, although more research is needed to complete the picture. We are still too involved in the actual task of liberation to study systematically the literatures not only of the Nguni but also of the Pa and the Khoikhoi. That such a task as we have before us involves the definition of our history and our literary heritage, is an indication of our deep awareness of the very problems this conference is convened for. It is for that reason that we regard the conference as a historical one, enabling both the African and Asian peoples to foster the essential understanding of the purposes of revolution. We regard it as a great opportunity to disseminate a heritage in a world that is gradually going insane. It is insane because in its worship of the iron gods it annihilates not only people in Vietnam, in South Africa, in Mozambique and elsewhere but also what has so long been built up as part of the general heritage.

As the theme of our subject develops it will become clear that the darkest ages in our history are those periods in which, by the arrogance of foreigners, we have been forced to swallow their local productions, indeed as if they were the only statement of mankind. The same imperialism is fond of referring to our civilization as no more than a disorganized entity having no value and no relevance to the civilization of the world. That same imperialism has destroyed our creative instruments and products. It is for this reason that the period that follows has particular significance, not only as a refutation of their claims but also in itself as an achievement of great excellence. This was the 19th century: our golden age of literature. The disturbances in the continent of Africa produced major heroic epics which recorded the great era of resistance against the colonialist aggressor. In the Cape alone, nine major wars were fought against the invaders; while these wars were going on the Zulus in the north were creating a military machinery as had never been known before in this part of the world. Because of the closeness between life and literature in African societies, these factors in themselves produced a feverish flowering of not only epic poetry but also satirical, lyrical and dramatic. The poets and storytellers not only told tales and recited poetry but also extended the scope of literature, which ceased merely to comment on everyday social events but became the true vehicle of social, political and historical analysis. Individuals ceased to project their own personal excellence but became symbols of resistance. In the case of the Zulu empire, individuals came to symbolize courage, fearlessness and prowess. This radical change in the literary idiom can be seen in the epic of Magolwane, one of the greatest traditional poets. Of Shaka's military campaigns he says:

Like piles and piles of mountain cairns
Folding like a giant wave of the sea
Which forever howls in the dark night
Like a vast field of poisonous millet grains
Like a chasm filled with black millipedes
Like a tiger, a leopard, a ferocious lion
Like a black mamba, a stampeding elephant.

Compare this with the earlier poems of the pre-Shakan period:

O thou whose body is beautiful
You are like an overgrown greenery
On which birds fall and die
Only the birds of paradise survive.

Note the idea of survival, not a phenomenon related to ethos and power but to individual external qualities of beauty.

Going through this whole 19th century period we come across numerous examples of the same epic quality. In the Cape for instance, the literary idiom assumes not only this epic quality but also, true to all resistance literature, uses a highly symbolic language. Its ultimate intention is not only to create a strong central authority but also to convey meanings that evoke the identity of those who constitute the resistance force.

The heights of literary genius are also reached by the Sotho people during the reign of their able monarch King Moshoeshoe I. Not only are the people called upon to resist the invader but also to sink their differences. Thus the house of Molapa becomes the subject of satire because of its divisive activities.

We must go back to Magolwane who aptly summarizes the literary and political achievements of this period. He ends his epic with a philosophical statement whose significance is true for all achievements and civilizations of mankind:

O my Lord, generations of men come and go
But our great works are indestructible
It is they that will remain eternally
Making generations of men stare and weep at ruins.

Thus did Magolwane bear witness to one of the greatest periods of our literary history.

At this point we may perhaps give a rough idea of the literary techniques used in traditional literature. Of course these differ according to period and according to the language structure. However, basic to all African traditional literature is the use of two levels of meaning. On the one level the form is descriptive and on the other symbolic and philosophical. Since central to all African literature is a realistic approach, all symbolism and description is based on items not of fantasy and fancy but everyday experience and reality.

This does not mean that African literature does not seek to convey its meanings through a mythological system. What it means is that the mythological system itself bears direct relationship to forms of reality as they are perceived in everyday existence. It also means that the embellishment of reality is achieved more through parallelization of concepts than through remodelling of reality; as in the animal stories for example, which project specific recognisable parallels between man and beast. This parallelization is deepened as a technique in the 19th century, precisely because in dealing with heroic subjects the African was concerned with conflicts whose significance was universal. Thus too, the human drama found its philosophical interpretations extended beyond the hitherto narrow confines of the clan or village. As the concern for philosophical summary became more and more urgent, the poets in particular developed a stanza form which became a vehicle of thought and description, for example:

The prattling women of Nomgabi
Prattling they claimed that he will never rule
But alas! it was Shaka's time to fill the earth.

These techniques, of course, cover wider areas of literature: the dramatised story form, the extended satirical form, the socially based lyric. All these can only be developed in a more detailed study which cannot be given in this brief summary. Suffice it to say that the techniques developed in this period have since become the most potent vehicles for conveying revolutionary thought.

Sometimes through the use of myths and legends the oppressor is identified with detestable characters. There is for example the work-poem found in every labouring group in South Africa:

The white men are scoundrels
They call us Jim boys
They the dirty swine.

They arrest us everywhere
They reap the harvest of manacled men
They arrest us everywhere.

The full dramatic meaning of these two short poems can only be conveyed in the dramatic context of the sound of picks and shovels.

The satirical form, too, has assumed new meanings relevant to the situation in South Africa. Thus the school children may be heard reciting about the tyrannical rule of the Boers.

But before we go into details of the modern period, let us look into the relationship between literature and the latter period of the conquest. It was not until the late 19th century that the resistance of the African people was broken. Even after that there continued isolated but significant pockets of resistance, like the Bambatha rebellion in 1906 in which 10,000 Africans died fighting bravely against the coloniser. These were glorified in the poetry of resistance, in which poets sang:

On the Sandlwane Battle
Son of Ndaba, you beat them (the whites)
Bending down on your knee
But alas I warn you Europeans have inhuman souls
Wait until they cross the Tukela river.

On the Division of the Land
The white vermin, my Lord,
Invades the lands of our forefathers
They, the adolescents who defecate
In the house like infants.

The white man carves the land
With blood-drenched knives
From north to south the sun bleeds . . .

Interpreting Africa
The unification of the white front in 1910 resulted in the creation of a unified oppressive machinery. The literature of this period is significant for its pathos and a sense of despair mixed with a nostalgia for the days of old. The temporary defeat of the African people stimulated a philosophy of deprivation. But this was only more apparent than real. A new intellectual elite was emerging whose belief was that the white man could be beaten on his own ground by the combined forces of all the African people.

Thus we find one of the most outstanding political documents, given by Dr. Seme in 1908, stressing the absolute necessity of the unity of the African people against the oppressor. The unity was not only of the local kind but encompassing the whole continent of Africa. The significance of the document, or rather the political views contained therein, lies not only in the dimensions of political interpretation of resistance, but also because such views became part of the literary mood of the period.

This was reflected in the numerous volumes of literature — translations, historical and political treatises — defining the African intellectual resistance movement. That these corporate works sought to interpret African political and historical thought is seen from the very titles: 'The Origin of the African Peoples' by Soga, 'Shaka's Page Boy' by Dube, 'African Political Organizations' by Dladla, and so on.

No Land — No Presses
To define this movement exactly, one must study the political and social

factors operating at the time. The formation of the Union of South Africa signified, as stated, the unification of the oppressive forces. The immediate task of these forces was to drive the African people from the land so that they became a landless mobile labour-pool available for the newly established industries. To ensure the total and universal implementation of this pro-gramme, a tax was imposed so that every able-bodied man would be forced to seek employment in the white man's cities.

The 1913 Land Act not only deprived the African of the right of owner-ship of land but, under the Urban Areas Act, the Africans were prohibited from owning any interest in land except with the express authority of the Governor-General. The immediate result was the restriction of the African population, which outnumbered the whites four to one, to only 12½% of the land area of South Africa. The position remains unchanged except for one-half percent added later as a 'compensation' for the loss of voting rights.

In spite of all this it took some time before the law took effect. What is then the significance of this Act to literature? Hitherto the African intelli-gentsia and others had been able to pawn their lands and buy printing presses and locate them on their land. Thus J.L. Dube, one of the early leaders of African intellectual resisters and first President of the African National Congress was able to establish 'Ilanga Lase Natal Press'. Through this press he published a newspaper which was one of the mouthpieces of the intellectual resistance movement.

Early African Press
In the Cape a more united and more vocal group of intellectuals established an African press through which 'Imvo Zabantu' and other works were pub-lished. Both 'Ilanga Lase Natal' and 'Imvo Zabantu' became not only the organs of debate about methods of resistance, but also involved in these debates the mass of the African people. They at once mobilised African opinion and exposed the most brutal forms of oppression perpetuated by the regime.

It was not only through this that political resistance of the African people was kept alive but also through literature produced from African-owned printing presses. It is to the credit of these intellectuals that they not only saw their destinies invariably tied up with those of their own people — despite endless attempts by the regime and missionaries to isolate them — but they also effected their beliefs by publishing in African languages. This meant that all literature productions were available to the general African populace.

The immediate effect then of the Land Act was that it deprived the Africans of the control of publication and left them at the mercy of the mission-owned presses. It also deprived the small land-owning group of the capacity to produce literature without too much dependence on the meagre earnings from white men's industries and schools. The result was a decline not only in literary output, which had been impressive, but also a decline in content. The novelettes produced failed to deal with social and political drama and remained soulless material which neither challenged the regime nor depicted the African situation. Instead the literature became no more than sentimental reportage of love situations between frozen and fleshless characters.

We can call this 'situational literature' since it dealt with situations without drawing any conclusions about their significance. Never in the whole period of our history has there been so much puerile, banal and purposeless literature. The writers, if we can call them such, pandered to the school market and purged their works of any slightly 'oppressive' (by missionary and government standards) paragraphs, words or sentences.

Such novelettes as *Nomsa* and such didactic literary omelettes as *Umendo kadukotela* vulgarised the very soul of the African people. No student read after completing his term of study: saturated with the infantility of these works, no student found anything to interest him in literature. Thus was born a whole generation of philistines whose only recourse was to the chapters and quotations of books long out of print.

Gimmicks and Chunks

They suffered also because the very intellectual isolation created a vacuum that was neither filled by European literature (which they had not been trained to understand) nor by traditional African literature (which they had been trained to despise as barbaric and depraved).

In all this, traditional African literature itself suffered a significant blow. The destruction of the African social and political units by colonialism meant that the very basis of our traditional literary productions was broken up. It is for that reason that though the tradition continued the literary products of our society showed neither genius nor purpose. Instead they became imitations of earlier epics and degenerated into eulogistic gimmicks in football matches. It is not unusual to hear whole chunks of plagiarized stanzas from the early epics modelled to suit the poetaster's needs.

All this is slightly misleading, since amidst all this decay there were signs of an awakening, an attempt at creating an idiom that by-passed the censorship. The whole picture cannot be fully known until liberation, since literally thousands of manuscripts lie buried in shelves, rejected by schools. Some principled writers refused to alter their manuscripts to suit the whims of a cruel regime, and thus remain unpublished to this day.

Censorship

Also on the traditional literary side the resistance is shown in the works already quoted. All these were harbingers of the great literary works of Dlomo, Mghayi, Vilakazi, Mofolo, etc. These writers produced not only historical novels but also poetry of resistance. To evade censorship they used literary nuances which could only be understood by those who knew African languages well. Mghayi, for instance, the great Xhosa poet, not only revived the traditional literary idiom but developed the structure to accommodate new literary ideas. By using double meanings he managed to compose virulent satires on the regime and the British empire.

186

Vilakazi, the great Zulu poet, viciously attacks the cruel system of migrant labour in the mines while appearing to be concerned with the muscular beauty of the former soldiers of the Zulu empire. Using a symbolic language he draws attention to the rusting qualities of mine bells which, in fact, are representations of the miners who are discarded soon after contracting silicosis. H.I.E. Dlomo similarly writes of the Valley of a Thousand Hills whilst, in fact, writing about the political denudations of African liberties.

It is in this period we see the re-emergence of nationally orientated literature. The literature is concerned with protest but as yet does not call the population to revolt. All the same this in itself is an achievement of great significance. For the very act of protest meant that the writers of this period were re-defining once more the very ethos of the African nation. All this does not mean that the regime had relaxed its laws. On the contrary since 1927 more laws of censorship had been passed. The 1927 Native Administration Act prohibited any matter or publication 'calculated to rouse hostility' between races. These sweet-sounding words actually meant that the government could censor any literature or newspaper which agitated for the rights of the oppressed.

The Riotous Assemblies Act of 1914, amended in 1930, prohibited publication of any words inciting public violence. This tightening-up of the law is a tribute to the very resistance which the government sought to stop. But such is the fate of all oppressive regimes that each law exposes loopholes in other spheres. The Suppression of Communism Act of 1950 and all its subsequent amendments not only make a definition of communism suitable to the regime's requirements, but also give power to ban any statements made by banned people. This has resulted in a large number of banned writers unable to publish anything whatsoever.

So one could go on *ad nauseum*, dealing with all the laws of censorship, laws preventing mixed meetings, laws preventing entry into 'Europeans only' theatres and places of public entertainment, laws dealing with the banning of newspapers: the list is almost endless. A writer in this context finds himself not only unable to publish but also crippled spiritually by the weight of the oppressive machinery.

Government Press

The Bantu Education Act, by bringing all schools under the direct authority of a government department, gave authority to that department to prescribe set-books for schools in all the provinces. This in practice has meant that books prescribed were those written by government-sponsored writers who penned ideological tracts orientating the African child towards acceptance of his inferior status in society. Side by side with this development has been the taking over of book publication by semi-government presses like Afrikaans Pers Beperk and Bantu Press.

All literature currently being published in South Africa for the African public and African schools is either the most poisonous and trite, or else the innocent mutterings of a politically unsophisticated romantic. Of the 30 volumes of poetry published, it is difficult to find anything of merit except in the works of such poets as 'Bulima Mgiyeke' or Seth Dlamini. The novel, if such a name can validly be used for these propaganda pamphlets, is no more than the structureless ramblings of demented minds. This is, of course, not the end of the story. Great writers are often stimulated by very harsh factors. But to know who they are we have to wait until liberation, for their works, as stated, remain unpublished.

Partly to avoid this censorship, partly as a result of accumulation, a new type of writer has emerged who writes in English. These writers, who are now mostly out of the country, represent a new form of resistance. Their works aim for a wider readership covering not only the South African audiences but the whole of the English-speaking world. They include such well-known names as Lewis Nkosi (perhaps the brightest star of this constellation); Alex la Guma, the undisputed great political-realist short-story writer; Ezekiel Mphahlele, the father and master of this school; Can Themba, Arthur Maimane, Nat Nakasa, Bloke Modisane, and Alfred Hutchinson, one of the greatest 'soul' writers South Africa has produced.

Almost all of them were on the staff of the now defunct *Drum*, a magazine started with good intentions but debased into one of the most frivolous literary puddles; while it stimulated writers to write socially-based comments, it swallowed them into its doctrine of crime sensationalism, beauty contest fads and shebeen ideologies. Writers who once worked for this magazine still bear the scars. One, in an attempt to rediscover himself, was driven to suicide. Others are still terrified of their *Drum* identity, and sometimes crawl as it were in the night to find torn roots of their umbilical cords. What *Drum* did is one of the most glaring tragedies of the colonial situation. It used the talents of its writers without adequate compensation. Its sensationalised reporting on African location life, so that from the grime and mire came laughing voices and suffering, was transformed by titillating fun.

Out of this school has survived, through sheer resistance, a genre of writers who are the true illustrious parallels of the earlier intellectuals. They are all living in exile outside South Africa.

We have not here dealt with the literature of the ruling circles. We regret the lack of time and space, for we feel that this literature is itself part of the story of liberation. The bulk of the literature is poor for the simple reason that its dimensions are limited by the concepts of baasskapism (race superiority) and apartheid. The settlers find it hard to reconcile their claim to being part of the African reality with the refutation found everywhere in their emigre literature. Most of it shows an extremely superficial experience. Only a few white writers escape this. I do not here include Campbell, the once popular fascist poet. I do include Nadine Gordimer, Olive Schreiner (writer of the *Story of an African Farm*), and Ruth First, the ceaseless South African political writer and stylist.

Unfortunately there are only a few of these writers in the Afrikaans language. Although in the Afrikaans language some outstanding works have been produced they, like the majority of white South African works, are confined within the tribal ethos. They show a narrowness and typically myopic view of the universe. African character is caricatured as simple, docile, or else treacherous and evil. There are, however, a few angry young writers like Breyton Breytenbach who have written with a new dynamic urgency. But Breytenbach has to live in Paris to experience the totality of human relations. This is the tragedy of the South African situation.

The literature of resistance has begun in earnest in South Africa to reflect the new values of revolution and resistance. Some of it is being clandestinely distributed in the country, or recited in the camps and prisons like Robben Island. As our resistance grows more powerful so shall the output of our literature. We intend to use everything at our disposal to win our freedom, and literature must, in our interpretation, define the very depths of our revolutionary action.

On Gris-gris

Eduardo Mondlane/Amilcar Cabral

> *Remarks by Dr. Eduardo Mondlane, President of FRELIMO,*
> *and Amilcar Cabral, Secretary-General of the PAIGC, in an article*
> *by Jean-Francois Kahn in* L'Express *(Paris), 8-16 February,*
> *1965. Translated from French.*

Eduardo Mondlane

The ancestral belief in invulnerability produced by the wearing of certain 'gris-gris' could be utilized for a revolutionary goal. One must distinguish between an instrument and a political attitude. The superstitious individual is the same in every community. At the time of the bombing in Rome, during the last war, there was a Catholic priest with a cross in every American plane, supposed to bless the town. In Mozambique, it is possible that certain animists have this same attitude. But the war goes on. Even if one has to make use of certain fetishes, it will still go on.

We must also attentively study the tribal phenomenon. We must know if a particular tribal group thinks of itself as being a political community. If the answer is yes, the revolutionaries must take such a fact into consideration, utilize it and transform it.

Amilcar Cabral

Animist religion presents us, revolutionaries, with both positive and negative factors. Thus, the fear of certain natural phenomena, such as rain or lightning, hinders our struggle. We must thus educate the masses and explain the meaning of rain and its advantages. Certain taboos constrain us also.

On the other hand, animism often allows us better to unite men in a specific goal. We are not against some fetish ceremonies. Thus, there are some tribes which cannot take on arms without first executing certain dances, or covering themselves with 'gris-gris'. We do not oppose this. We simply try to explain to them that this does not stop the bullets.

Our Culture and the New Man

Agostinho Neto

From an interview by Julia Herve with Dr. Agostinho Neto, President of the MPLA, published in Algerie-Actualite *(Algiers), No. 337, 2-8 April, 1972.*

Herve: The struggle is conducted on two fronts: to the struggle against Portuguese colonialism, you add a fight against obscurantism, fetishism, magic, religion? Are you thinking of participating in the creation of this 'new man', the object of the Cuban revolution?

Neto: We believe that the revolution will create this 'new man'. The anti-colonialist actions which we undertake contribute to its creation. There are two aspects of our struggle: on the one hand, our aim is to destroy the colonial structure, on the other it is to build our country. For the attainment of the latter, we need men, since they are the ones who may ensure us with some kind of social organization. The programme of our movement includes an educational stage designed to alter the mentality of our people.

However, when dealing with cultural aspects rooted in our people for centuries, these cannot be erased from their life overnight. Certain popular habits are good, some are not. We are concerned with keeping and reviving those Angolan cultural practices which have been despised or destroyed through centuries of colonization. Music, dance, and art are not evolving today, because they have been stifled by colonialism in its attempt to force its cultural tradition upon us.

There are also some habits which are not positive. Our people is very religious. Certain religious practices are not adapted to modern life, even if they still exist. Our movement has been combating fetishism through education. Religious sentiment is still very strong and we respect it since we feel that our people will gain knowledge during the years of struggle.

In looking at what our action has accomplished in the past ten years, we realize that we have trained numerous cadres in our schools, and through participation in the struggle. There are no fetishists in the ranks of our organization, for instance. The militants of the MPLA will be the motors of our revolution. The creation of the 'new man' is the greatest and the most difficult task to be accomplished by us.

Protest Against the Name, Namibia
SWANU

*Petition from the National Executive of the South West African
National Union (SWANU) sent to U Thant, Secretary-General
of the United Nations from Windhoek on 15 September, 1968.*

Dear Mr. Secretary-General,
The National Executive Committee of the South West Africa National Union
after a careful study of the numerous pronouncements from the outside,
particularly the United Nations, has decided to draw your attention to a
decision taken recently by the United Nations. This decision concerns the
renaming of our country 'Namibia'.

Much has been said, done and even claimed in our name, the people of
South West Africa, without any prior consultation with the people, or at
least without subsequent appeal to them.

In 1920 we were not consulted when our country was placed under the
South African Administration as a Mandate under the defunct League of
Nations. Again in 1945 we were not consulted, but were presumed to welcome the new arrangements. The list does not end there, but these two
instances will suffice.

The South African regime treats our people as chattels best suited for the
menial and most difficult work without adequate compensation and above
all without pretence of consulting us or finding out our views or wishes. This
position we know and we do not expect otherwise from the South African
racist regime. Hence, our total and unequivocal rejection of its administration
in our country. Our resistance against the forcible removal from our 'Old
Location' to the Apartheid-designed Katutura is an apt demonstration of our
stand against Apartheid and foreign rule.

Through the local Newspapers and the Party representatives abroad, we
learned that we have now been christened with a new name, namely 'Namibia'. There might be nothing wrong in the name as such, but as leaders of the
South West Africa National Union, we expect that our people should have
been asked first before the christening ceremony was staged. Yet, the United
Nations merely passed a resolution giving us a new name, and for that matter
it is claimed to be our wish — the wish of our people.

We are aware that South West Africa is a colonial geographical designation.
But the colonialists never pretended to work for our interest and wishes. Yet,
today, we find the body which says it works for the well-being of our people,
renaming South West Africa without seeking their views on such an important matter. If it is the wish of some member-States of the United Nations,
notably the African States, that our country should be given a new name
that is more African or sounds like an African name, we do appreciate such
wishes. But, we demand that the final word on such an important issue should
be that of the people of this country. We are tempted to put the question,
what next will be decided or done in our name?

The name 'Namibia' is an imposition of the United Nations upon the people of this country and as such it is most unacceptable to us. The people regard the name as synonymous with 'Bantustans' thrust upon them by the United Nations. To insist upon calling the UN Council for South West Africa, 'Namibia' is tantamount to declaring war upon those who are against your dictatorship. Will there be any difference, then, between the United Nations and the regime of South Africa concerning the people of this country?

Hoping that the matter will receive your serious consideration, we remain

Sincerely yours,
National Executive Committee
South West Africa National Union
(SWANDU).

Why Namibia?

SWAPO

Statement in SWAPO's Namibia News *(London), I,*
8-9, October-December 1968.

South West Africa is a misnaming of our country. It is a general geographical description which could equally apply to other countries such as Angola. The name is reminiscent of colonial arbitrariness. As such, it can only be understood in terms of colonial logic whose main premise is territorial acquisition and expansion. When the Germans arrived in 'South West Africa' in the 1870s they had an idea that to the north of that territory they came to colonize lies the Portuguese colony of Angola. They knew also that to the north was the Dutch-English controlled South Africa. The German colonialists did not, however, know precisely where the boundaries of these two colonies were in relation to their intended colony of 'South West Africa'. Thus, they thought it wise to simply give their colony such a general name with a view to expanding it gradually in that region as vastly as the neighbouring colonial powers could allow. The original German colonial settlement was established in the central part of 'South West Africa', sometimes referred to as Hereroland or Damaraland. But as the time went on this colonial possession was expanded to include Namaqualand to the south and beyond Onamutoni to include Ovamboland to the north.

The South West African People's Organization considers the name 'South West Africa' an inappropriate delineation of our territorial image. Against this background, SWAPO has adopted Namibia as the logical name of our country. The choice of the name Namibia is not necessarily governed by historical nostalgia. Rather, it is predicated on some essential features of the geographical nature of our national territory. This name is derived from the

'Namib' in the coastal desert of 'South West Africa'. !Namib, a Nama or Damara word, literally means the 'enclosure'. '!' represents the click stress in pronunciation. The Namib runs 850 miles from the Cunene River on the Namibia-Angola border to the Orange River to the South African-Namibia border, with a width varying from 30 to 80 miles. It constitutes a natural shield to this country and it is important to recall that Portuguese navigators sailed along the 'South West African' coast as early as the 15th century but were unable to penetrate into the interior because of this grossly disencouraging shield. It should also be remembered that coastal peoples throughout Africa had been the immediate victims of European colonialism and slavery. It is equally significant to remember that 'South West Africa' was among the last territories in Africa to be colonized. As Noel Mostert has put it:

It was this Coastal Namib Desert,
Running like a narrow white moat
Along almost the entire length of the
South West shore, that helped seal off
The interior and those living there
From any prying new-comers.

From the defence point of view, the Namib has thus played such a historical role to the communities of 'South West Africa'. It can be of the same importance to an independent nation. Though bare of vegetation, the Namib is desert where diamonds have been found lying upon the ground as thick as plums under a tree. The Luderitz district of the Namib is one of the richest alluvial sources of diamonds in Africa.

The Namib Desert rolls down to a freezing sea which is chilled by the cold Benguela current which comes up from the Antarctic to form off this coast, one of the world's richest fishing grounds. Here whales, seals, land penguins come ashore from the Antarctic icy water to walk on the Namibian coast. The fabulously productive fishing industries of Walvis Bay and Luderitz Bay are graphic testimonies to the extraordinary significance of the Namib. Remarking upon the Namib, Walter Fitzgerald wrote: 'It possesses two of the finest natural harbours in the subcontinent, Walvis Bay and Ludritz. The former facing the north, is well sheltered and deep enough to allow large vessels to go alongside.' Walvis is, indeed, a very busy port today where a great number of cargo ships from all over the world enter daily.

Furthermore, the various sorts of fishes which run off the coast and the tens of thousands of guano producing birds which cloud the sky constitute such a vivid versatility of the Namib, unknown of any other desert in the world. Conceived from these perspectives, the Namib, we believe, is not just a wasted land of the dunes, but a resourceful region. The natural defence shield — 'enclosure', the rich fishing ground, and the diamond fields of the Namib Desert are valuable attributes of our national territory. This is the reason why we have chosen to call our country Namibia — the land of the Namib.

The United Nations and the OAU have both embraced Namibia as the

name of that nation. The adoption of this name by the African nations and
the UN is in conformity with the principles of self-determination. For, it is
we, the people of Namibia, who must ultimately shape our own destiny *and
identity. And we call it Namibia.*

Revolutionary Education
FRELIMO

*From the document, 'Shaping the Political Line' published in
FRELIMO's* Mozambique Revolution *(Dar es Salaam), 25 June,
1972.*

The setting up of an education programme entailed immense difficulties. The
few schools which existed in our country were run by missionaries whom the
Portuguese evacuated from the war zones at the beginning of the struggle in
order to turn the buildings into barracks. We had practically no teachers, we
had access to those who knew only how to read and write in order to start
our courses. It was only slowly, through a system of seminars, that we succeeded in developing and raising the standard of new teachers.

The need for an educational programme was felt even in the military field.
In fact, at a certain stage of the development effort, the administration of the
commercial centres, all the many and varied tasks of national reconstruction
could not be implemented without the spread of a certain level of knowledge.
Thus, simultaneously with the literacy courses in the army, we organised
accelerated courses of 6 months, one year and two years in order to enable
the more capable militants to finish primary education and take on bigger
responsibilities. Afterwards, people were selected to go to our secondary
school on the basis of the level of political consciousness which they had
demonstrated, on their dedication to the revolution and on their intellectual
capacity. This system of selection proved highly successful; it reduced dramatically the number of failures as compared with those students who had
attended more conventional schools.

The contents of the curriculum also demanded deep reflection and further
elaboration. It was obvious that we had to eliminate subjects with a clear
colonialist colour. (The history of Portugal, for example.) But the development of the educational work also showed that we could not organise our
system by a mere touching up of an essentially Portuguese system. Our
general line had to be conditioned by more fundamental questions: what is
the objective of our education? In what way does it distinguish itself from
the two other forms of education prevailing in our society, i.e. traditional
and colonial education?

Again the answer to these two questions had to come from the general
development of the struggle and from the political growth of the

organisation. It was the need for a new life and a more precise definition of our objectives in the liberated zones which gave to our education programme, its form and content. Our education, as our President said in the message he addressed to the Second National Conference of the Department of Education and Culture in August, 1970, 'must give us a Mozambican personality which assumes our reality and assimilates critically and without servility the ideas and experiences of other people of the world at the same time transmitting to them the fruit of our reflection and practice'.

It is necessary in turn to identify precisely the content both of traditional and colonial education in order to fight against their effects in our mentality and in our social life.

In traditional society, given the low level of knowledge which characterises it, superstition takes the place of science and blocks any scientific analysis of the physical and social milieu in favour of the supernatural. Through one of its mechanisms for survival, traditional education aims at creating in the new generation's passivity and respect towards acquired ideas; it encourages the belief in the infallible wisdom of the older generations personified in the elders. With regard to women, tradition tries to justify historically women's submission to men.

Mental Scars

Colonial education is concerned with teaching only to the extent that it facilitates further exploitation. It aims at reinforcing division within the colonised society by separating those who are educated and those who are not. Among the former it encourages a feeling of shame and later a despising of their culture and traditions. The marks left by this type of education is an even greater obstacle in the establishment of the new types of relations we want to create among people. Moreover, even when the struggle against the policy of assimilation does become clear on the plane of principle, it retains many more subtle effects and manifestations. For one may strongly reject the idea of becoming 'a black Portuguese', but it is nonetheless certain this idea will continue to breed an inferiority complex among many Mozambicans. The conviction that our traditional culture has no value has been for a long time deeply embedded in the minds of many of our people. For these reasons it has been necessary to launch an intensive and self-conscious combat against this mentality. It was with this aim in mind that the Department of Education and Culture organises cultural seminars where an inventory is made of the cultural wealth of our people.

Today a new culture is being developed based on traditional forms with a new content dictated by our new reality. This reality is constituted first of all by the liberation struggle itself, but also, by the common effort of Mozambicans originating from different places and tribes who are united in the struggle for the construction of a new Mozambique. From this point of view, culture plays an important role in the reinforcement of national unity. The dances which are performed today in the liberated regions are no longer dances of Cabo Delgado, or Tete or Niassa. The militants from other regions there bring their way of living, their dances, their songs, and from this a new culture, national in its form and revolutionary in content, is born.

Destined Leaders

Revolutionary education must aim at destroying the corrupt ideas and habits inherited from the past; develop the scientific spirit in order to eliminate superstition; promote the emergence of a national culture; liquidate individualism and elitism.

These are not abstract problems: a hard struggle had to be waged inside the organisation against those tendencies when a superiority complex which was the result of an elitist mentality developed in our secondary school. Imbued with the ideas acquired in the colonialist society that those who had education were destined to be leaders, some pupils of the secondary school contemptuous of the masses, refused to participate in the war which they considered as a non-intellectual activity, they preferred to sit back and wait for victory in comfort.

The problem which is posed today is whether the progress of our country is the task of a few or whether it must be the result of the effort of the whole people. The answer which springs from the practice of our liberation struggle is obviously the latter. Without the active and responsible participation of the masses what could the few dozen FRELIMO militants have done? Our choice leads us also to reject formal academic education as the only legitimate kind of learning and to emphasise instead broader and more permanent forms of education. This shift in emphasis is also necessary if we are to undertake the general education activity which is implicit in our political programme.

It is obvious that such cultural conceptions bring potential political contradictions to the fore, both domestically and on the international plane. For the 'enlightened' minority which would lead our country would be the best guarantee of the maintenance of exploitation and the preservation of foreign interests in Mozambique. It is therefore not surprising that, as with other fighting organisations, Mozambican students in the western countries are subjected to all the reactionary pressures and influences which promote elitist sentiments. This remains for us a continuing problem.

One method which we have adopted in order to discourage the development of such elitist ideas is the encouragement of a liaison between the student and the masses. Thus, one of the most important innovations in our school syllabus has been the introducing of productive activities. Moreover, this has a second benefit beyond the crucial socio-political aspect which we have been underlining: it also ensures that primary education is at least partly operational, i.e. that it brings some benefits to the students and to their families by including the teaching of such artisan skills as carpentry, mechanics, tailoring, etc.

The education programme faces other difficulties as well, among them the resistance on the part of parents to sending their daughters to school. Parents tend to consider their daughters in terms of the wealth they will gain from dowries at the time that the girls marry. The risk that the girl's chance for a profitable marriage will be spoilt by her going to school makes many parents refuse to send their daughters there. And initiation rites have a similarly negative role. In many regions, after the initiation rites, the girls must stay at home awaiting marriage, a practice which means the definitive cessation of their education. The Political Commissariat and the Women's Detachment are involved in the work of mobilising people and explaining the advantage of education in order to change this negative attitude of the parents towards their daughters.

The Role of Culture in the Struggle for Independence
Amilcar Cabral

A paper prepared by the Secretary-General of the PAIGC, for the UNESCO Meeting of Experts on the Concept of 'Race', 'Identity' and 'Dignity', held in Paris in July 1972.

The struggle of peoples for national liberation and independence has become a tremendous force for human progress and is beyond doubt an essential feature of the history of our time.

Objective analysis of imperialism as a fact or historical phenomenon that is 'natural', even 'necessary', to the economic and political evolution of a great part of mankind, reveals that imperialist rule, with its train of misery, pillage, crimes and its destruction of human and cultural values, was not a purely negative reality.

The huge accumulation of capital in a half dozen countries of the northern hemisphere as the result of piracy, sack of other people's property and unbridled exploitation of their labour, did more than engender colonial monopoly, the sharing-out of the world and imperialist dominion. In the rich countries, imperialist capital, ever looking for higher profits, heightened man's creative capacity. Aided by the accelerated progress of science and technology, it profoundly transformed the means of production, stepped-up the social organization of work and raised the standard of living of vast sections of the population.

In the colonized countries, colonization usually arrested the historical development of the people — when it did not lead to their total or gradual elimination. Here imperialist capital imposed new types of relationships within the indigenous society whose structure became more complex. It aroused, fomented, inflamed or resolved social contradictions and conflicts.

With the circulation of money and the development of the domestic and foreign markets, it introduced new elements into the economy. It led to the birth of new nations out of ethnic groups or peoples at varying stages of historical development.

It is no defence of imperialist domination to recognize that it opened up new worlds to a world whose dimensions it reduced, that it revealed new phases in the development of human societies and, in spite of or because of the prejudices, discriminations and crimes it occasioned, helped to impart a deeper knowledge of mankind, moving as one, as a unified whole amid the complex diversity of its various forms of development.

Imperialist rule fostered a multilateral, gradual (sometimes abrupt) confrontation on the different continents not only between different men but between different societies.

The practice of imperialist rule – its affirmation or its negation – demanded and still demands a more or less accurate knowledge of the people dominated and their historical background (economic, social and cultural). This knowledge is necessarily expressed in terms of comparison with the dominating power's own historical background.

Such knowledge is an imperative necessity for imperialist rule which results from the usually violent confrontation of two different identities, distinct in their historical backgrounds and antagonistic in their functions. Despite its unilateral, subjective and often unjust character, the search for such knowledge contributed to the general enrichment of the human and social sciences.

Indeed, man has never shown such interest in learning about other men and other societies as during this century of imperialist domination. An unprecedented amount of information, hypotheses and theories was thus accumulated concerning subjugated peoples or ethnic groups, especially in the fields of history, ethnology, ethnography, sociology and culture.

Concepts of race, caste, clanship, tribe, nation, culture, identity, dignity and many more besides have received increasing attention from those who study man and the so-called 'primitive' or 'evolving' societies.

More recently, with the upsurge of liberation movements, it has been found necessary to analyse the characteristics of these societies in terms of the struggle that is being fought, so as to determine which factors spark off or restrain this struggle. Researchers generally agree that, in this context, culture takes on special importance. Any attempt to throw light on the true role of culture in the development of a liberation (pre-independence) movement can be seen as making a helpful contribution to the general struggle of peoples against imperialist rule.

Because independence movements are as a rule marked even in their beginnings by increased cultural activity, it is taken for granted that such movements are preceded by a cultural 'renaissance' of the dominated people. Going a step further, culture is regarded as a method of mobilizing the group, even as a weapon in the fight for independence.

From experience of the struggle of my own people and it might be said of all Africa, I feel that this is a too limited, if not erroneous, conception of the vital role of culture in the development of liberation movements. I think it comes of generalizing incorrectly from a real but restricted phenomenon that appears at the level of colonial elites or diasporas. Such a generalization is unaware of or disregards an essential factor – the indestructibility of cultural resistance by the mass of the people to foreign rule.

With a few exceptions, the era of colonization was too short, in Africa at least, to destroy or significantly depreciate the essential elements in the culture and traditions of the colonized peoples. Experience in Africa shows that (leaving aside genocide, racial segregation and apartheid) the one so-called 'positive' way the colonial power has found for opposing cultural resistance is 'assimilation'. But the total failure of the policy of 'gradual assimilation' of colonized populations is obvious proof of the fallacy of the theory and of the peoples' capacity for resistance.

On the other hand, even in settlement colonies, where the overwhelming majority of the population is still indigenous, the area of colonial and particularly cultural occupation is usually reduced to coastal strips and a few small zones in the interior.

The influence of the colonial power's culture is almost nil outside the capital and other urban centres. It is only significantly felt within the social pyramid created by colonialism itself and affects more particularly what may be called the indigenous petty bourgeoisie and a very limited number of workers in urban centres.

We find then that the great rural masses and a large fraction of the urban population, totalling over 99 per cent of the indigenous population, are virtually isolated from any cultural influence by the colonial power. This implies that not only for the mass of the people in the dominated country but also for the dominant classes among the indigenous peoples (traditional chiefs, noble families, religious leaders) there is usually no destruction or significant depreciation of culture and traditions.

Repressed, persecuted, humiliated, betrayed by certain social groups which have come to terms with the foreigner, culture takes refuge in villages, in forests and in the minds of the victims of domination, weathering all storms to recover all its power of expansion and enrichment through the struggle for liberation.

That is why the problem of a 'return to the source' or a 'cultural renaissance' does not arise for the mass of the people; it could not, for the masses are the torch-bearers of culture; they are the source of culture and, at the same time, the one entity truly capable of creating and preserving it, of making history.

For an accurate appreciation of the true role of culture in the development of the liberation movement, a distinction must therefore be made, at least in Africa, between the situation of the masses who preserve their culture and of the social groups that are more or less assimilated, uprooted and culturally alienated.

Even though marked by certain cultural features of their own indigenous community, native elites created by the colonizing process live materially and spiritually the culture of the colonialist foreigner with whom they seek gradually to identify themselves in social behaviour and even in their views of indigenous cultural values.

Over two or three generations at least under colonization, a social class has been formed of government officials, employees in various branches of the economy (especially trade), members of the liberal professions and a few urban and agricultural landowners. This indigenous lower middle class, created by foreign rule and indispensable to the colonial system of exploitation, finds itself placed between the mass of workers in the country and in the towns and the minority of local representatives of the foreign ruling class.

Although its members may have more or less developed relations with the mass of the people or the traditional chiefs, they usually aspire to a way of life similar to, if not identical with, that of the foreign minority. Limiting their relations with the masses, they try to become integrated with that minority, often to the detriment of family or ethnic bonds and always at personal cost.

But despite apparent exceptions, they never succeed in crossing the barriers imposed by the system. They are prisoners of the contradictions of the social and cultural reality in which they live, for they cannot escape their condition as a 'marginal' class. This marginality is the real social and cultural drama of the colonial elites or indigenous petty bourgeoisie. While living conditions and level of acculturation determine its intensity, this drama is always lived at the individual, not the community, level.

Within the framework of this daily drama, against the background of the usually violent confrontation between the mass of the people and the ruling colonial class, a feeling of bitterness, a frustration complex, develops and grows among the indigenous lower middle class. At the same time, they gradually become aware of an urgent need to contest their marginal status and to find an identity. So they turn towards the other pole of the social and cultural conflict in which they are living — the mass of the people.

Hence the 'return to the source', which seems all the more imperative as the sense of isolation and frustration of this lower middle class grows. The same holds true for Africans dispersed in colonialist and racist capitals.

It is not by chance, then, that theories or movements such as Pan Africanism and Negritude (two pertinent expressions based mainly on the notion that all Black Africans are culturally identical) were conceived outside Black Africa. More recently, the Black Americans' claim to an African identity is another, perhaps desperate, expression of this need to 'return to the source', though it is clearly influenced by a new factor — the winning of independence by the great majority of African peoples.

But the 'return to the source' neither is nor can be in itself an act of struggle against foreign (colonialist and racist) rule. Nor does it necessarily mean a return to traditions. It is the denial by the indigenous petty bourgeoisie of the superiority claimed for the culture of the ruling power over the culture of the dominated people with which this petty bourgeoisie feels the need to identify.

This 'return to the source', then, is not a voluntary step; it is the only possible response to the irreconcilable contradiction between the colonized society and the colonial power, between the exploited masses and the foreign exploiters.

When the 'return to the source' goes beyond the individual to find expression in 'groups' or 'movements', this opposition turns into conflict (under cover or open), the prelude to the pre-independence movement or struggle for liberation from foreign yoke.

This 'return to the source' is thus historically important only if it involves both a genuine commitment to the fight for independence and also a total, irrevocable identification with the aspirations of the masses, who reject not only the foreigner's culture but foreign rule altogether. Otherwise it is nothing but a means of obtaining temporary advantages, a conscious or unconscious form of political opportunism.

It should be noted that this 'return to the source', whether real or apparent, is not something that happens simultaneously and uniformly within the lower middle class. It is a slow, discontinuous, uneven process, and its development depends on each person's degree of acculturation, material conditions of life, ideological thinking and individual history as a social being.

This unevenness explains the splitting of the indigenous petty bourgeoisie into three groups in relation to the liberation movement: a minority which, even though it may want the end of foreign rule, hangs on to the ruling colonial class and openly opposes the liberation movement in order to defend and secure its own social position; a hesitant or undecided majority; another minority which helps to create and to direct the liberation movement.

But this last group, which plays a decisive role in developing the pre-independence movement, does not really succeed in identifying itself with the mass of the people (with their culture and their aspirations) except through the struggle, the degree of identification depending on the form or forms of the struggle, the ideological content of the movement and the extent of each person's moral and political awareness.

Culture has proved to be the very foundation of the liberation movement. Only societies which preserve their culture are able to mobilize and organize themselves and fight against foreign domination. Whatever ideological or idealistic forms it takes, culture is essential to the historical process. It has the power to prepare and make fertile those factors that ensure historical continuity and determine a society's chances of progressing (or regressing).

Since imperialist rule is the negation of the historical process of the dominated society, it will readily be understood that it is also the negation of the cultural process. And since a society that really succeeds in throwing off the foreign yoke reverts to the upward paths of its own culture, the struggle for liberation is above all an act of culture.

The fight for liberation is an essentially political fact. Consequently, as it develops, it can only use political methods. Culture then is not, and cannot be, a weapon or a means of mobilizing the group against foreign domination. It is much more than that. Indeed, it is on firm knowledge of the local reality, particularly the cultural reality, that the choice, organization and development of the best methods of fighting are based.

This is why the liberation movement must recognize the vital importance not only of the cultural characteristics of the dominated society as a whole but also of those of each social class. For though it has a mass aspect, culture is not uniform and does not develop evenly in all sectors, horizontal or vertical, of society.

The attitude and behaviour of each class or each individual towards the struggle and its development are, it is true, dictated by economic interests, but they are also profoundly influenced by culture. It may even be said that differences in cultural level explain differences in behaviour towards the liberation movement of individuals of the same social class.

It is at this level, then, that culture attains its full significance for each individual — comprehension of and integration within his social milieu, identification with the fundamental problems and aspirations of his society and acceptance or rejection of the possibility of change for the better.

Whatever its form, the struggle requires the mobilization and organization of a large majority of the population, the political and moral unity of the different social classes, the gradual elimination of vestiges of tribal or feudal mentality, the rejection of social and religious taboos that are incompatible with the rational and national character of the liberating movement. And the struggle brings about many other profound modifications in the life of the people.

This is all the more true because the dynamics of the struggle also require the exercise of democracy, criticism and self-criticism, growing participation of the people in running their lives, the achievement of literacy, the creation of schools and health services, leadership training for rural and city workers, and many other achievements that are involved in the society's 'forced march' along the road of cultural progress. This shows that the liberation struggle is more than a cultural fact, it is also a cultural factor.

Among the representatives of the colonial power as well as in their home countries, the first reaction to the liberation struggle is a general feeling of surprise and incredulity. Once this feeling, the fruit of prejudice or of the planned distortions typical of colonialist news, is surmounted, reactions vary with the interests, the political opinions and the degree to which colonialist and racist attitudes have crystallized among the different social classes and individuals.

The progress of the struggle and the sacrifices imposed by the need to take colonialist repressive measures (police or military) cause a split in metropolitan opinion. Differing, if not divergent, positions are adopted and new political and social contradictions emerge.

From the moment the struggle is recognized as an irreversible fact, however great the resources employed to quash it, a qualitative change takes place in metropolitan opinion. The possibility, if not the inevitability, of the colony's independence is on the whole gradually accepted.

Such a change is a conscious or unconscious admission that the colonized people now engaged in the struggle have an identity and a culture of their own. And this holds true even though throughout the conflict an active minority, clinging to its interests and prejudices, persists in refusing the colonized their right to independence and in denying the equivalence of cultures that right implies.

At a decisive stage in the conflict, this equivalence is implicitly recognized or accepted even by the colonial power. To divert the fighters from their objectives, it applies a demagogic policy of 'economic and social improvement', of 'cultural development', cloaking its domination with new forms. Neo-colonialism is, above all, the continuation of imperialist economic rule in disguise, but nevertheless it is also the tacit recognition by the colonial power that the people it rules and exploits have an identity of their own demanding their own political control, for the satisfaction of a cultural necessity.

Moreover, by accepting that the colonized people have an identity and a culture, and therefore an inalienable right to self-determination and independence, metropolitan opinion (or at least an important part of it) itself makes significant cultural progress and sheds a negative element in its own culture — the prejudice that the colonizing nation is superior to the colonized one. This advance can have all-important consequences for the political evolution of the imperialist or colonialist power, as certain facts of current or recent history prove.

If culture is to play its proper role, the liberation movement must lay down the precise objectives to be achieved on the road to the reconquest of the rights of the people it represents — the right to make its own history and the right to dispose freely of its own productive resources. This will pave the way to the final objective of developing a richer, popular, national, scientific and universal culture.

It is not the task of the liberation movement to determine whether a culture is specific to the people or not. The important thing is for the movement to undertake a critical analysis of that culture in the light of the requirements of the struggle and of progress; to give it its place within the universal civilization without consideration as to its superiority or inferiority, with a view to its harmonious integration into the world of today as part of the common heritage of mankind.

9. Conclusion

Editors' Introduction
The conclusion is of course the beginning. In 1961, Chief Alfred Lutuli received the Nobel Prize for Peace. He addressed the world. In 1972, Samora Machel sent a message to his comrades. In 1973, the PAIGC proclaimed the independence of Guinea-Bissau. The words speak to the present and to the future. We end with a reprise by Agostinho Neto on the theme of this book, 'who is the enemy?'.

This is What We Stand For

Alfred Lutuli

> *From the speech by Chief Alfred Lutuli, President-General of the ANC, upon accepting the Nobel Prize for Peace in Stockholm on 11 December, 1961.*

The true patriots of South Africa, for whom I speak, will be satisfied with nothing less than the fullest democratic rights. In government we will not be satisfied with anything less than direct individual adult suffrage and the right to stand for and be elected to all organs of government. In economic matters we will be satisfied with nothing less than equality of opportunity in every sphere, and the enjoyment by all of those heritages which form the resources of the country which up to now have been appropriated on a racial 'whites only' basis. In culture we will be satisfied with nothing less than the opening of all doors of learning to non-segregatory institutions on the sole criterion of ability. In the social sphere we will be satisfied with nothing less than the abolition of all racial bars.

We do not demand these things for peoples of African descent alone. We demand them for all South Africans, white and black. On these principles we are uncompromising. To compromise would be an expediency that is most treacherous to democracy, for in the turn of events the sweets of economic, political and social privileges that are a monopoly of only one section of a community turn sour even in the mouths of those who eat them. Thus apartheid in practice is proving to be a monster created by Frankenstein. That is the tragedy of the South African scene.

Many spurious slogans have been invented in our country in an effort to redeem uneasy race relations – 'trusteeship', 'separate development', 'race federation' and elsewhere 'partnership'. These are efforts to side-track us from the democratic road, mean delaying tactics that fool no one but the unwary. No euphemistic naming will ever hide their hideous nature. We reject these policies because they do great offence to man's sublime aspirations that have remained true in a sea of flux and change down the ages, aspirations of which the United Nations Declaration of Human Rights is a culmination. This is what we stand for. This is what we fight for.

In bringing my address to a close, let me invite Africa to cast her eyes beyond the past and to some extent the present with their woes and tribulations, trials and failures, and some successes, and see herself an emerging continent, bursting to freedom through the shell of centuries of serfdom. This is Africa's age – the dawn of her fulfilment, yes, the moment when she must grapple with destiny to reach the summits of sublimity saying – ours was a fight for noble values and worthy ends, and not for lands and the enslavement of man.

Africa is a vital subject matter in the world of today, a focal point of world interest and concern. Could it not be that history has delayed her rebirth for a purpose? The situation confronts her with inescapable challenges, but more importantly with opportunities for service to herself and mankind. She evades the challenges and neglects the opportunities to her shame, if not her doom. How she sees her destiny is a more vital and rewarding quest than bemoaning her past with its humiliations and sufferings. The address could do no more than pose some questions and leave it to the African leaders and peoples to provide satisfying answers and responses by their concern for higher values and by their noble actions that could be

... footprints on the sands of time;
Footprints, that perhaps another,
Sailing o'er life's solemn main,
A forlorn and shipwrecked brother,
Seeing, shall take heart again.

Still licking the scars of past wrongs perpetrated on her, should she not be magnanimous and practise no revenge? Her offers of friendship scornfully rejected, her pleas for justice and equality spurned, should she not seek to turn enmity to harmony?

Though robbed of her lands, her independence and opportunities – this, oddly enough, often in the name of civilization and even Christianity, should she not see her destiny as being that of making a distinctive contribution to human progress and human relationships with a peculiar new African flavour enriched by the diversity of cultures she enjoys, thus building on the summits of present human achievement an edifice that would be one of the finest tributes to the genius of man? She should see this hour of her fulfilment as a challenge to labour on until she is purged of racial domination, and as an opportunity of reassuring the world that her national aspiration lies, not in overthrowing white domination to replace it by a black caste, but in building a non-racial democracy that shall be a monumental brotherhood, a 'brotherly community' with none discriminated against on grounds of race or colour.

What of the many pressing and complex political, economic and cultural problems attendant upon the early years of a newly-independent State? These, and others which are the legacy of colonial days, will tax to the limit the statesmanship, ingenuity, altruism and steadfastness of African leadership and its unbending avowal to democratic tenets in statecraft. To us all, free or not free, the call of the hour is to redeem the name and honour of Mother Africa. In a strife-torn world, tottering on the brink of complete destruction by man-made nuclear weapons, a free and independent Africa is in the making, in answer to the injunction and challenge of history: 'Arise and shine for thy light is come'. Acting in concert with other nations, she is man's last hope for a mediator between the East and West, and is qualified to demand of the great powers to 'turn the swords into plough-shares' because two-thirds of mankind is hungry and illiterate; to engage human energy, human skill and human talent in the service of peace, for the alternative is unthinkable – war, destruction and desolation; and to build a world community which will stand as a lasting monument to the millions of men and women, to such devoted and distinguished world citizens and fighters for peace as the late Dag Hammarskjold, who have given their lives that we may live in happiness and peace. Africa's qualification for this noble task is incontestable, for her own fight has never been and is not now a fight for conquest of land, for accumulation of wealth or domination of peoples, but for the recognition and preservation of the rights of man and the establishment of a truly free world for a free people.

A Revolution is Like a Bushfire
Samora Machel

From the message of the President of FRELIMO to the people of Mozambique on the occasion of the 8th anniversary of the beginning of armed struggle, 25 August 1972.

It is correct to compare a revolution with a bushfire. It starts hesitantly, timidly. It has to overcome difficulties to affirm itself, to spread and to grow. Once it catches on the flames leap and spread and nothing can stop them. This is what is happening with our revolution in Mozambique.

When we started we were weak, inexperienced and divided. We had a correct line, but it was difficult for us to implement it. There were contradictions among us. Many of our militants were still dominated by their personal, selfish interests and they tried to put them over and above the interests of the people. We were not united. Ambition, corruption, tribalism and racism prevailed among some of our comrades. But the struggle grew and its very growth eliminated these evils. Today in FRELIMO there is solid and firm unity, the more solid in that it has not been achieved in support of a person, but of an idea, that of the *total* independence of Mozambique. It is still more firm in that all the aspects and implications of this idea, that is our ideology, are understood and followed by all the militants in our organisation.

Proclamation of Independence
Guinea Bissau People's National Assembly

Proclamation of the State of Guinea-Bissau by the People's National Assembly held in the Boe region, 24 September, 1973.

The current era of man's history is characterized by the struggle of peoples for their full emancipation from colonialism, imperialism, racism and all other forms of domination and oppression hampering human development and dignity, peace and progress.

In the liberated areas of Guinea-Bissau, our people, guided by the Partido Africano da Independencia da Guine e Cabo Verde (PAIGC) under the enlightened leadership of its founder and No. 1 militant, Amilcar Cabral, has, in the course of 17 years of political and armed struggle, constructed a new life and now possesses a constantly-evolving administrative organization, social and cultural services, a judicial system, a steadily developing economy and national armed forces.

The visit of a United Nations Special Mission to the liberated areas of Guinea-Bissau from 2 to 8 April 1972 served to confirm to the international community what has been attested to by dozens of impartial, honest observers from every continent: the self-determination of our people and the *de facto* existence of an efficiently functioning State structure.

In flagrant violation of modern international law, the Portuguese colonialists are still encroaching upon some portions of our national territory. The United Nations has repeatedly recognized the illegality of the Portuguese presence, the inalienable right of our people to freedom and sovereignty, and the legitimacy of its struggle against Portuguese colonialism.

On the basis of the historic resolution 1514 (XV) of 14 December 1960 concerning the granting of independence to colonial countries and peoples, the United Nations General Assembly and the Security Council have reaffirmed the inalienable right of our people to self-determination and independence, particularly in General Assembly resolution 2918 (XXVII) of 14 November 1972 and Security Council resolution 322 (1972) of 22 November 1972. Furthermore, on the proposal of the Special Committee on Decolonization, the Fourth Committee of the United Nations General Assembly at its twenty-seventh session recognized PAIGC, the liberation movement of Guinea-Bissau and the Cape Verde Islands, as the only and authentic representative of the people of that territory.

The People's National Assembly, which is the result of PAIGC's successes in the fight against Portuguese colonialism, was constituted on the basis of the principle that power derives from the people and should serve the people. The Assembly is composed of representatives elected by universal and direct suffrage by secret ballot, being the expression of the sovereign will of the people of Guinea-Bissau.

At its meeting of 24 September 1973 in the Boe region, the People's National Assembly, expressing the sovereign will of the people *solemnly proclaims the State of Guinea-Bissau.*

The State of Guinea-Bissau is a sovereign, republican, democratic, anti-colonialist and anti-imperialist State whose primary objectives are the complete liberation of the people of Guinea-Bissau and Cape Verde and the forging of a union between those two territories for the purpose of building a strong African homeland dedicated to progress. The arrangements for this union will be determined, after these two territories are liberated, in accordance with the will of the people.

The State of Guinea-Bissau assumes the sacred duty of taking action to expedite, by every means, the expulsion of the forces of aggression of Portuguese colonialism from that part of the territory of Guinea-Bissau which they still occupy and to intensify the struggle in the Cape Verde Islands, which form an integral and inalienable part of the national territory of the people of Guinea-Bissau and Cape Verde.

In due course, the People's Assembly of Cape Verde will be established in the Cape Verde Islands, with a view to the creation of the supreme body having full sovereignty over the people of Guinea and Cape Verde: the People's National Assembly of Guinea and Cape Verde.

The State of Guinea-Bissau regards the strengthening of the links of solidarity and soldierly brotherhood between our people and all peoples of the Portuguese colonies as one of the fundamental principles of its foreign policy; it stands in solidarity with the peoples struggling for their freedom and independence in Africa, Asia and Latin America and with all Arab peoples fighting against Zionism.

The State of Guinea-Bissau is an integral part of Africa and strives for the unity of the African peoples, respecting the freedom of those peoples, their dignity and their right to political, economic, social and cultural progress.

As regards international relations, the State of Guinea-Bissau wishes to maintain and develop ties of friendship, co-operation and solidarity with its neighbours – the Republic of Guinea and the Republic of Senegal – with all independent African States and with all States throughout the world which recognize its sovereignty and support the national liberation struggle of our people. These relations shall be based on the principles of peaceful co-existence, mutual respect for national sovereignty, non-aggression, non-interference in internal affairs and mutual advantage.

The State of Guinea-Bissau assumes responsibility for promoting the economic advancement of the country, thereby creating the material basis for the development of culture, science and technology, with a view to the continuing improvement of the social and economic living standards of our population and with the ultimate aim of achieving a life of peace, well-being and progress for all our country's children.

Having as a foundation our heroic People's National Liberation Army, the State of Guinea-Bissau will provide our national armed forces with all necessary means to accomplish the task of bringing about the complete liberation of our country, and defending the achievements of our people and the integrity of our national territory.

From the historic moment of the proclamation of the State of Guinea-Bissau, authorities and organs of the Portuguese colonial State which exercise any political, military or administrative authority in our territory are illegal, and their acts are null and void. Consequently, from that moment on, the Portuguese State has no right to assume any obligations or commitments in relation to our country. All treaties, conventions, agreements, alliances and concessions involving our country which were entered into in the past by the Portuguese colonialists will be submitted to the People's National Assembly, the supreme embodiment of State power, which will proceed to review them in accordance with the interests of our peoples.

The State of Guinea-Bissau affirms the principle that it is fighting against Portuguese colonialism and not against the Portuguese people, with which our people wishes to maintain a friendly and co-operative relationship.

The State of Guinea-Bissau adheres to the principles of non-alignment. It supports the settlement of international disputes by negotiation and, to that effect and in accordance with the resolutions of the highest international organs, it declares its willingness to negotiate a solution which will put an end to the aggression of the Portuguese colonial Government that is illegally occupying part of our national territory and committing acts of genocide against our populations.

The frontiers of the State of Guinea-Bissau delimit the territory situated between latitudes 12°20' and 10°59' north and between longitudes 16°43' and 13°90' west, that is to say bounded by the Republic of Senegal to the north, the Republic of Guinea to the south and east and the Atlantic Ocean to the west. The territory consists of a mainland part, a string of coastal islands and all the islands comprising the Bijagos archipelago and covers a land area of 36,125 square kilometres plus the respective territorial waters and corresponds to the area of the region formerly designated as the colony of Portuguese Guinea.

The State of Guinea-Bissau appeals to all the independent States of the world to accord it *de jure* recognition as a sovereign State in accordance with international law and practice. It expresses its determination to participate in international life, particularly the United Nations, where our people will be able to make their contribution to solving the fundamental problems of our times both in Africa and in the world.

Who Is the Enemy? . . . What Is Our Objective?
Agostinho Neto

A lecture delivered by the President of the MPLA, at the University of Dar es Salaam on 7 February, 1974.

It is with the greatest pleasure that I am speaking before the always deeply interested audience of this University, whose preoccupation, on the part of both students and lecturers, shows a desire for a profound understanding of our continent and of the different factors affecting its development. This is a preoccupation worthy of the country's future leaders and of those who are forming them, which fact transforms the great pleasure of this meeting into a special honour.

I should like briefly to outline the fruit of my personal experience, the fruit of reflection on the national liberation struggle on our continent. This experience is simply an expression of a need experienced in Africa over the past five centuries, and most especially in the last decades, the need for each and every one of us to feel free. It is also a broader expression of the common desire of men in this world to regard themselves as free, as capable of releasing themselves from the shackles of a society in which they weaken and die as human beings.

In my opinion, the national liberation struggle in Africa cannot be dissociated from the present context in which it is taking place; it cannot be isolated from the world. A workers' strike in England, the imposition of fascism on the Chilean people or an atomic explosion in the Pacific are all phenomena of this same life that we are living and in which we are seeking ways to a happy existence for man in this world. This universal fact is however rendered particular in Africa through current political, economic and cultural concepts.

The historical bonds between our peoples and other peoples in the world are becoming ever closer, since there can be no other trend on earth. Isolation is impossible and is contrary to the idea of technical, cultural and political progress.

The problem facing us Africans now is how to transform unjust relations with other countries and peoples in the world, generally relations of political and economic subordination, without this transformation taking place to the detriment of the social progress which must of necessity be injected into action to win freedom, and without which one's behaviour would be that of a man coming out of one form of discrimination only to fall into another as negative as the first, as a simple inversion of the intervening factors. And within this same African society, the national liberation movement also seeks to ensure that the internal socio-economic forces, that is, those that evolve within each country, are restructured in the direction of progress.

In Africa we are making every effort to put a final end to paleo-colonialism, which barely exists today in the territories dominated by Portugal, contrary to the general belief, since they are in fact dominated by a vast imperialist partnership which is unjustly protecting the selfish interests of men, economic organisations and groups of countries.

The so-called white minority racist regimes are merely a consequence and a special form of paleo-colonialism in which links with the metropoles have become slack and less distinct in favour of a white minority dictatorship.

This visible, clear and open form of colonialism does not prevent the existence on our continent of another more subtle form of domination which goes by the name of neo-colonialism, in which he who exploits is no longer identified by the name coloniser, but acts in the same way at various levels.

However, internal forms of subjugation caused by fragmentation into small ethnic or linguistic groupings, by the development of privileged classes endowed with their own dynamism, are also forms of oppression linked with the visible forms known as colonialism old or new, and racism. They easily ally themselves with imperialism and facilitate its penetration and influence.

These phenomena are universal and they are found or have been found in all societies in the world, but at the present time they are acute and very tangible in Africa, and it is here that they most concern us Africans, as well as other nations with which we have relations either of subjugation or cooperation.

Colonial and racist domination and oppression are exercised in different ways and at different levels. They do not take place in a uniform way on our continent, they do not always use the same agents, and they do not always act on the same social stratum or on the same type of political or economic organisation.

For this reason, everyone, whether coloniser or colonised, feels in a different way this phenomenon which is today anachronistic and which it is desired to replace by other kinds of relations (and we Africans are not yet very clear or very much in agreement on these new kinds of relations).

Whereas for some people colonialism meant and still means forced labour, to others it is a racial discrimination, while for others it is economic segregation and the impossibility of political advancement. But the plunder of African lands by the colonisers, the enslavement of the worker, corporal punishment and the intensive exploitation of the wealth that belongs to us are forms of the same colonialism; and the capacity of each person to apply himself to the dynamics of solving the colonial problem, with greater or lesser intelligence and clarity, depends on a broad understanding of all these factors.

And, as previously stated, action against colonialism is closely linked with and part of something else of an apparently internal nature, but which is in fact as universal as the first, which is the need for social transformations, so that man may be truly free in every country and every continent in the world.

The way in which this aspect of the problem is tackled is also very important to the stand taken and the line to be followed in the liberation process.

These two crucial problems of our continent and of our era are therefore closely interconnected with relations with foreign peoples, on the one hand, and with the relations among the ready forces within each country.

The correctness of attitude and the emotional intensity with which we embark upon action for liberation depend on how we see the world, how we foresee our country's future and the extent to which we feel in our skin the action of the foreign forces.

The national liberation struggle in our era is therefore influenced not only by the historical factors determining colonialism, neo-colonialism or racist regimes, but also by its own prospects, its objectives and the way each person sees the world and life.

Reaction to foreign domination, whether individual, collective or organised, must of necessity be influenced by the two factors mentioned, which have to do with both past and future history.

This is why the importance of the national liberation movements is much greater than is generally admitted, because through their activity they are transforming themselves into accelerators of history, of the development of the society within which they are acting and also outside it, imparting fresh dynamism to social processes to transcend the present stage, even that in politically independent countries.

The different types of colonisation in Africa have endowed us Africans with different ways of seeing the problem of liberation, and it is natural that it should be thus, since our consciousness cannot draw upon material to form itself except from the field of lived experience and from our possibilities of knowing the world.

Sometimes we differ in our concepts and, hence, in the practical implementation of combat programmes, and the line taken in action for liberation does not always fulfil the twofold need to concentrate both on transforming the relations between peoples and intrinsically transforming the life of the nation.

Hence the need to see the problem clearly and to provide clear answers to the following specific questions: Who is the enemy and what is the enemy? What is our objective?

It is obvious that the answers to these questions do not depend simply on the desire to be free. They also depend on knowledge and on a concept of the world and life, on lived experience. This means that they cannot be dissociated from acquired political ideas, from ideological positions which generally result from the origins of each and every one of us. Without wishing to go into an analysis of the Angolan problem in its specific aspects, I should nevertheless like to clarify the ideas I have just put forward and shall put forward later, basing myself on my own experience.

Angola is a vast country which today has a very low population density and which has been colonised by the Portuguese since 1482. This is the generally accepted idea. However, as far as colonisation is concerned, Portugal did not succeed in dominating all of our territory on its first contact. It took centuries before it was able to impose its political and economic rule over the whole of our people. And I wish again to emphasise that neither is it true that Angola is dominated only by Portugal. The world is sufficiently enlightened on this point to know that the political and economic interests of several world powers are involved in Angola. Portugal's administration has not prevented the presence of its partners, a presence which has been there for centuries. For example, Great Britain, the country with the largest volume of capital investments in Angola, and the United States of America, with growing economic interests and longing to control our country's strategic position, as well as other countries of Europe, America and Asia, are competing for the domination of our people and the exploitation of the wealth that belongs to us.

To think that Angola, Mozambique, Guinea and other colonies are dominated by small and backward Portugal today is to be as mistaken as to think that French society is now in the feudal era (the reference to France is merely by way of example).

Small and backward Portugal is not the chief factor of colonisation. Without the capital of other countries, without growing investments and technical cooperation, without complicity at various levels, radical transformations would already have taken place many years ago.

Therefore, if we can say that Portugal is the manager of a series of politico-economic deals, we will see that it is not our principal enemy but merely our direct enemy. At the same time, it is the weakest link in the whole chain established for domination of the peoples. If we look at Portugal itself, at the internal picture it presents, we see a society which is still striving to transcend an obsolete form of oligarchic government, incapable of abandoning the use of violence against its people for the benefit of just a few families, with a peasant class struggling in the most dire poverty in Europe, and where every citizen feels himself a prisoner in his own country. The Portuguese themselves are right when they say that their country is today one of the greatest disgraces of Europe and the world.

We can now give an answer to the question: Who is the enemy and what is his nature? The enemy of Africa is often confused with the white man. Skin colour is still a factor used by many to determine the enemy. There are historical and social reasons and lived facts which consolidate this idea on our continent.

It is absolutely understandable that a worker in the South African mines who is segregated and coerced, and whose last drop of sweat is wrung from him, should feel that the white man he sees before him, for whom he produces wealth, is the principal enemy. It is for him that he builds cities and well-paved roads and maintains hygienic and salubrious conditions which he himself does not have.

Consciousness, as I have said, is formed chiefly from one's experience of life. The experience of South Africa could lead to this immediate conclusion, which is to a certain extent logical and emotionally valid.

All the more so in that the society created by the colonialists, to come back to the case of Angola, created various racial defence mechanisms which were made to serve colonialism. The same poor, wretched and oppressed peasant who is exploited in his own country is the object of special attention when he establishes himself in one of 'its' colonies. He is not only imbued with a lot of jingoism, but he also starts to enjoy economic and social privileges which he could never have before. Thus he becomes a part of the system. He starts to get a taste for colonialism and becomes a watchdog of the interests of the fascist oligarchy.

However, deep in their hearts both the watchdog and the exploiter nonetheless feel themselves slaves of the system as a whole.

We can therefore say today that the phenomenon of colonial or neo-colonial oppression in our continent cannot be seen in terms of the colour of individuals.

The same system that oppresses and exploits the peasant in Portugal also oppresses and exploits the Angolan citizen, using different motivation, different techniques, but always with the same goal – to exploit. And the establishment of just relations is possible between Portuguese men and Angolan, Mozambican and Guinean men, that is, the establishment of relations which prevent the exploitation of one man by another. The racial factor will play only a secondary role, and for a little time more, once relations between master and slave are ended.

An ideological understanding of this problem also makes it easier to solve once the objectives of the liberation struggle are defined.

In special conditions there are already cases where the racial problem is overcome. This is what happens in the war. There are conscious Portuguese who desert to join the nationalist ranks in one way or another.

Our experience of clandestine struggle showed that there can be such racial cooperation in the struggle against the system.

And what do we really want basically?

I do not think that the national liberation struggle is directed towards inverting systems of oppression in such a way that the master of today will be the slave of tomorrow. To think in this way is to go against the current of history. Attitudes of social revenge can never be what we want, which is the freedom of men.

And I should like again to emphasise that the liberation struggles are not aimed solely at violently correcting the relations between men and especially the production relations *within the country* – they are an important factor for the positive transformation of our entire continent and the whole world.

The national liberation struggle is also a means of overthrowing a whole unjust system of oppression existing in the world.

Let us look at the question pragmatically:

We do not find a single country in Africa which does not maintain preferential relations with its former metropole, even through the absorption of the inevitable cultural values of a regime of a colonial type. What is more, the forms of exploitation do not end and neither, consequently, do the forms of racial discrimination, accentuated to a greater or lesser degree. In such cases, liberation is not yet complete.

Under independence in which there is not merely apparent political independence, but also economic and cultural independence, where respect for true national values exists, so as to make it possible to abolish exploitation, I believe that man would find true freedom.

To answer our question, we would say that the enemy is colonialism, the colonial system, and also imperialism, which sustains the former, to the point of being the principal enemy.

These enemies use on their own behalf all the contradictions they can find in the dominated society: racial, tribal, class and other factors. On them they build their foundation for exploitation and maintain it, changing its appearance when it can no longer be maintained.

Thus, in Africa formal political domination can no longer prevail, but no one is yet free from economic domination. It is present there, and it is for this very reason that I am very pleased by the formula adopted by some political parties in power in Africa when they say that they too are national liberation movements. This expresses the full significance of the phenomenon of liberation.

This broader concept of national liberation has vitally important consequences as regards the necessary cooperation between the oppressed of the world.

I shall therefore go on to say that national liberation must be a stage for the achievement of a vaster form of liberation, which is the liberation of man.

If one loses sight of this idea, dynamism disappears and the essential contradictions in a country remain.

The Angolan experience has already shown that pure anti-racism cannot permit the full development of the liberation struggle. For centuries our society has had within it white people who came as occupiers, as conquerors, but who had time to establish roots, to multiply, and to live for generations and generations on our territory. This white population dominates the urban centres, giving rise to the fact of people who are racially mixed, making our society interlinked in its racial components.

If the liberation struggle overlooks the realities of the country, and if formulations are taken up which are pleasing to nationalists who are sincere but not over-concerned about the aspect of the people's socio-historical development, it weakens itself and cannot attain its political and human objectives.

Everyone in a country who wants to participate in whatever way in the liberation struggle should be able to do so.

The preoccupation in Africa of making the liberation struggle a racial struggle of blacks against whites is not only superficial, but we can say that it is reactionary and that this view has no future at the very time when we see more contact between blacks and whites on the continent than in the era of colonialism.

215

The expanded relations with socialist countries and with countries which are against colonialism (in its old form), and the so-called relations of co-operation with the former metropoles have brought to Africa a noteworthy number of Europeans, Americans and Asians, more than there have ever been in any era of Africa's history.

Therefore, to pose the problem as one of black against white is to falsify the question and deflect us from our objective.

What do we want?

An independent life as a nation, a life in which economic relations are just both between countries and within the country, a revival of cultural values which are still valid for our era.

The literary concept of negritude, born of philosophico-literary trends which have had their day, like existentialism and surrealism, posed with discernment the problem of arousing the cultural consciousness of the black man in the world, irrespective of the geographical area to which he had been dispersed.

Like the idea of Pan-Africanism, the concept of negritude started at a certain point to falsify the black problem.

It is and was correct to heighten the essence of cultural values which black people took to all the continents, and predominantly to the American continent. Our culture must be defended and developed, which does not mean that it must remain stagnant.

Basically, and as various thinkers have asserted, the national liberation struggle is a struggle for culture. But I do not believe that cultural links in any way prevent political compartmentalisation.

This has been an equivocal point in many alleged demonstrations of national liberation.

I cannot fail to express my full political identification with the struggle of the black peoples of America where they are, and to admire the vitality of descendants of Africans who today are still oppressed and segregated in American society, especially in the United States. I say *especially* in the United States, because I do not very much believe in the full freedom of blacks or the national equality in Brazil of which they talk so much and are trying to convince us.

The social advancement of the black American has been noteworthy, to the extent that today the black American distinguishes himself in Africa not only by his comportment but also by his intellectual and technical level.

Only rarely do the physical characteristics of black Americans allow any doubt as to their country of origin. Thus, the phenomenon of miscegenation has produced a new kind of man. The type that the ordinary man in Angola calls a white man or a mulatto is a black man in the United States.

There is therefore no physical identity and there are strong cultural differences, as there could not fail to be.

Therefore, without confusing origins with political compartments, America is America and Africa is Africa.

Today we are all linked in solidarity in a liberation struggle against oppressors who have the same colour, but tomorrow there will certainly be different social personalities to be preserved. And the evolutionary process of mankind through which differences are obliterated cannot but bring about an even greater mingling of the now antagonistic ethnic groups in the United States. America has its own life, just as Angola and Mozambique have their own life. Although we have to identify with each other as black men in defending our values, I cannot conceal my sometimes ill-founded concern at the way some of our brothers from the other side of the Atlantic have a messianic desire to find a Moses for a return to Africa. For many this theory is certainly out of date.

But I should like to return to the question of knowing who is our enemy.

As stated previously, according to my understanding the first reactions against a system of oppression stem from the way one lives, from the way one feels this oppression. I cited the case of South Africa.

I do not wish to ignore at this moment the pressure that is exerted on the liberation movements to maintain so-called *black purity*. The case of America, where the racial struggle is the most apparent to the blacks, is often cited. What I am saying should not be taken as criticism of our brave black American brothers, who know better than anyone how to orient their struggle, how to envisage the transformation of American society so that man will be free there.

But allow me also to reject any idea on the transformation of the national liberation struggle in Angola into a racial struggle.

I would say that in Angola the struggle *also* assumes a racial aspect since discrimination is a fact. The black man is exploited there. But it is fundamentally a struggle against the colonial system and its chief ally, imperialism.

I also reject the idea of black liberation, since the unity of Africa is one of the principles universally accepted by the OAU, and knowing that in Africa there are Arab peoples, that there are some areas which are not black. The problem cannot be purely racial. So long as there is imperialism, it will be possible to continue colonialism.

And as I have said, for us they are the enemies.

What we want is to establish a new society where black and white can live together. Naturally, and so as not to be misinterpreted, I must add that the democratic process must be exercised in such a way that the most exploited masses (who are black) have control of political power, since they can go furthest in establishing proper rights for all.

A people's struggle for political power, for economic independence, for the restoration of cultural life, to end alienation, for relations with all peoples on a basis of equality and fraternity — these are the objectives of our struggle.

These objectives are set by defining who is the enemy, by defining who are the people and what is the character of our struggle, which is a revolutionary struggle affecting not only the foundations of the colonial system but also the foundations of our own society, as a nation and as a people.

But can such liberation take place at this stage?

Let us see.

We are in a period in which the imperialist forces are deploying themselves on the African scene with dynamism and tenacity. Together with the Portuguese colonialists, with the racist regimes in Southern Africa, imperialism is present on our continent. Its influence can be felt. Its activity is causing alarm in the life of Africa. Neo-colonialism is a fact. Everywhere in Africa there is still the need to struggle for independence, whether political in some areas, economic in others, or cultural almost everywhere.

Imperialism is doing everything it can to maintain sources of raw materials and cheap labour. This is a phenomenon which is being debated not only in Africa but in the whole of the so-called third world.

In a world divided into blocs, among which it was customary to distinguish between the socialist bloc and the capitalist bloc, non-alignment has arisen to try to seek a balance and to defend the less developed.

And within this division, it is the socialists who hold high the banner of internationalism and in fact give the most support to the liberation movements.

But today the socialist camp is divided, weakened by irreconcilable ideological concepts, and the relations of solidarity which made these countries an impenetrable iron fortress have broken down and are taking a long time to be restored.

The relations of solidarity have changed and conflicts of greater or lesser importance have marred the avowed ideal of socialism.

Thus, in the same way as a number of African countries have on their markets products from countries dominated by the enemy, from South Africa, Portugal and Rhodesia, we see with great concern the increase by some socialist countries of commercial and cultural relations with especially Portugal.

So, let us be realistic, the national liberation struggle in Africa does not have very sound bases in the international arena, and it is not political or ideological affinities that count, nor even the objectives themselves, for in most cases other interests dominate relations between the liberation forces and the world.

We are in another era. The world is changing and we have to take note of this fact.

Thus, there are many cracks through which the enemy can penetrate. However, an essential factor we must recognise is that the national liberation struggle is today a cause which few people fail to support, with greater or lesser sincerity. Political independence for the African majority is an attainment of our time.

And since various political currents and ideological trends are involved, with sometimes antagonistic interests, the liberation movements find themselves at grips with the problem of their political and ideological independence, the problem of preserving their personality, which must reflect the social image of the country.

To preserve independence is not easy, and sometimes the struggle is affected by our own contradictions. And contradictions can stem from different concepts from which our definition of who is the enemy and of our objectives derives.

Some would like to see the liberation movement take the direction of a class struggle, as in Europe. Others would like to see it racist, Don Quixote tilting at a windmill with a white skin. Others would like to see it tribalised, federalised, according to their idea of a country which they do not know. Others, idealists, would like to see us heading along the path to political compromise with the enemy.

These efforts to transform the liberation movements into satellites of parties in power, subject to unacceptable paternalism, are caused by the fact that most of the liberation movements conducting an armed struggle have to do so from outside their countries.

Exile has its effects.

'The worst thing the Portuguese did to us,' said one of my most intelligent friends, 'was to oblige us to wage a liberation struggle from abroad.' I agree.

The Organisation of African Unity, which has done something, especially politically, to promote the national liberation movements, will still have to help them enough for them to be independent, respecting the conventions and the programmatic involvement of different organisations, in accordance with the realities of the country.

The dialogue between independent Africa and dependent Africa is still not satisfactory, and for this very reason the political battles are not taking place with the required force.

We cannot digress on the various nuances of political action to demonstrate our shortcomings, but I do not want at this time to give the idea of having had any critical intention in my appraisal of the period we are going through in this phase of liberation.

I will merely say that we could, for example, cooperate on economic matters so as to wage the battle in this field too. With regard to Portugal, its plunder of our resources, like oil, coffee, diamonds, iron, etc., products which are marketed by international bodies in which Africans participate, could be prevented or at least decreased.

And what harm would there be in involving the liberation movements in discussions on the crucial problems of our times which will certainly affect the development of our continent, like for example the broader association of Africa with the Common Market, or problems of European security?

And the problem of Southern Africa? Will we be permitted to discuss it exhaustively one day?

Finally, we could go on much longer reflecting on our lived experience in this national liberation struggle.

I shall end here, thanking you Mr. Chairman and all the ladies and gentlemen and comrades for your attention.